The Art of

Natural
Family
Planning®

Student Guide
Second Edition

This text is an integral part of The Couple to Couple League's (CCL) Natural Family Planning instructional course. Natural Family Planning is best learned through a class series taught by a certified CCL teacher or through CCL's Home Study Program. For information on how to get in touch with a certified CCL teacher, visit the CCL website at **www.ccli.org**.

The Art of
Natural
Family
Planning®

Student Guide
Second Edition

Foreword by John T. Bruchalski, M.D., FACOG

The Couple to Couple League
International, Inc.
4290 Delhi Avenue
Cincinnati, OH 45238-5829

Book Design by Scott Bruno of b graphic design
Cover Photo by Ron Rack of Rack Photography

Permission to Publish:
Permission to publish is a declaration that this book is considered to be free of doctrinal or moral error. It is not implied that those who have granted the Permission to Publish agree with the contents, opinions or statements expressed.

Rescript
In accord with the *Code of Canon Law*, I hereby grant my permission to publish *The Art of Natural Family Planning® Student Guide.*
Reverend Joseph R. Binzer
Vicar General
Archdiocese of Cincinnati
July 8, 2008

USCCB Approval:
The Couple to Couple League's NFP Programs meet the standards of and have been formally approved by the United States Conference of Catholic Bishops (USCCB).

Cataloging data
        L.C. 2007933434

The Art of Natural Family Planning Student Guide, Second Edition
The Couple to Couple League
Foreword by John T. Bruchalski, MD, FACOG
Natural Family Planning
Birth Control
Breastfeeding
Sexual Morality

ISBN 978-0-926412-30-9

Published by The Couple to Couple League International, Inc.
4290 Delhi Avenue
Cincinnati, OH 45238-5829
U.S.A.
800-745-8252
www.ccli.org
info@ccli.org

Printed in the United States
10 9 8 7 6 5 4

Table of Contents

Foreword F

It is a tremendous honor to be asked to write the foreword to the *Student Guide* of the Couple to Couple League's course in Natural Family Planning. This manual comes at a pivotal time in our understanding of marriage and sexuality.

Pope John Paul II's **Theology of the Body** is becoming *user friendly*. Exiting the academic, scholarly and theological circles, this revolutionary and liberating language is being incorporated into something as foundational as Natural Family Planning (NFP).

It has been decades since Woodstock and legalized abortion, and married couples have experienced firsthand the trauma and failure of the contraceptive, no-consequences approach to sexual relations and family life. Families want and deserve better, and they are actively looking for an approach that is relevant to their time but is grounded in the belief of strong, stable families, and a more accurate and truthful understanding of the language of their bodies. *Our Bodies, Ourselves*, the bible of the sexual revolution, has failed miserably as a guide; **Theology of the Body** and NFP are ready and more than able to replace it.

From my perspective as the Founder of the Tepeyac Family Center, I see a "perfect storm" of medicine, sociology and theology battling the accepted dogma of the contraceptive mentality. And now, CCL has brought together experts on marital sexuality and fertility awareness and offers a program that creates a paradigm shift in the way NFP is presented in the English language. To understand and relate to our culture, language is crucial, foundational and critical to the way CCL approaches the subject of sex and marriage. The language of CCL's new course leads couples, physicians, clerics, and scholars toward the fountain of truth and invites them to take a drink, and then drink deeply.

Much has happened over these last four decades. In our medical practice and in our outreach here at the Tepeyac Family Center, we are experiencing more and more women of all ages seeking quality obstetrics and gynecologic care that respects their dignity as women. *It's time for the day of the MD-deity to end*, and we hope that the day for pills and potions, gadgets and devices is soon to be over. Women are seeking cooperative, ecologically sound medical advice regarding their sexuality and fertility. The answer for these women is NFP, which empowers them to make virtuous, character-building, critical decisions, in prayerful cooperation with their husbands, by listening and understanding the language that their bodies speak. This updated book and course provides them with the reasons and resources they need in a new and dynamic way.

Finally, as a member of the Advisory Council for the Couple to Couple League, I have watched CCL's program grow from its inception and am impressed with its approach and quality. At the same time, there are new studies acknowledging the effectiveness of sympto-thermal methods of NFP like the program taught by CCL. Without a doubt, this *Student Guide* comes at a time when many medical professionals, married and engaged couples, and clergy are seeking quality, accurate and understandable instruction on NFP presented in a manner that respects the dignity of each human person and the dignity of each family.

Every couple preparing for marriage — regardless of their religious affiliation — could benefit from this course. What couple does not want their marriage to be everlasting and filled with growth and maturity? Every medical professional who deals with marital sexuality would benefit by becoming familiar with this NFP program and learning how to respond to questions in ways that cooperate with and nurture sexuality, fertility and relationships, rather than destroy, cut-off, or suppress normal and healthy physiologic processes. Our first commandment in medicine is to *do no harm!* Every cleric who prepares couples for marriage needs to have this book to help him show couples that the secret to healthy marriages is mutual respect and openness to life.

This is a defining moment in the understanding of marriage, family and the dignity of the human person. In the "perfect storm" battling against the emptiness of the contraceptive mentality, CCL's response in the form of this *Student Guide* and NFP course has the potential to change the marital and medical landscape by changing hearts, minds and souls, person to person; couple to couple...The way all revolutions really take place. Congratulations, CCL!

John T. Bruchalski, M.D., FACOG
Founder, Tepeyac Family Center
Chairman and President Divine Mercy Care

Preface P

In the Spring of 2004, The Couple to Couple League (CCL) surveyed its cadre of volunteer teachers and promoters and gathered feedback from couples attending class and diocesan family life offices, in an effort to best assess our student text and teaching process. This book, now in its second edition, and how we now teach Natural Family Planning (NFP), is a result of that analysis.

With this new edition, we have not changed the Sympto-Thermal Method of NFP. We have, however, clarified some of our rules, and improved the classroom experience based on additional feedback from our Teaching Couples. As its previous edition, this text follows directly along with CCL's classroom presentation.

Much of the information on the electronic screens from which our teachers instruct is "built" directly into this guide so you can follow along page by page. There are hands-on exercises integrated throughout each of the classes to help you understand the concepts better, and the book is in full color to provide a better learning experience. While this book is accompanied in the class setting by a dynamic classroom presentation with embedded animation and video clips, it is simple yet complete enough to use as a stand-alone text.

So what is Natural Family Planning (NFP)? You will learn very early in Class 1 that NFP is fertility awareness, which is simply knowledge — the knowledge of a couple's fertility. It is a means of reading the body's signs of fertility and infertility, whereby, married couples can virtuously apply that knowledge to either postpone or try to achieve a pregnancy. The foundation of NFP is to understand how to "read" the language of the body to determine the fertile and infertile times of a woman's cycle. But *The Art of Natural Family Planning®
Student Guide* presents this in the context of the Catholic Church's vision for sexuality and marriage.

As Dr. Bruchalski alludes to in the foreword, this vision is explained in a way that is easy to understand and applies to everyone regardless of faith — that we are made in the image and likeness of God, that we have an innate dignity, and that natural family planning respects that dignity. This is introduced in Class 1, along with the anatomy and physiology of the female cycle, and the interaction of hormones and how they lead to measurable signs of fertility. The class concludes with how to identify the post-ovulatory infertile phase of a woman's cycle.

In Class 2, we go further in defining the phases of a woman's cycle to include identifying the pre-ovulatory infertile and fertile phases. We also explain how NFP can be used to help achieve a pregnancy. Class 2 concludes with a discussion on the Catholic Church's vision of marriage and sexuality to include responsible parenthood — the virtuous application of NFP.

Lastly, Class 3 briefly overviews a few other methods of NFP which provide the basis for CCL's single-sign rules that are occasionally used when all the signs of fertility may not be available, as well as applying NFP in special situations, such as stress or illness. Class 3 highlights behaviors that attack human dignity, like contraception, and finishes with the benefits of breastfeeding and its effect on fertility.

It is our belief that both the format of this book, as well as the League's approach to teaching NFP will enable thousands of couples to learn and properly practice NFP and realize its many benefits in their marriages!

The Art of Natural Family Planning® Student Guide is the result of years of planning and production work, which has truly been a collaborative effort. Many individuals have contributed to the development of this text; CCL has special thanks for the following individuals.

Gerri Laird, Bob Laird and Father Richard Hogan spent months writing, reviewing, editing, and reediting the first edition of this book, and Mike Manhart, Ph.D. and Andy Alderson edited the second edition. Ann Gundlach has been the final editor of both editions. Scott Hofmann dedicated countless hours to the design of many of the illustrations both in this book and in the course visuals. CCL is also thankful for the technical writing and research of Vicki Braun, the medical advice and oversight of Jack Burnham, M.D., John Bruchalski, M.D., and Marie Anderson, M.D., and the graphic design of Scott Bruno.

Lastly, our Volunteers deserve thanks for their valuable feedback on both the *Student Guide* and the NFP class.

Class 1

1 Introduction

This first class is divided into six lessons: *Introduction, Anatomy and the Female Cycle, Measurable Signs of Hormonal Interactions, Interpreting the Signs of Fertility, Theology of the Body as It Relates to Sexuality,* and *Getting Started.*

This *Introduction* will summarize the Class 1 lessons.

Summary: Class 1 Lessons

Lesson 2, *Anatomy and the Female Cycle,* provides a brief overview of male and female anatomy, and the female cycle. Generally, men are fertile from their teenage years until their death, while women are fertile for only a few days each month from their teenage years to midlife. Important to the use of NFP is understanding the process by which a woman becomes fertile and infertile every month or so. This lesson explains that there are four hormones related to the changes that occur in a healthy, fertile woman during her menstrual cycle.

In addition to causing the internal changes a woman experiences from one menstruation to the next, the same hormones also create other observable external effects.

Lesson 3, *Measurable Signs of Hormonal Interactions,* teaches the observable changes in cervical mucus, basal body temperature and the cervix. This lesson also introduces the CCL chart on which a couple will record these observable changes.

Lesson 4, *Interpreting the Signs of Fertility,* teaches a couple how to interpret the observable signs to determine their state of fertility. It also introduces the Sympto-Thermal Rule

(ST Rule), which is used to identify the beginning of Phase III of the female cycle: the time of infertility after ovulation. By identifying the boundary between Phase II, the fertile time, and Phase III, an infertile time, couples will know when it is possible to conceive a child and when a child most likely will not be conceived.

Lesson 5, *Theology of the Body as It Relates to Sexuality*, introduces material on the moral teachings of the Catholic Church regarding sexuality and procreation. (These teachings were common to all Christian denominations prior to 1930.)

The central concept of Lesson 5 is that the human body is the expression or manifestation of the human person. It is through our bodies that we each communicate to others who we are, what we are thinking and choosing, and what we are feeling and sensing. The human body speaks a language that can be read and understood. One of the most important aspects of our "body language" is our sexuality, i.e. our maleness and femaleness. By understanding the design God built into our personhood, we come to know ourselves, and spouses come to know each other in a very profound way.

Lesson 6, *Getting Started*, helps couples get started practicing NFP the day after Class 1 by observing, recording and interpreting their signs of fertility. It provides guidelines for applying NFP in the first cycle and after using hormonal contraceptives, and it reminds couples that there are two supplemental classes and books provided by CCL: one for the postpartum time and another for premenopause.

The lessons are interspersed with practical exercises intended to reinforce the information taught. These exercises will help couples properly record and interpret the signs of fertility. The proper interpretation of these signs will enable couples to apply their knowledge of NFP to their marriages as they decide to hope for a child or to postpone pregnancy.

Those who are attending the classes will complete certain exercises in class, as well as some homework between classes. Those using the *Home Study Course* will use additional data and directions in the Appendix to complete the exercises, and check their work against the provided answers.

Remember that teaching couples are generally available before and after NFP classes to answer questions or address any concerns that may arise. For those using the *Home Study Course,* CCL's central office is available to answer questions or discuss concerns. The office can be contacted by phone, e-mail or through the CCL website (see page iv).

What is Natural Family Planning (NFP)?

The human body speaks more than one language. One of these languages is the bodily language of love, spoken in a unique way through our sexuality. In this class, you will learn the language of sexuality by observing, recording and interpreting the bodily signs of human fertility, the essence of NFP.

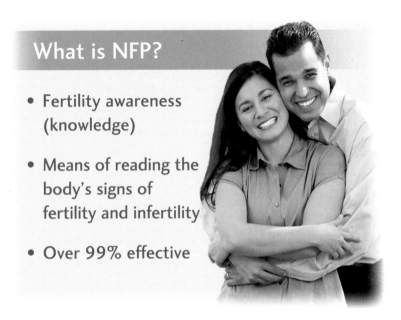

What is NFP?

- Fertility awareness (knowledge)

- Means of reading the body's signs of fertility and infertility

- Over 99% effective

Natural Family Planning is **fertility awareness**, the knowledge of a couple's fertility; it is a means of reading the body's signs of fertility and infertility. Applying this knowledge through the Sympto-Thermal Method (STM) is over 99% effective in postponing pregnancy. A married couple's virtuous application of this knowledge either to try to achieve a pregnancy or to postpone a pregnancy is called **responsible parenthood**.

After finishing Class 1, couples should:

- know how to observe, record and interpret the signs of fertility

- know how to identify the boundary between the most fertile time (time of ovulation) and the most infertile time of the female cycle (time after ovulation)

- understand that the human body speaks a language

- be acquainted with the language of the body spoken through human fertility

- be able to apply what was learned

Notes

Anatomy and the Female Cycle 2

Lesson 2

The human body is indeed "fearfully and wonderfully made."[1] As we study male and female anatomy, we can see how our bodies were designed to complement each other. A man produces sperm, but the sperm by itself doesn't produce a new life. A woman has eggs or ova, but by themselves can't produce a new life. Only when a sperm unites with an egg or ovum, does a new life begin. A male body does not complement another male body, and a female body does not complement another female body. But a male and a female body were made to complement each other in the marital embrace. Their anatomies fit perfectly with each other. Thus God created man and woman to complement each other physically, as well as emotionally and spiritually.

In this lesson, we will first examine male anatomy, and then female anatomy. The last and longer section of this lesson will study the female reproductive cycle.

---

[1] Psalm 139:14.

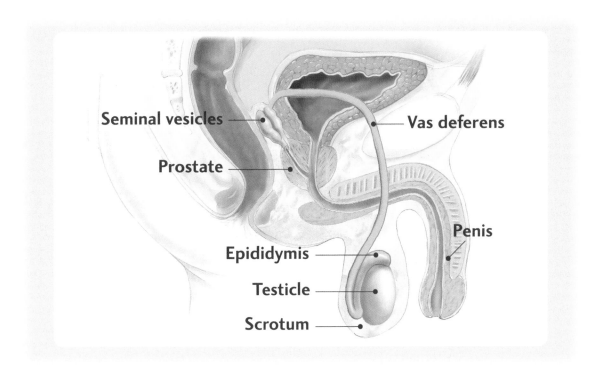

Male Anatomy

Looking first at the male reproductive system, the **penis** is the external male sex organ used to ejaculate semen and to convey urine outside the body. **Semen** is composed of sperm and seminal fluid (discussed below). **Sperm** are produced in the two **testicles** located in a sac or pouch called the **scrotum**, exterior to the body's torso in the groin area. Sperm are very sensitive to heat and need to be produced and nurtured in an environment cooler than normal body temperature. Locating the testicles on the outside of the torso, then, is a protective mechanism for healthy sperm production — part of God's perfect design.

Attached to each testicle is the **epididymis**, which acts as a storage vessel for sperm after they have been produced in the testicle. While in the epididymis, the sperm further mature. When they are released, the sperm are transported through the **vas deferens** to the seminal vesicles. Both the **seminal vesicles** and the **prostate gland** aid in sperm life by producing some of the fluids that comprise the seminal fluid.

The prostate gland, located at the base of the bladder, produces the majority of the **seminal fluid** responsible for keeping the sperm alive. Seminal fluid contains sugars and other nutrients, which both feed the sperm and provide a swimming medium.

Once healthy young men reach **puberty**, they constantly produce sperm. When a man ejaculates, his seminal fluid contains approximately 200–500 million sperm.

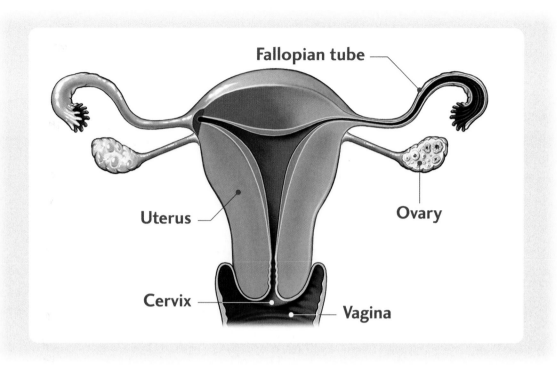

Fallopian tube

Uterus

Ovary

Cervix

Vagina

Female Anatomy

In contrast to the male, all of the major female reproductive organs are internal. A front view diagram of the female anatomy more easily illustrates the internal female reproductive organs. Note a woman's two ovaries. Each **ovary** is roughly the shape of an almond. Inside the ovaries are thousands of immature **eggs** or **ova**, each within a sac or container called a **follicle**. At birth, a female has all the eggs or ova that she will ever have — several hundred thousand. Once she reaches puberty, the ovaries begin to release eggs from the follicles, usually one egg per menstrual cycle. (Her ability to conceive is linked to the release of the eggs.) In the illustration above, the ovary seen on the right depicts the development of a follicle within a particular cycle.

Extending from either side of the upper end of the uterus are the **Fallopian tubes**. The free end of each Fallopian tube has loose finger-like projections, specifically designed to pick up the egg from the ovary once it is released. The Fallopian tube then transports the egg to the uterus.

The **uterus** (womb) is a muscular, pear-shaped organ. When a woman is having menstrual cycles, the inner lining (**endometrium**) builds up in the early part of each cycle (depicted in the illustration as a reddish-colored layer inside the uterus). The purpose of this lining is to provide a place for a newly conceived life to implant and receive nourishment.

At the base or bottom of the uterus is the **cervix**, the opening to the uterus, which extends into the **vagina**. The vagina is the organ that connects the uterus and cervix to the outside of the body. Both the cervix and important glands lining the cervix are activated at various times during the reproductive cycle.

Not shown on the diagram are the exterior parts of the female genital organs, called the **vulva**. This includes the **labia** (inner and outer folds of skin), **clitoris** (which plays an important role in female sexual response), and the vaginal opening.

Female Cycle

The female menstrual cycle can be divided into three phases. **Phase I** begins on the first day of menstrual bleeding. Following **menstruation**, which usually lasts three to five days, a woman normally experiences some days without any signs of fertility. Phase I is a time of infertility, and its length will vary with each individual woman, and even from cycle to cycle.

Phase II begins as soon as a woman's daily observations detect the onset of signs of fertility, and this fertile time lasts until several days after the time of **ovulation** (when an egg is released from the ovary). In a normal, healthy woman, Phase II will typically last approximately eight to 12 days.

The post-ovulation time is called **Phase III**. It is a time of infertility, and typically accounts for the last one-third of a healthy woman's cycle. This part of the cycle is generally consistent in length from cycle to cycle.

Notes

The three phases of the female cycle are the result of **hormones** — chemical messengers that are produced in one part of the body and transported by the bloodstream to another part of the body to bring about some physiological activity. Indeed, it is the interplay or interaction of a number of hormones that produces these three different phases of the female cycle.

Let us look at four key hormones in the physiological processes that enable the female reproductive system to function properly. Two are produced by the **pituitary gland**, a small gland at the base of the brain, and two are produced within the female reproductive organs.

Follicle Stimulating Hormone (FSH)

Follicle stimulating hormone (FSH) is released by the pituitary gland during Phase I of a woman's menstrual cycle. This hormone affects the ovaries and initiates the transition process from Phase I to Phase II. It is FSH that stimulates the immature follicles (or egg containers) in the ovaries to produce mature eggs. Usually, only one of the eggs fully matures and is ultimately released. (In rare cases, a second follicle will mature and release a second egg, but always within 24 hours of the first.) It is FSH, then, that initiates the changes in follicles that will eventually result in ovulation. As the follicle grows and develops, it produces a second key hormone — estrogen.

Estrogen

As **estrogen** increases it causes changes in a woman's body:

- the glands that lie within the cervix produce mucus that is essential for sperm survival

- the **cervical os** — the opening of the cervix — opens slightly and softens in order to allow sperm to enter

- the lining of the uterus — the endometrium — builds up with blood and tissue so that if a pregnancy occurs, the newly conceived child will have an adequate endometrial lining in which to implant

- a feedback message is sent to the pituitary gland to cause a surge in another hormone from the brain — luteinizing hormone (LH)

Luteinizing Hormone (LH)

Luteinizing hormone (LH), traveling from the pituitary gland to the ovary, signals the release of the egg from the mature follicle (**ovulation**). Once the egg is released from the ovary, the follicle, now an empty container, turns into a structure known as the **corpus luteum** (Latin for "yellow body"). The corpus luteum has a new and very important function: in addition to continuing to produce estrogen, it also now produces progesterone.

Progesterone

Progesterone has a number of effects on a woman's reproductive system. Progesterone:

- causes the cervix to close and harden

- continues to enrich blood and tissue in the endometrial lining

- causes the mucus that is being produced by the cervical glands to thicken, dry up, and/or disappear

- affects a woman's **basal body temperature** (her waking, resting temperature), which rises and remains elevated for about two weeks until the next menstruation

- sends feedback to the pituitary gland to suppress any further ovulations in that cycle

If a pregnancy has not occurred, then the progesterone level remains high until the beginning of the next cycle, when it drops and the brain receives a signal to start a new cycle.

This remarkable orchestration of four hormones — two from the brain (FSH and LH), and two from the ovary (estrogen and progesterone) — enables the female menstrual cycle to function for decades from the time of **menarche** (onset of menstruation) to **menopause** (when the female menstrual cycles end).

It is interesting to note that FSH and LH are also produced by the pituitary gland in men. FSH plays a role in sperm maturation, and LH is involved in the secretion of testosterone, the primary male hormone.

Notes

To review, Phase I begins with a woman's menstruation or period, which is triggered by a drop in progesterone, as the corpus luteum from the previous cycle ceases to function. Phase I is an infertile time of the cycle.

Phase II, the fertile time, begins when estrogen, produced by maturing follicles in the ovaries, reaches a threshold level, resulting in observable mucus production, opening and softening of the cervix, as well as the build-up of the lining of the uterus. Continuing increases in estrogen persist and the combination of high estrogen and a surge of LH, released from the pituitary, results in the release of an egg from a mature follicle. The now empty follicle is called the corpus luteum and immediately begins producing progesterone, which causes the mucus to dry, the cervix to close and harden, and the temperature to rise.

Phase III begins several days after ovulation and is an infertile time of a woman's cycle.

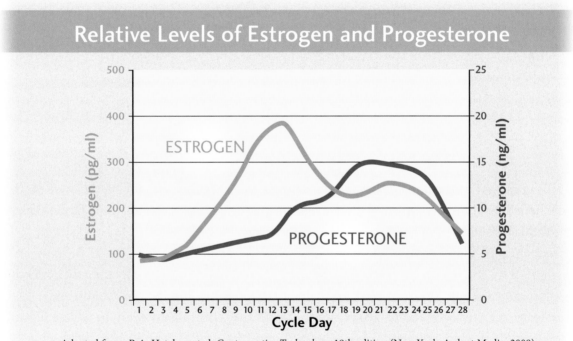

Adapted from: R.A. Hatcher, et al, *Contraceptive Technology*, 19th edition (New York: Ardent Media, 2009).

This graph depicts the levels of estrogen and progesterone at various times during the cycle. Notice that estrogen (green line) builds up during the first half of the cycle, and then drops off somewhat after the release of the progesterone following ovulation. It is easy to see that estrogen is the more dominant hormone of the two before ovulation; whereas, progesterone (blue line) is more dominant after ovulation.

It is important to note that, although one hormone is dominant in each half of the cycle, both hormones are still present throughout the cycle. A woman's body continually produces some of each of the hormones, but in differing amounts at different times. In fact, in the second half of the cycle there is still a relatively significant amount of estrogen being produced; but in comparison, progesterone production surpasses it, and hence, is the dominant hormone at that time.

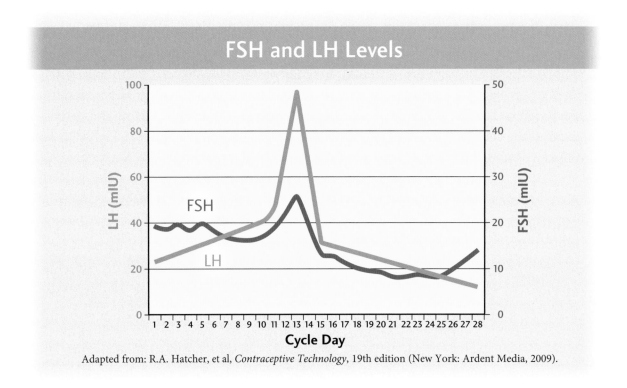

Adapted from: R.A. Hatcher, et al, *Contraceptive Technology*, 19th edition (New York: Ardent Media, 2009).

This graph shows the levels of the pituitary hormones, FSH and LH, during the cycle. Both of these hormones are at their highest levels during the early and middle parts of the cycle, with FSH (red line) at a higher level than LH (orange line) very early in the cycle. Both reach their peak amounts about mid-cycle in a typical 28-day menstrual cycle. In shorter or longer cycles, the peak amounts of FSH and LH would occur approximately two weeks before the onset of the next period. As ovulation approaches and the levels of estrogen increase, the influence of estrogen produced by the ovary signals the brain to release higher levels of LH. It is this surge of LH around mid-cycle that triggers the release of the egg from the follicle in the ovary, or ovulation. After this point, both FSH and LH play a less prominent role.

This description of how four key hormones relate to a woman's anatomy and to the phases of her menstrual cycle points out the scientific principles that form the basis for NFP. *Natural Family Planning is based on observable scientific facts.*

The four hormones discussed are responsible for the changes that occur in the female cycle. However, they also produce observable signs that most women can detect. By recognizing these observable signs, every woman who has a healthy menstrual cycle can usually identify when she is fertile and infertile. The next lesson teaches the three key measurable signs: cervical mucus, the basal body temperature and the cervix.

Measurable Signs of Hormonal Interactions 3

Lesson 3

The three phases of the menstrual cycle are the result of four hormones – estrogen, progesterone, luteinizing hormone (LH), and follicle stimulating hormone (FSH). These hormones have other observable effects as well. The Sympto-Thermal Method of NFP taught in this course is based on three key signs: the cervical mucus, basal body temperature and the cervix. These are easily noticed by any woman who has learned to watch for them.

As these signs are observed, they should be recorded on the chart included with this course (see next page). The chart provides a daily record that can be used to identify boundaries between the phases of the cycle. In knowing the phase boundaries, couples will know when they are fertile and infertile.

Notes

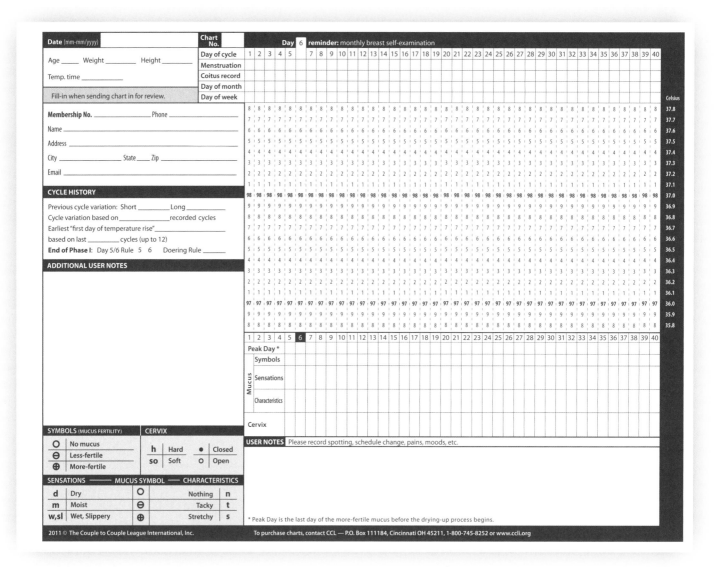

The NFP Chart

It is best to be as thorough as possible when recording information on the chart.

Date

Record the month(s) and year each time you begin a new chart.

Age/Weight/Height

A record of this information is essential if anyone else (e.g., NFP teaching couple, physician) needs to review the chart.

Temperature Time

Record the time that you normally take your basal body temperature each day.

Date (mm-mm/yyyy)	Nov-Dec 2011		Chart No.					Day	6	reminder: monthly breast

Date (mm-mm/yyyy) **Nov-Dec 2011**	Chart No.					Day 6	reminder: monthly breast

Age **23** Weight **120lbs** Height **5'5"**

Temp. time **7:00 a.m.**

Day of cycle	1	2	3	4	5		7	8	9	10	11	12	1
Menstruation													
Coitus record													
Day of month													
Day of week													

Fill-in when sending chart in for review.

Membership No. **963905**   Phone **555-555-1234**

Name **Joan Smith**

Address **12 Broadway Blvd.**

City **St. John**   State **KS** Zip **67576**

Email **joansmith4nfp@gmail.com**

CYCLE HISTORY

Previous cycle variation: Short _____ Long _____

Cycle variation based on _____ recorded cycles

Membership Number

This area is for contact information needed by any NFP teacher who may review the chart. Always include the CCL membership number (highlighted below), which can be found following "CCLID #" on your mailing label of the *Family Foundations* magazine. Chart review and assistance are provided to current CCL members who received CCL instruction through a class series or the *Home Study Course.*

```
*********************************3 DIGIT 481
P-3  P-12
CCLID # 963905    EXP DATE 8/1/2022
JOAN SMITH
12 BROADWAY BLVD
ST JOHN KS 67576-1001
IIIˌIˌˌIIˌIIˌIˌIIIIˌIIIˌIˌIIˌIˌˌIIIˌIIˌˌIIIˌIˌII
```

Family Foundations

A guide to the
FIRST YEAR OF MARRIAGE
THE DOCTOR IS IN
A GUY'S GUIDE TO NFP
HOW-TO'S: CATHOLIC STYLE

Day of cycle	1	2	3	4	5		7	8	9	10	11	12	13	14	15	16	17	18	19	20	21	22	23	24	25	26	27	28	29
Menstruation	X	X	X	/	•																						X		
Coitus record					✓		✓								✓	→													
Day of month	16	17	18	19	20	21	22	23	24	25	26	27	28	29	30	31	1	2	3	4	5	6	7	8	9	10			
Day of week	Th	F	S	S	M	T	W	Th	F	S	S	M	T	W	Th	F	S	S	M	T	W	Th	F	S	S	M			

Chart Number

Numbering charts makes it easier to track cycles of experience. Start with "1," if this is your first cycle using NFP. If experienced with another type of NFP chart or system, number the CCL chart with the next sequential number.

Day of cycle

Day 1 of the cycle is the first day of menstruation. If your period starts anytime before midnight, the entire day becomes Cycle Day 1 of the next cycle. Note that the chart holds data for up to 40 days. If a cycle becomes longer than 40 days, continue on another chart and change the numbers to "41, 42, etc."

If you are new to NFP, it is quite possible that you will begin your first chart mid-cycle. If this is the case, estimate how many days it has been since your last menstrual period started, and mark that as the first day of the cycle. If your menstrual period actually started a day or two earlier or later than you estimated, it does not matter. With the beginning of the next cycle, everything will be accurate.

Note that each chart has a reminder to make a breast self-examination every month on Cycle Day 6.

Menstruation

A new cycle begins with menstruation, thus the day before your period starts is the last day of the previous cycle. You will also see a drop in temperature around this time as the previous cycle is ending and the new cycle is beginning.

When recording menstruation, use an "X" for normal or heavy flow, a slash "/" for lighter flow, and a dot "•" for very light flow or spotting. For example, if your next period starts on Cycle Day 27, an "X" or "/" should be recorded on Cycle Day 27, which becomes the first day of the new cycle. The previous cycle would then be 26 days in length.

Note that some women experience spotting before their next period — this is recorded on the current cycle. When the flow increases to light or heavy, or spotting is associated with the temperature drop, the new cycle begins.

Coitus record

Coitus is another term for marital relations. Coitus is used because it is a less familiar term, especially to children who may see the chart.

The days of marital relations are recorded with a check mark on the chart in the coitus row.

You can choose whether or not to keep a complete record of your marital relations. However, for interpretation, it is best to record at least the last coitus in Phase I, any coitus in Phase II and the first coitus in Phase III.

Day of month/Day of week

These notations link the monthly cycle with the calendar, and provide important clues about events that may influence the cycle (vacations, holidays, an upcoming wedding, etc.). It is very helpful to note weekends on the chart because habits change on weekends. Write the first letter of the day of the week (M–T–W, etc.) in the day of the week row.

Notes

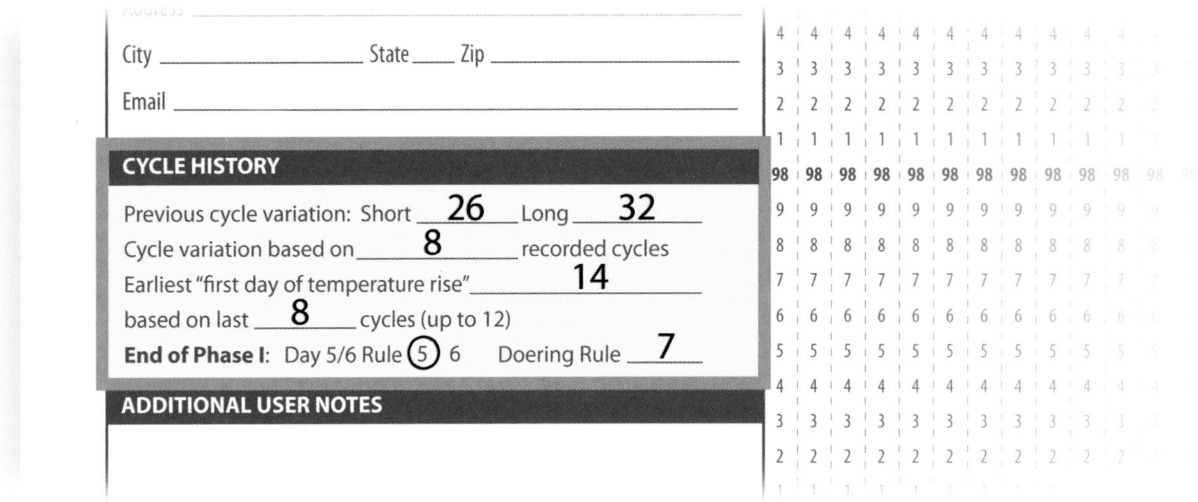

City _____ State _____ Zip _____

Email _____

CYCLE HISTORY

Previous cycle variation: Short ___**26**___ Long ___**32**___

Cycle variation based on ___**8**___ recorded cycles

Earliest "first day of temperature rise" ___**14**___

based on last ___**8**___ cycles (up to 12)

End of Phase I: Day 5/6 Rule ⑤ 6   Doering Rule ___**7**___

ADDITIONAL USER NOTES

Cycle History

This box is used to record data from past cycles that is needed when calculating the length of Phase I in future cycles.

The "Previous cycle variation" line is used to record the shortest and longest cycles a woman has experienced.

This information should be updated at the start of each new cycle on the new chart. For example, if your previous shortest cycle was 26 days and you experience a 24-day cycle, the 24-day cycle becomes the new shortest cycle on your next chart. Similarly, if you have a longer cycle than previously noted, that cycle becomes the new longest cycle and should be noted on the new chart of your next cycle.

The remaining lines in the Cycle History box track information necessary for applying certain rules that will be explained in Class 2.

Notes

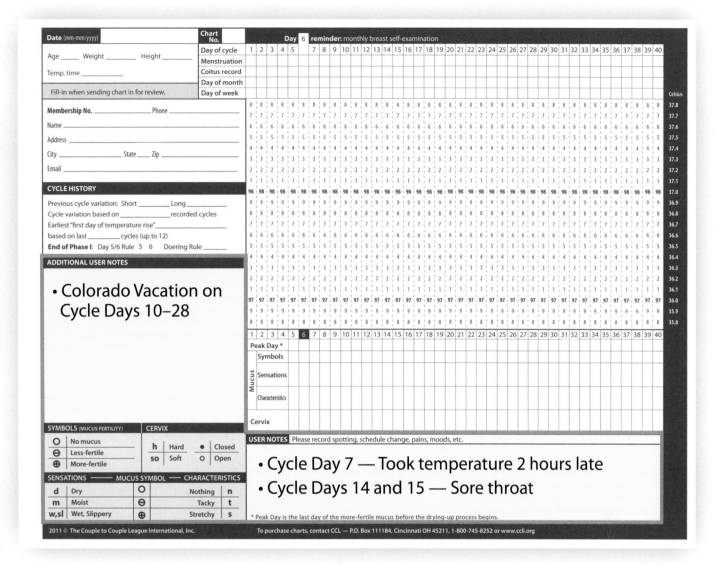

User Notes and Additional User Notes

These areas are used to record any significant changes in lifestyle during the cycle. Note any medications taken, illnesses, trips, changes in sleeping arrangements, or stressful situations that occur. Label the comments by cycle day. These areas can also be used to record more specific information about the daily mucus observations.

Notes

Key Observable Signs

These next sections will provide detailed information about the key observable signs of fertility — cervical mucus, temperature and cervix. If you are new to this information, it may seem very personal and possibly embarrassing. While this is a very natural reaction, it is good to remember that God has given us these common signs of fertility, and it is important for both married and engaged couples to understand them.

The Mucus Sign

Cervical mucus appears in response to estrogen and:

- is a natural fluid of the body just like tears or saliva
- is healthy, clean and necessary for the proper functioning of a woman's reproductive system
- is an aid to fertility
  - provides a swimming medium for sperm
  - provides nutrients for sperm
  - enables sperm to survive for days in a woman's cervix area where the sperm temporarily "take up residence" while waiting for ovulation
- helps filter out abnormal sperm so they do not reach the egg

Identify mucus

- What you feel and sense (sensations)
- What you see and touch (characteristics)

When there is no mucus, sperm life is very short, measured in hours, because the normal vaginal environment is very acidic and hostile to sperm.

Women can easily learn to become aware of their cervical mucus. This awareness is comprised of two facets: **sensations**, which are what a woman feels and senses; and **characteristics**, which are what she sees and touches.

Identifying Mucus Sensations — What You Feel and Sense

Identifying mucus sensations is accomplished in two ways: by awareness of what you feel and sense throughout the day, and by awareness of what you feel and sense when you wipe during your bathroom visits.

One way to sense mucus is to detect feelings of dryness, moistness, or wetness as you go about your normal activities throughout the day. These sensations will occur around the vulva area, and may first be noticeable when bending over, walking or going up the stairs as the folds of the labia move against each other. You may notice a feeling of dryness; a feeling of being moist, sticky or damp; or a feeling of wetness similar to what occurs just before your period starts — as if something is running. (Sometimes mucus can become so fluid it seems like water. This watery sensation is very fertile.)

Identify mucus

- What you feel and sense (sensations)
  — Awareness throughout day
  — Awareness when you wipe

It takes a lot less mucus to be able to "feel" or "sense" it than it does to actually "see" it.

A second way to detect mucus sensations is through an awareness of what you feel and sense when you wipe with toilet paper each time you use the bathroom. You may notice that it feels rough, scratchy and dry. Or, you may notice that it feels lubricative or slippery — similar to your hands after applying lotion. Once you begin to regularly assess these two sensations of mucus — throughout the day and when wiping — you will be amazed at your ability to detect even slight changes.

Be attentive to the sensations of mucus as soon as your period subsides, or by Cycle Day 5, whichever comes first. (In the early part of the cycle, you may only notice mucus sensations one time on a particular day.)

Notes

Recording Mucus Sensations

To record the sensations that you feel, place the following letter(s) in the Sensations row on your chart at the end of the day:

- Record "**d**" when you have a sensation of dryness throughout the day
- Record "**m**" when you have a sensation of moistness, stickiness, or dampness at any time during the day
- Record "**w**" when you have a sensation of wetness at any time during the day
- Record "**d**" when you have a sensation of dryness when wiping each time you use the bathroom
- Record "**sl**" when you have a sensation of slipperiness when wiping at any time during the day

Note that you only record "d" if you feel completely dry the entire day and when wiping. For example, if you have dry sensations most of the day, but also feel wet and/or slippery at least one time, you record "w" and/or "sl" respectively. *It is important that you always record the most fertile sensation detected each day.* (This will be explained in Lesson 5.)

Recording Mucus Sensations › Practice

	1	2	3	4	5	6	7	8	9	10	11	12	13	14	15	16	17	18	19	20	21	22	23	24	25	26	27	28	29	30
Peak Day *																														
	Symbols																													
Mucus	**Sensations**																													
	Characteristics																													

If you are attending the classes, you will complete this exercise in class. If you are using this Student Guide as a Home Study Course, see page 165 in Appendix A for the data to be recorded on the above practice chart. After completing the exercise, check your answers on page 177 in Appendix B.

Identifying Mucus Characteristics — What You See and Touch

In addition to identifying the presence of mucus through sensations, you can identify the characteristics of mucus by seeing it and/or checking its qualities. If mucus is present, there will be a residue remaining on the toilet paper after wiping. If you observe mucus on the toilet paper, check its characteristics.

Mucus characteristics can be classified in three ways:

- **Nothing**: no mucus is observed.

- **Tacky**: mucus that is thick in appearance and may have some stretch, but typically breaks when pulled apart (it is not as elastic as stretchy mucus); also described as sticky, gummy, thick, pasty, creamy, or clumpy.

- **Stretchy**: mucus that stretches repeatedly when pulled apart; also described as very elastic, thin, stringy, and resembling raw egg-white.[1]

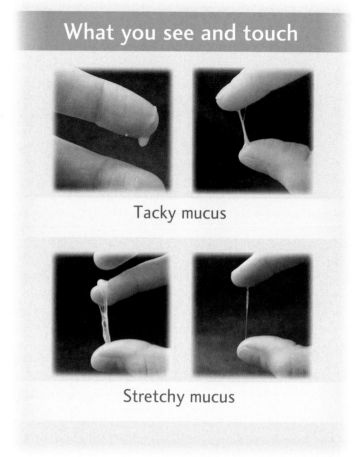

What you see and touch

Tacky mucus

Stretchy mucus

When your mucus discharge first starts in each cycle, it tends to be thick or tacky, and it will not stretch very far. Later in Phase II, the mucus becomes fluid and stretchy.

Observing Mucus Characteristics

Observing mucus characteristics is very simple.

1. Check for mucus at each bathroom visit. Be sure to begin your mucus observations as soon as your period lessens, or by the fifth day after menstruation begins (Cycle Day 5), whichever comes first. Some women may not have much mucus, or may only notice it once during the day. Therefore, checking with each bathroom visit increases your chance of observing it.

> Start checking for mucus as soon as your period lessens, or by Cycle Day 5, whichever comes first

---

[1] For additional pictures of mucus, see Reference Guide, pages 237–240.

2. Use folded, white, unscented toilet paper.

3. Wipe from front to back before or after you urinate or have a bowel movement. (Some women cannot adequately detect mucus characteristics after going to the bathroom. Thus, checking before going may provide more useful information.) Visible mucus sits on the paper, whereas urine soaks into the paper.

4. If there is enough mucus present on the toilet paper, pick some up between the thumb and forefinger or lift it with an edge of the paper and test its elasticity by seeing if it can be pulled apart.

5. Determine the mucus characteristic:

   - Is it tacky or sticky? (*tacky*)

   - Does it stretch just a little and break? (*tacky*)

   - Does it stretch repeatedly without breaking when pulled apart? (*stretchy*)

   - Is it thin and stringy? (*stretchy*)

   - Does it resemble raw egg white? (*stretchy*)

> Mucus sits on the tissue paper; urine soaks in.

Recording Mucus Characteristics

To record the characteristics that you observe, place one of the following letters in the Characteristics row on your chart at the end of the day.

- Record "**n**" for *nothing* — no mucus is observed.

- Record "**t**" for *tacky* — sticky, gummy, thick, pasty, creamy, clumpy, breaks when stretched repeatedly.

- Record "**s**" for *stretchy* — elastic, stringy, resembles raw egg-white, stretches repeatedly when pulled apart.

Note that if you do not observe any mucus, then you record an "n" (for "nothing"). If you notice tacky mucus once, you should record a "t." Similarly, if you notice stretchy mucus even once during the day, you should record an "s." *Remember that it is important to always record the most fertile observation each day.* (This will be explained in Lesson 5.)

Notes

1	2	3	4	5	6	7	8	9	10	11	12	13	14	15	16	17	18	19	20	21	22	23	24	25	26	27	28	29	30
Peak Day *																													
	Symbols																												
Mucus	**Sensations**	d	d	d	d	m	m	w	w sl	w sl	w sl	m	m	d	d	d	d	d	d	d	d	d	d	d	d	d	d
	Characteristics																												

If you are attending the classes, you will complete this exercise in class. If you are using this Student Guide as a Home Study Course, see page 166 in Appendix A for the data to be recorded on the above practice chart. After completing the exercise, check your answers on page 177 in Appendix B.

The Temperature Sign

The basal body temperature is the temperature of the human body at rest or upon awakening, unaffected by food, drink or activity. A woman's basal body temperature rises slightly after ovulation in response to progesterone, so recording the basal body temperature throughout the menstrual cycle provides important information.

Take your temperature at the same time every day (or at least within one-half hour of your waking time). Make a note on your chart if you take your temperature earlier or later than this acceptable interval. Note: Getting up briefly during the night (i.e., to care for an infant) will not affect your normal waking temperature, as long as you get a minimum of six hours of sleep in total and have rested again for at least one hour before taking your temperature.

With a digital thermometer, you can take your temperature in a minute. To maintain accuracy, it is a good idea to stay in bed while you take it. Some models beep differently when taking the temperature than when the reading is complete. Check your model's directions for details.

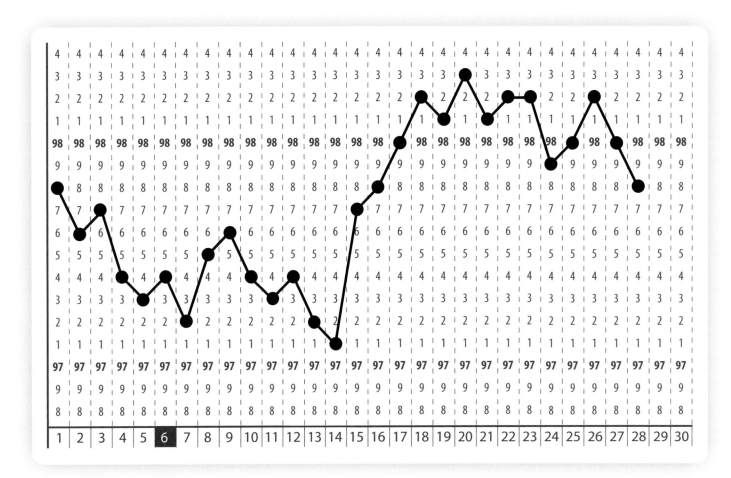

Recording the Temperature

After taking your temperature, record it on the chart. With a digital thermometer, it is not necessary to record your temperature immediately since the thermometer will hold the temperature until it is reset. If your thermometer measures hundredths of a degree, or if your temperature falls between the numbers on a glass thermometer, round it down to the next tenth of a degree or disregard the hundreths place altogether. Measuring to a hundreth of a degree is not necessary.

Note regarding Celsius temperatures: The Celsius temperatures on the right side of the temperature graph are not meant to equal the Fahrenheit temperatures. If you want to use the Celsius readings, ignore the Fahrenheit numbers.

For temperatures when doing shift work, or when changing time zones, see the Reference Guide, p. 247–248.

The Cervix Sign

The third key observable sign is the cervix, and it is an optional sign with regard to the Sympto-Thermal Method of NFP. The structure of the cervix is sometimes compared to the narrow end of a pear with the stem removed. It has an indentation or dimple where the cervical opening, or os, is located.

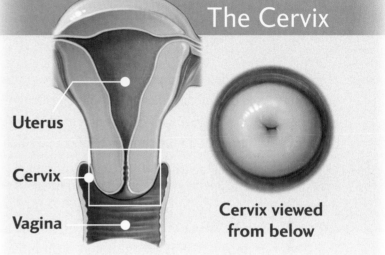

Like cervical mucus, the cervix changes in response to both estrogen and progesterone. It is closed and hard (i.e., it feels similar to end of your nose) until the beginning of the fertile time.

As ovulation approaches, the cervix undergoes the following changes in response to the hormone estrogen:

- it opens slightly
- the tip becomes softer (i.e., it feels like your facial lips)

These are gradual changes that usually occur over a period of a week or more.

The cervix changes in response to estrogen and progesterone

- Closed and hard until the beginning of Phase II

- Opens and softens in response to estrogen

- Closes and hardens during Phase III in response to progesterone

After ovulation, in response to progesterone, the cervix closes and hardens again. When the cervix closes completely and the mucus thickens in the cervical canal after ovulation, sperm migration decreases and other organisms cannot enter the uterus. These post-ovulation changes occur faster than those preceding ovulation, and usually coincide with changes in the other fertility signs.

Observing the Cervix

Even though the cervix is an internal organ, you can learn to observe the changes in your cervix by performing a personal examination. This requires inserting your finger through the vaginal canal and gently touching the cervix.

There are techniques listed in the Reference Guide (page 210) for checking the cervix. Find what works best for you, and use this same procedure each time.

Use special care when examining the cervix because it is a delicate part of the body. Keep your fingernails trimmed so that you do not accidentally injure it. Make sure your hands are clean: preferably, wash with mild, unscented, non-deodorant soap, as residues from chemical perfumes, deodorants and so forth can irritate the vaginal tissues of some women.

Like checking for mucus, you should start to make the cervix observation when your period lessens, or by Cycle Day 5, whichever comes first. Check the cervix once or twice a day when you visit the bathroom, but only in the afternoon or evening. The cervix exam should not be done in the morning because the muscles that support the uterus contract a bit during the night as you sleep, thus making the cervix harder to reach; the muscles stretch a bit after you have been up and around for a while.

Also, do not make the cervix observation right after a bowel movement because that may cause the cervical os to open a bit or change its position.

Although the cervix observation is optional, it can be a helpful sign that:

- provides a woman with a more complete picture of her fertility
- can reduce the number of days of abstinence
- can help during times of transition, such as postpartum (after eight weeks) or premenopause

Recording the Cervix Sign

In the Cervix row of the chart:

- Record a "•" if the cervix is closed
- Record a "O" if the cervix is open
- Record an "**h**" if the cervix is hard
- Record "**so**" if the cervix is soft

You can vary the diameter of the circle to denote the amount of openness.

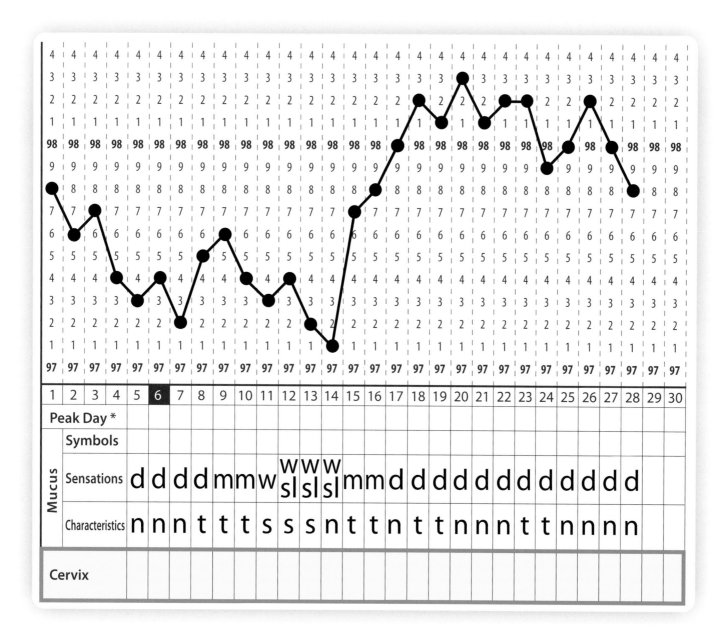

If you are attending the classes, you will complete this exercise in class. If you are using this Student Guide as a Home Study Course, see page 167 in Appendix A for the data to be recorded on the above practice chart. After completing the exercise, check your answers on page 178 in Appendix B.

Other Less Common Signs

In addition to the three key observable signs, many women experience one or more less common signs of fertility. They may notice an additional change in the cervix — it may rise around the time of ovulation. Other symptoms women may experience during Phase II could include:

- increased libido
- breast tenderness
- abdominal bloating
- swelling of the vulva
- ovulation pain

If you become aware of any of these less common signs, be sure to record them in the User Notes area of the chart. These signs are individual and personal, but they will help you understand the unique way in which your body communicates its fertility.

Conclusion

The Sympto-Thermal Method of NFP encourages both the husband and the wife to communicate on a very intimate level. Both spouses become actively involved in reading the language of the body. For instance, in some households the husband takes his wife's temperature each morning; in others he might remind his wife to take her temperature each morning. And some husbands record all of the information on the chart at the end of each day. What they have learned is that active involvement of both husband and wife in observing and recording the data engages the couple in deeper communication. They develop an awe in the beauty of their creation as male and female. They love each other as they are at any given moment, and their sexual intimacy is an experience that is profound, holy and good.

The next lesson will teach the rules for interpreting the key observable signs.

Interpreting the Signs of Fertility

4

Lesson 4

You have already learned that the signs of fertility change throughout the cycle based on changing levels of hormones. For example, as ovulation approaches and passes, cervical mucus appears and disappears; daily temperatures will shift from a lower to a higher level; and the cervix changes in significant ways that can help confirm the other two signs. You have also learned how to observe and record these changes.

Now you will learn to interpret these observations in order to determine the fertile and infertile times of your cycle. Scientific research and the collective experience of thousands of couples practicing NFP over several decades have led to the development of guidelines — or "rules" — for identifying the phases of the cycle. Knowing these rules and applying them to the evidence on the chart is the "art" of Natural Family Planning.

Interpreting the Mucus Sign

- The **absence** of mucus sensations **and** characteristics usually indicates **infertility**

- The **presence** of mucus sensations **or** characteristics usually indicates **fertility**

- Two types: **less-fertile** and **more-fertile**

Interpreting the Mucus Sign

The absence of cervical mucus usually is a sign of infertility, and the presence of mucus usually indicates fertility.

As you know from previous lessons, the cycle progresses from menstruation to ovulation in response to hormones. The level of estrogen rises, which causes the cervix to produce mucus. The mucus coats the vaginal walls, and gradually becomes more liquefied, watery or runny, and some of it flows outside the body. The more liquefied the mucus, the better it can help sperm reach the egg. After ovulation, when progesterone levels increase, the mucus becomes thicker, and it usually dries up. Although there are many qualities of mucus produced by this change in hormone levels, the mucus basically falls into two categories: less-fertile and more-fertile.

Less-Fertile Mucus — Sensations

As soon as estrogen levels reach a certain point, cervical mucus can be felt or sensed. For many women, the first thing they notice is a slight sensation of moistness, dampness or stickiness on the labia. As ovulation approaches, these sensations become more pronounced. It should be noted that while mucus characteristics may be easier to detect, the mucus sensations are just as important as what is visible on the toilet paper. In fact, because mucus can be sensed at much smaller quantities than what is necessary to see it, this awareness of the presence of mucus sensations can be key in knowing the earliest onset of Phase II.

Less-Fertile Mucus — Characteristics

When estrogen levels begin to rise, the mucus produced is usually "tacky" and does not stretch easily. Instead, it tends to break when pulled apart. Women have described it as sticky, gummy, thick, pasty, creamy, clumpy, or having some stretch, but thicker than the more-fertile

Less-fertile mucus characteristics:

- Breaks easily
- Tacky and very little stretch

type of mucus. There are several ways to describe it, and each woman finds her own way to do so.

Note that we have not called this mucus "non-fertile or infertile." It is still a sign of some estrogen activity, and pregnancy can occur from sexual relations when less-fertile mucus is present prior to ovulation in normal menstrual cycles.

More-Fertile Mucus — Sensations

As the estrogen level continues to increase and reach its highest level right around the time of ovulation, the amount of water in the mucus increases as well. The mucus can thin or liquefy so much that it literally runs out of the vagina. Thus, many women will experience a strong feeling or sensation of wetness, and/or slipperiness when wiping. In fact, sometimes no mucus is visible at all, and a woman just senses a strong feeling of wetness and/or feels very slippery.

More-Fertile Mucus — Characteristics

With higher levels of estrogen, the mucus characteristics change as well. The mucus becomes stretchy, thin, stringy, or may resemble raw egg white. Notice the qualities of the mucus in the photos on the right. More-fertile mucus develops elasticity; in other words, a woman can stretch it repeatedly without breaking it.

More-fertile mucus characteristics:

- Resembles raw egg-white
- Stretchy

The highly fertile characteristics of stretchy, thin, and stringy mucus will normally accompany the more-fertile sensations of wetness outside the vagina or slipperiness when wiping. If these signs do not seem to coincide on a regular basis, contact a CCL teaching couple or the CCL central office for assistance.

Mucus Symbols

The daily goal of observing mucus is to identify the most-fertile type of mucus felt or seen throughout the day, and record your observations with a symbol. At the end of the day, take into account the record of both sensations and characteristics, and classify those recordings as "no mucus," "less-fertile" or "more-fertile."

Note that a woman could easily observe more than one type of mucus during a single day. For example, she could experience less-fertile mucus in the morning and more-fertile mucus in the evening, or no mucus in the morning and less-fertile mucus later that day. When deciding on a symbol, consider only the "most-fertile" mucus sensation and/or characteristic observed that day.

Charting the Mucus Sign

Symbols for mucus

◯	No mucus	d, n
⊖	Less-fertile	m, t
⊕	More-fertile	w, sl, s

- Record "◯" for No mucus, if the day was totally without mucus, including no sensation of mucus.

- Record "⊖" for Less-Fertile, if all the mucus observed was a less-fertile type.

- Record "⊕" for More-Fertile, if any of the more-fertile mucus was present, either through a sensation or a characteristic.

These symbols will be important in helping identify the change to the infertile time after ovulation, Phase III.

Notes

Recording Mucus Symbols › Practice

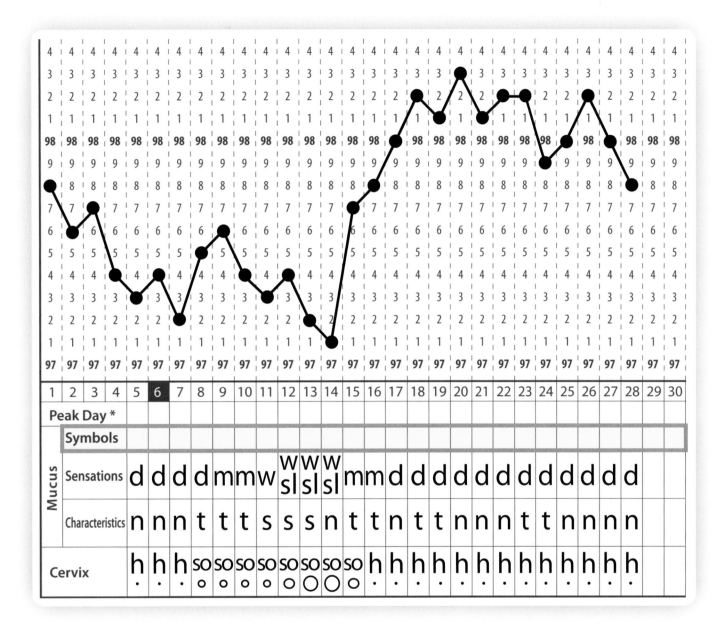

	1	2	3	4	5	6	7	8	9	10	11	12	13	14	15	16	17	18	19	20	21	22	23	24	25	26	27	28	29	30
Peak Day *																														
Symbols																														
Mucus Sensations	d	d	d	d	m	m	w	w sl	w sl	w sl	m	m	d	d	d	d	d	d	d	d	d	d	d							
Characteristics	n	n	n	t	t	t	s	s	s	n	t	t	n	t	t	n	n	n	t	t	n	n	n							
Cervix	h ·	h ·	h ·	so ∘	so ∘	so ∘	so ∘	so ∘	so ∘	so ◯	so ◯	so ∘	h ·	h ·	h ·	h ·	h ·	h ·	h ·	h ·	h ·	h ·	h ·	h ·						

If you are attending the classes, you will complete this exercise in class. If you are using this Student Guide as a Home Study Course, apply a symbol to each cycle day on the chart and then check your answers on page 179 in Appendix B.

Standard Mucus Pattern

You have learned how to interpret the mucus sign on each individual day; now you will learn how to interpret the mucus pattern within a cycle.

Typically, a woman may first notice sensations of mucus — a moist, damp, or sticky feeling — while going about her daily activities, or when she wipes with toilet paper before or after using the bathroom. This can occur as early as a week or so before ovulation. These sensations are distinctly different from the dry feeling she typically observes after the end of her period, and they become stronger with more pronounced wetness present while estrogen builds until ovulation occurs. The wet feelings reach a peak right around ovulation.

The slippery feeling may not be noticeable to a woman until several days after she first notices wetness, as the mucus changes more with increasing amounts of estrogen being produced. Note that the wet and slippery sensations are usually very pronounced at the time of ovulation.

The characteristics of mucus are tacky and stretchy. A woman will typically experience tacky mucus first for a few days before she observes the stretchy, stringy type of mucus. Again, the mucus changes characteristics over several days as ovulation approaches because of the increase in estrogen. Closer to ovulation, the mucus acquires the more-fertile characteristics, such as stretchy, stringy, elastic, or resembling raw egg white.

Peak Day

At ovulation, as the progesterone levels begin to rise, the mucus changes: the highly wet and/or slippery sensations change dramatically, as do the stretchy mucus characteristics. A woman may yet feel some sensations of mucus (i.e., moist, damp, or sticky), but the more pronounced wet and/or slippery sensations will have disappeared, or she may feel totally dry. The visible characteristics of mucus change as well: the mucus thickens, becomes denser or more opaque and may eventually disappear altogether. This is referred to as the start of the drying up process — the point at which more-fertile mucus sensations and characteristics are no longer present. In fact, when this process occurs, the start of it is usually very dramatic. A woman will notice a distinct change in her mucus sensations and characteristics. At one time, it produces a very wet or slippery sensation, and appears stretchy, thin, or stringy, and then — almost from one bathroom visit to the next, or from one day to the next — she will note that it has changed. No longer does she have a highly wet sensation or a slippery feeling, nor is the mucus as elastic or stringy as it was before. There will be a BIG change. She may even comment to herself, "Wow, I can really tell a difference!"

> When the drying-up process starts, it is usually very dramatic. A woman can notice a difference from one bathroom visit to the next, or from one day to the next.

Peak Day is the last day of the more-fertile mucus before the drying-up process begins

Symbols		⊕	⊕	⊕	⊕	⊕	⊕	⊕	⊕	○	○	⊖
Sensations	w	w	w	w	w	sl	w sl	w sl	d	d	d	
Characteristics	n	t	t	t	s	s	s	s	n	n	t	

After the change continues for two to three days, a woman can then establish her **Peak Day** of mucus. Peak Day is the last day of the more-fertile mucus before the drying-up process begins. It is frequently the day of ovulation. Research shows that ovulation almost always occurs ± three days of Peak Day.[1]

Peak Day is easily spotted on the chart as it will be the last day with a more-fertile mucus symbol (⊕) prior to days of less-fertile mucus symbols (⊖) and/or no mucus symbols (○). When determined, Peak Day should be noted with a "**P**" placed on the chart in the Peak Day row.

It is important to remember two things about Peak Day. First, it happens after a build-up of mucus from less-fertile to more-fertile over several days. Second, Peak Day is identified in retrospect; in other words, after it has happened. A woman will not know at the time that a particular day of more-fertile mucus will be the last one in that cycle. It is not until a drying-up process has been underway that a Peak Day can be confirmed.

The drying-up process begins when a woman notices a distinct *change* in her mucus from the highly wet and/or slippery sensations (w, sl) to something less than that (m). Stretchy mucus (s), if present, will thicken, and become more dense or opaque, but may still stretch some (t). Remember to note the amount of stretch on your chart.

---

[1] Thomas W. Hilgers, Guy E. Abraham and Denis Cavanaugh, "Natural Family Planning: I. The peak symptom and estimated time of ovulation." *Obstetrics and Gynecology* 52:5 (November 1978) 575–582; Table 3, 579.

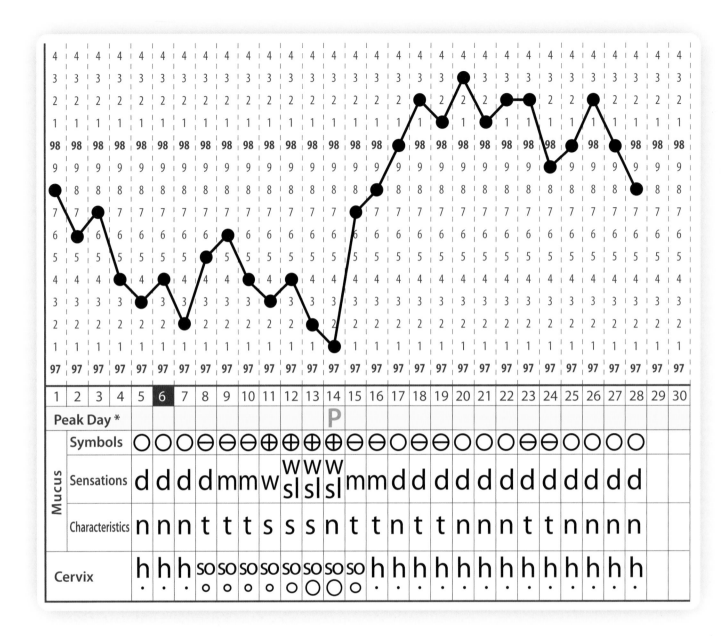

In the chart above, you can see that Peak Day is identified with a "**P**" on Cycle Day 14, the last day of the more-fertile mucus before a drying-up process began. The last day of more-fertile mucus was identified by looking at the Symbols row on the chart. In this case, Cycle Day 14 is the last of several days with a more-fertile mucus symbol, and it is followed by a change to less-fertile or drying-up mucus. Therefore, Peak Day is Cycle Day 14.

Notes

Identifying Peak Day › Practice 1, 2, 3

⌄ Practice 1

Day	1	2	3	4	5	6	7	8	9	10	11	12	13	14	15	16	17	18	19	20	21	22	23	24	25	26	27	28	29	30	31	32	33
Peak Day *																																	
Symbols	○	○	○	○	○	⊖	⊕	⊖	⊕	⊕	⊖	⊖	⊖	⊖	⊖	⊖	⊖	⊖	⊖	⊖	⊖	⊖	⊖	⊖	⊖	⊖							
Sensations	d	d	d	d	d	m	w	sl	sl	sl	sl	m	d	d	d	d	d	d	d	d	d	d	d	d	d								
Characteristics	n	n	n	n	n	t	t	t	s	s	t	t	t	t	t	t	t	t	t	t	t	t	t	t	t								
Cervix																																	

⌄ Practice 2

Day	1	2	3	4	5	6	7	8	9	10	11	12	13	14	15	16	17	18	19	20	21	22	23	24	25	26	27	28	29	30	31	32	33
Peak Day *																																	
Symbols	○	○	○	○	⊕	⊖	⊕	⊕	⊕	⊕	⊕	⊕	⊕	⊕	⊕	○	○	○	○	⊖	○	⊖	○	⊖	○	○	○	⊖	⊖	⊖			
Sensations	d	d	d	d	w	d	w	sl	sl	sl	sl	sl	w	w	d	d	d	d	d	d	d	d	d	d	d	d	d	d	d	d			
Characteristics	n	n	n	n	n	t	t	s	s	s	s	n	n	n	n	n	n	n	n	t	n	n	t	n	n	n	t	t	t				
Cervix																																	

⌄ Practice 3

Day	1	2	3	4	5	6	7	8	9	10	11	12	13	14	15	16	17	18	19	20	21	22	23	24	25	26	27	28	29	30	31	32	33
Peak Day *																																	
Symbols	○	○	○	○	○	○	⊕	⊖	⊕	⊕	⊕	⊕	⊕	⊕	○	○	○	○	○	○	○												
Sensations	d	d	d	d	d	d	sl	d	sl	sl	w	sl	sl	sl	sl	d	d	d	d	d	d	d											
Characteristics	n	n	n	n	n	t	t	t	s	s	s	s	s	n	n	n	n	n	n	n													
Cervix																																	

*If you are attending the classes, you will complete this exercise in class. If you are using this Student Guide as a Home Study Course, find Peak Day on the three charts above and place a "**P**" for that day in the Peak Day row of each chart. Check your answers on page 179 in Appendix B.*

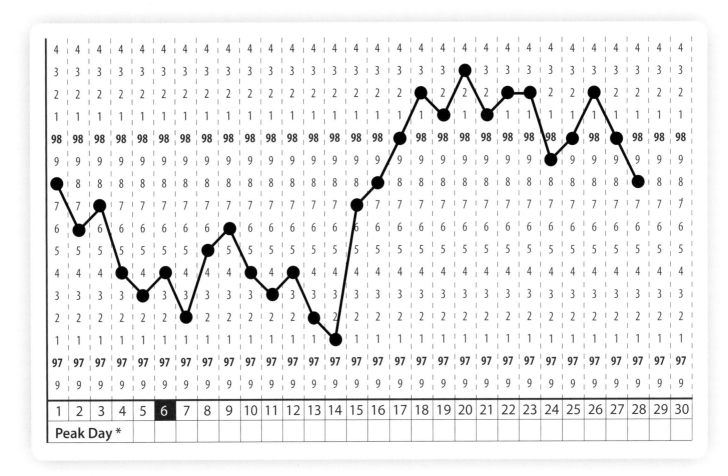

Interpreting the Temperature Sign

- The cycle has a shift in temperature after ovulation caused by the increase of progesterone

- Typical cycle has two temperature levels — low prior to ovulation; high after ovulation

- A thermal shift indicates that ovulation has already occurred

- Scientific knowledge dates back to 1930s

Recall that progesterone is released by the corpus luteum, the empty egg sac left in the ovary after ovulation. The increasing presence of progesterone in a woman's system causes changes to her metabolism, increasing her basal body temperature slightly. On the chart, the increase of progesterone can be seen because there will be two distinct temperature levels in the cycle — a lower one before ovulation and a higher one after ovulation — and the difference is usually about 0.4° Fahrenheit (F).

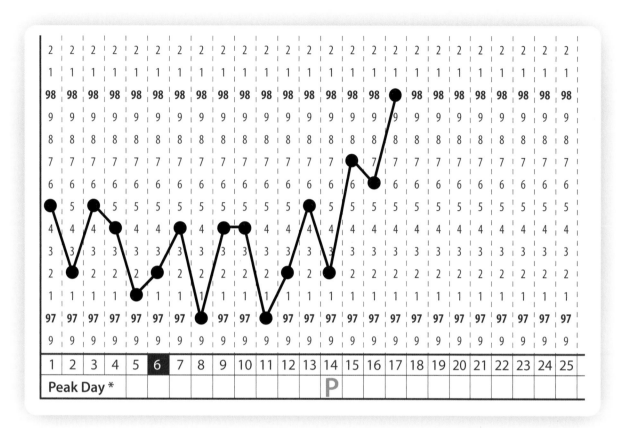

This **thermal shift** signals that ovulation has already occurred. The science behind the temperature sign is well-established. It was first noticed in the nineteenth century. Then during the 1930s, Fr. Wilhelm Hillebrand of Germany documented this finding in women's cycles. At that time, it was determined that three days of sustained higher temperatures above a lower pattern indicated that ovulation had taken place, and that a woman was no longer fertile.

In the above chart, it is clear from this woman's temperature pattern that by Cycle Day 17 there is a distinct temperature rise. Now, you will learn how to interpret this temperature pattern.

Finding the lower level of temperatures is the key to identifying the rise and determining that a thermal shift has occurred.

Begin by looking for three temperatures that are higher than the six previous normal temperatures. To be certain that the three rising temperatures are indeed part of a true rise (connected to ovulation), look for these temperatures close to Peak Day. (Abnormal temperatures — such as a high temperature from a fever — will be discussed later.)

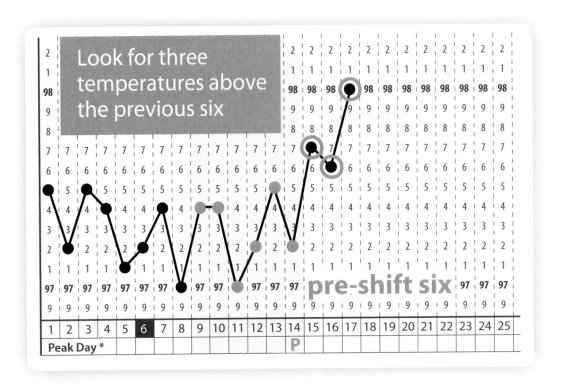

In this chart, the temperatures for Cycle Days 15, 16, and 17 are above the temperatures for Cycle Days 9–14, and they are near Peak Day. The six lower temperatures before the temperature rise are used to determine the lower temperature level. These six lower temperatures are called the **pre-shift six**.

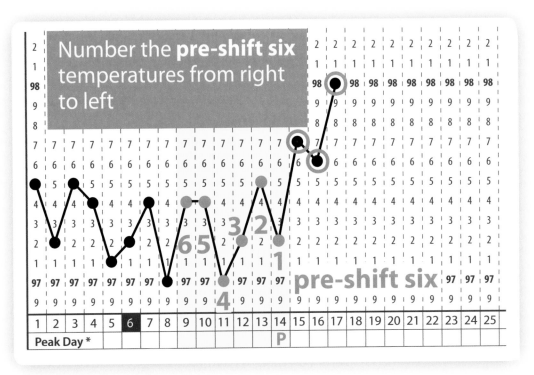

Once the pre-shift six are determined, number them backwards on the chart from right to left.

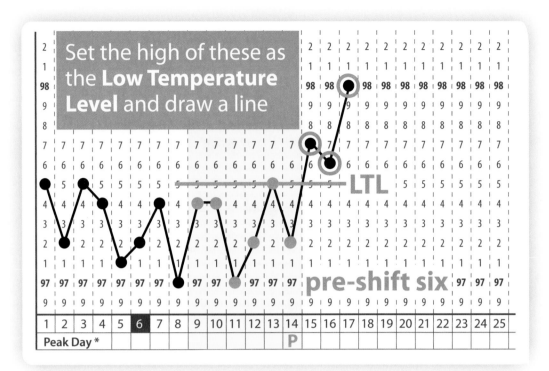

Next, find the highest of those six temperatures and draw a horizontal line through it. This is the **Low Temperature Level (LTL)** — the highest of the pre-shift six. From this base, the degree of temperature rise can be accurately measured.

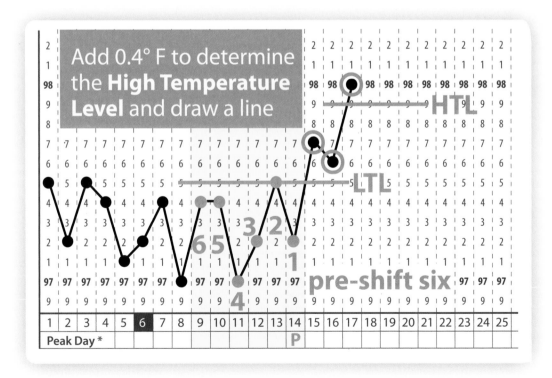

A horizontal line is drawn 0.4° F above the LTL. This is called the **High Temperature Level (HTL)**.

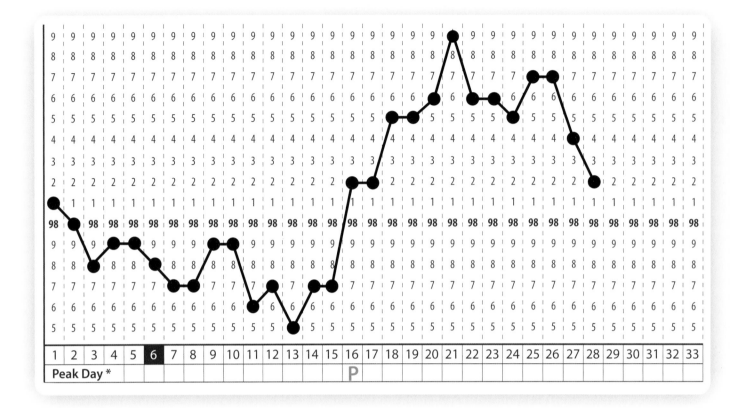

If you are attending the classes, you will complete this exercise in class. If you are using this Student Guide as a Home Study Course, follow the steps below, then check your answers on page 179 in Appendix B.

Steps to follow when interpreting the temperature sign:

- Identify the thermal shift by finding three temperatures near Peak Day that are higher than the previous six temperatures — the pre-shift six.

- Number the pre-shift six from right to left.

- Draw a horizontal line at the highest temperature of the pre-shift six. This becomes the Low Temperature Level (LTL).

- Add 0.4° F to the LTL and draw another horizontal line. This becomes the High Temperature Level (HTL).

Notes

Interpreting the Cervix Sign

Interpreting changes in the cervix is a bit more straightforward than interpreting the temperature sign. Recall that the cervix undergoes changes during the cycle. Early in the cycle, as well as after ovulation, the cervix is closed and hard. Therefore, a closed and hard cervix is a sign of infertility.

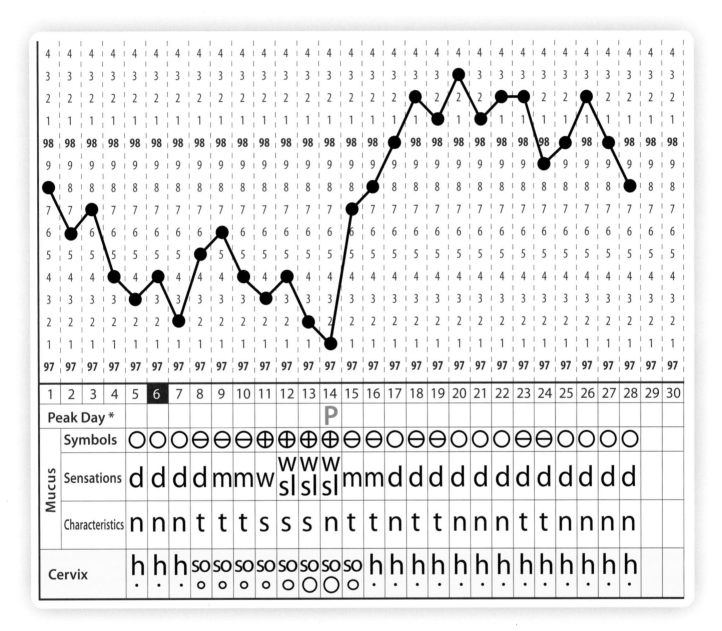

As ovulation approaches, the higher level of estrogen causes the cervix to open up and soften. This is a definite sign of fertility. The above chart shows that the cervix is closed and hard toward the beginning of the cycle (Cycle Days 5–7) — a sign of infertility. On Cycle Day 8, it begins to open, with increasing openness on Cycle Days 12–14, all signs of fertility. By Cycle Day 16 it is closed and hard, and it remains closed and hard for the rest of the cycle — a sign of infertility.

Notice that in the Cervix row of the chart, the cervix is shown as either closed or open and as either hard or soft. Both the closed/open signs and the hard/soft signs are necessary when using the cervix observation to help determine the start of Phase III.

The Sympto-Thermal Rule

Now it is time to put all the information together to determine the time of post-ovulation infertility, or Phase III. With the tools you have learned in recording and interpreting the signs, it is possible to determine the infertile time after ovulation with amazing accuracy and effectiveness. The rule that follows is called the Sympto-Thermal Rule (ST Rule), and when used properly it is at least 99% effective in determining the start of Phase III infertility.[2]

RULE

Sympto-Thermal Rule

Phase III begins on the evening of:

1. The third day of drying-up after Peak Day, combined with

2. Three normal post-peak temperatures above the LTL, and

3. The third temperature at or above the HTL or the cervix closed and hard for three days.

If the above conditions are not met, then Phase III begins after waiting an additional post-peak day for another temperature above the LTL.

It is important to note that if the cervix sign is used, the cervix must be both closed and hard for three days, i.e., not in the process of closing or hardening, for the identification of Phase III.

[2] P. Frank-Herrmann, et al. "The effectiveness of a fertility awareness based method to avoid pregnancy in relation to a couple's sexual behaviour during the fertile time: a longitudinal study," *Human Reproduction* 22(5) (2007):1310–1319.

This chart illustrates a typical application of the ST Rule.

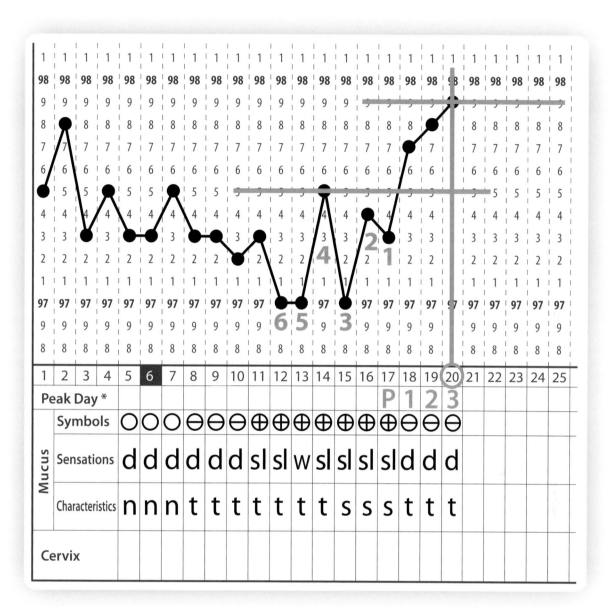

Notes

To apply the Sympto-Thermal Rule, follow these steps:

1. Find Peak Day and number the three days of drying-up after it from left to right.

2. Close to Peak Day, find three temperatures that are higher than the six preceding temperatures.

3. Number the pre-shift six from right to left.

4. Draw the Low Temperature Level (LTL) on the highest of the pre-shift six temperatures.

5. Draw the High Temperature Level (HTL) at 0.4° F above the LTL.

6. Find the third of three normal post-peak temperatures that are all above the LTL ("post-peak" means temperatures occurring after Peak Day). If this third temperature is at or above the HTL, Phase III begins on the evening of that day.

7. If the third normal post-peak temperature does not reach the HTL, check the cervix sign (if recorded). If there are three days of a closed, hard cervix, then it is not necessary for the third normal post-peak temperature to reach the HTL. Phase III begins on the evening of that day.

8. If the requirements in steps #6 and #7 are not met, wait for an additional normal post-peak temperature above the LTL; Phase III begins that evening.

9. After you apply the ST Rule and determine the start of Phase III, draw a vertical phase division line through the temperature dot on the first day of Phase III.

In the chart on the previous page, Phase III begins on the evening of Cycle Day 20, as indicated by following steps #1 through #6. The next chart illustrates an application of the ST Rule using the cervix observations (step #7).

Notes

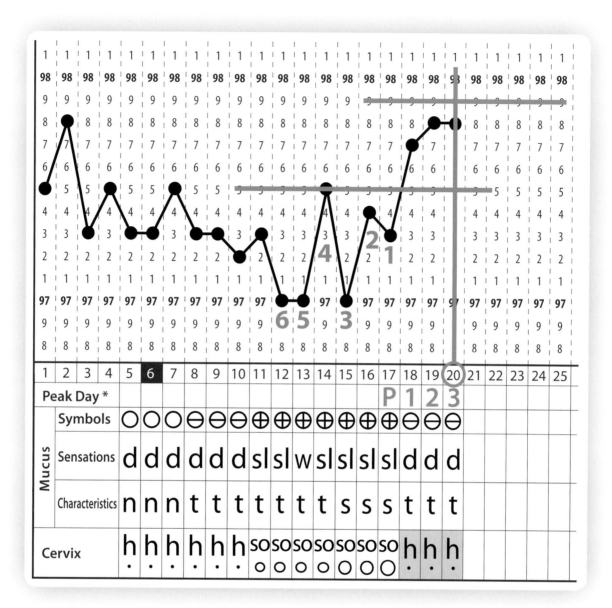

In this example, even though the temperature on Cycle Day 20 did not reach the HTL, there are three days of closed, hard cervix. Thus, Phase III still begins on the evening of Cycle Day 20.

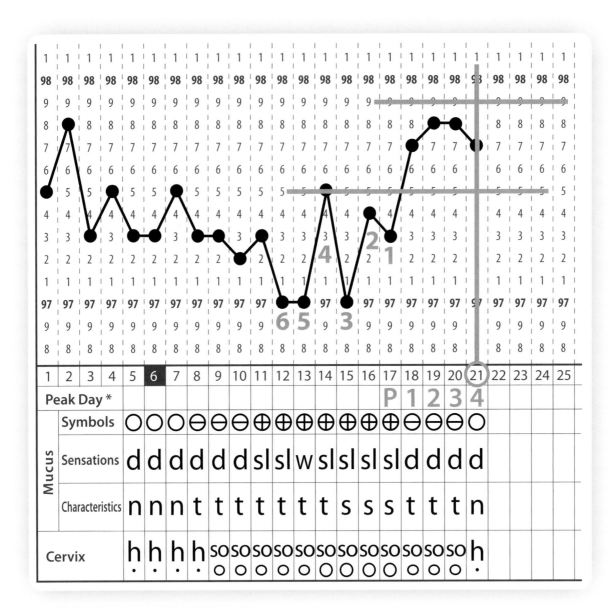

When These Conditions Are Not Met

Sometimes the temperature sign lags behind the mucus sign; or the cervix takes longer to close and harden, or is not observed at all. When this happens, it is still possible to determine the beginning of Phase III, but not on the third day past the Peak Day. In such situations, it is necessary to **wait for an additional normal post-peak temperature above the LTL** (none need reach the HTL).

In the example above, Phase III begins on the evening of Cycle Day 21, as indicated by following steps #1–8 on page 48.

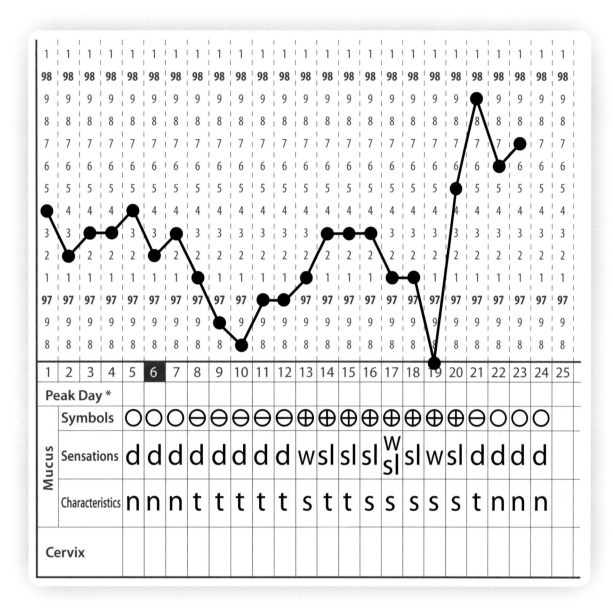

If you are attending the classes, you will complete this exercise in class. If you are using this Student Guide as a Home Study Course, apply the ST Rule by following the steps outlined on page 48 for each of the three practice charts, and determine the beginning of Phase III. Check your interpretations on pages 180–182 in Appendix B.

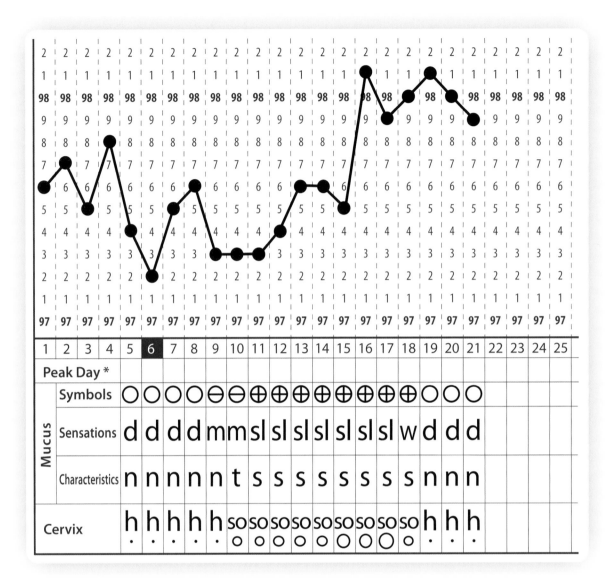

	1	2	3	4	5	6	7	8	9	10	11	12	13	14	15	16	17	18	19	20	21	22	23	24	25
Peak Day *																									
Symbols	○	○	○	○	⊖	⊖	⊕	⊕	⊕	⊕	⊕	⊕	⊕	⊕	○	○	○								
Sensations	d	d	d	d	d	m	m	sl	sl	sl	sl	sl	sl	sl	w	d	d	d							
Characteristics	n	n	n	n	n	t	s	s	s	s	s	s	s	s	n	n	n								
Cervix	h·	h·	h·	h·	h·	so○	so○	so○	so○	so○	so○	so○	so○	so○	h·	h·	h·								

(Mucus) label spans Symbols, Sensations, Characteristics rows.

Notes

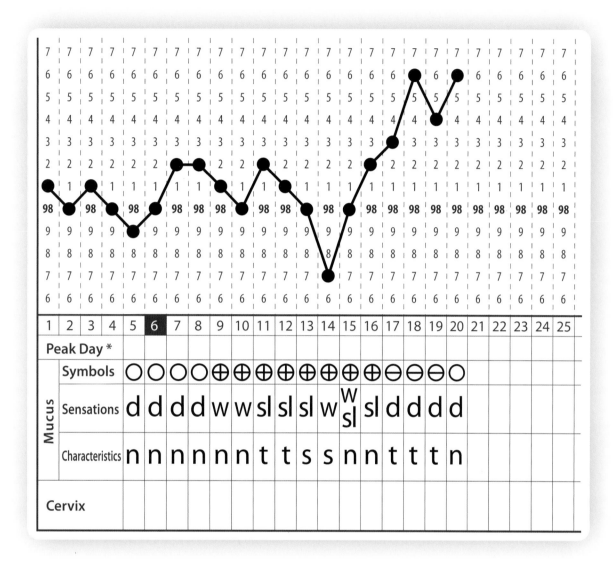

	1	2	3	4	5	6	7	8	9	10	11	12	13	14	15	16	17	18	19	20	21	22	23	24	25
Peak Day *																									
Mucus — Symbols				○	○	○	○	⊕	⊕	⊕	⊕	⊕	⊕	⊕	⊕	⊖	⊖	⊖	⊖	○					
Mucus — Sensations				d	d	d	d	w	w	sl	sl	sl	sl	w	W/sl	sl	d	d	d	d					
Mucus — Characteristics				n	n	n	n	n	n	t	t	s	s	n	n	t	t	t	n					
Cervix																									

5 Theology of the Body as It Relates to Sexuality

Lesson 5

There are a lot of misconceptions about what the Catholic Church teaches regarding marriage and sexuality. The Church has a wonderful vision for marriage and teaches that the marital embrace, the unique joining of husband and wife, is an incredible gift from God. Popes throughout history have written on this, but no pope has written more than John Paul II.

There are two vital works by Pope John Paul II (1978–2005) that pertain to sexuality, marriage and family life: the *Theology of the Body* and *The Apostolic Exhortation on the Family*.[1] The *Theology of the Body* is a series of addresses given at the Wednesday papal audiences in Rome from September 1979 to November 1984. The Wednesday papal audiences provide an opportunity for visitors and pilgrims to Rome to see and hear the Pope. John Paul II decided to use many of his Wednesday audiences to present a series of addresses devoted to one central theme. The first of these series was the *Theology of the Body*.

---

[1] See Pope John Paul II, *Man and Woman He Created Them: A Theology of the Body,* translated by Michael M. Waldstein (Boston: Pauline Books & Media, 2006). See also Pope John Paul II, *The Apostolic Exhortation on the Family* (*Familiaris Consortio*), also known as *The Role of the Christian Family in the Modern World* (Boston: Pauline Books & Media, 1981). Most of the following text is based on Richard M. Hogan's, *Is NFP Good?* and his *The Human Body…a sign of dignity and a gift* (Cincinnati: Couple to Couple League, 2005). Additional reading on this subject can be found in Richard M. Hogan's and John M. LeVoir's, *Covenant of Love*, 2nd edition (San Francisco: Ignatius Press, 1992) and Richard M. Hogan's, *The Theology of the Body in John Paul II: What It Means, Why It Matters*, (Ijamsville, MD: Word Among Us Press, 2007).

The Holy Father issued *The Apostolic Exhortation on the Family* (sometimes entitled *The Role of the Christian Family in the Modern World*) on November 22, 1981. It is without a doubt the most extensive document on the family that the Church has ever written.

Historical Background

On July 25, 1968, Pope Paul VI (1963–1978) issued his encyclical letter, *On Human Life*.[2] In this document, the Pope taught that contraception, sterilization and abortion were serious sins against life and marriage. The Pope based his teaching on the way God had created each and every human being, and was stating for the modern world what had been consistently taught by the Church throughout history. Unfortunately, Pope Paul VI's teaching in *On Human Life* met with tremendous opposition both within the Catholic Church and outside of it as well. Priests, theologians, and even some bishops bitterly opposed the teaching against contraception. It is fair to say that *On Human Life* was the most disputed document issued by a pope in centuries. Outside the Church, the teaching was considered to be rather quaint and hopelessly outdated.

The teaching of Pope Paul VI was sound, but it encountered the culture of the 1960s, a time of social and moral upheaval characterized by protests and the sexual revolution. College students protested against the U.S. government for an end to the Vietnam War. There were demonstrations by the civil rights movement and social justice groups, and the drive for equality for women. The mood of society was one of resistance and even rebellion against authority.

In the early 1960s, the contraceptive pill was developed and marketed. The Pill was hailed as the liberation of women from the toil of pregnancy and the pains of childbirth. Freed from the "threat" of pregnancy, the cry of the sexual revolution was heard in almost all segments of society.

Meanwhile, within the Catholic Church, the Second Vatican Council met from 1962 to 1965. The Council was viewed around the world as a meeting that would renew the Church in its teaching, its liturgy and in its mode of operation. The mood within the Church was not much different from the mood in the culture. Everything was changing, and one way to effect change was by putting pressure on the decision-makers. One instance of this pressure was the leaking of a confidential report on the question of the contraceptive pill. Pope John XXIII (1958–1963) had asked a commission of bishops and experts to study the question of contraception in light of the new Pill. Pope Paul VI expanded the commission. The commission issued two reports — both were to be confidential. However, these were leaked to the press. The majority report advised the Pope that

---

[2] Pope Paul VI, *On Human Life* (*Humanae Vitae*) (Boston: Pauline Books & Media, 1968).

the teaching on contraception could change. The minority report held the opposite opinion. When these reports became public, pressure mounted on the Pope to change the teaching.

Protest and the climate of change, combined with great expectation that the Church would change its teaching on the question of contraception, created a culture within the Church similar to that in the wider culture.

When the encyclical was issued, it might well be compared to a man standing on a train track trying to stop a roaring locomotive at more than a hundred miles an hour. In a certain sense, Paul VI's teaching, while **prophetic** and absolutely consistent with the Gospel, had almost no hope of a legitimate hearing.

Also, the encyclical was structured in a mode of thought that dated back to the thirteenth century, to the teaching of St. Thomas Aquinas (1225–1274). Since people no longer looked at the world or themselves as St. Thomas did, it became very difficult — even for those who wished to promote Paul VI's teaching — to convey it to young people, and engaged and married couples. There needed to be a new approach, a new way to convey the teaching of Pope Paul VI in *On Human Life*.

Vision for Sexuality and Marriage

Actually, a new approach to all of the Church's teaching on sexuality, marriage and family life was needed to convey the wondrous vision that the Church had always promoted to the modern culture. In the Book of Genesis, God invites all human persons to enter into a union of love in marriage, which is to mirror the love of God in the Trinity. Once the contraception question was posed and the Church said, in effect, "No," the positive side of the Church's teaching on marriage and family life was no longer adequately conveyed.

It seems that whenever the Catholic Church is asked about a sexual act, the answer is a definitive "No." A couple may ask, can we contracept? "No." Can we use in vitro fertilization? "No." The Church seems always to be saying "No." But the "No" of the Church is not even half the story. What the Church tries to uphold is that human persons are called in marriage to become a reflection of God Himself. The "No" is to those things unworthy of human persons. In effect, the Church is saying to us: "Do not look down. Do not settle for what is unworthy of you and is in effect a degradation of human dignity. Look to the vision, to the stars, to see what God has intended human persons to be and what God has intended for all spouses." The "Yes" of the Church to the vision of marriage and family life is far more important than the "No." A new formulation to teach what Pope Paul VI taught in *On Human Life* and to convey the Church's wonderful vision of marriage and family life was essential.

Theology of the Body

In his *Theology of the Body* addresses, John Paul II gave us a new formulation for the Church's teaching on human sexuality. Together with the *Apostolic Exhortation on the Family* and the last third of the *Theology of the Body* addresses, he also gave us a new way of understanding the authentic love of husband and wife. This new formulation not only emphasizes the positive teaching of the Church on sexuality and family life, but it also gives everyone a new way of understanding why the various "No's" of the Church to the sexual sins, including contraception, are essential to human dignity.

John Paul begins his considerations with the affirmation that human beings are the only earthly creatures God created in His image and likeness. As human beings, we are different from the animals and plants because we are persons, beings endowed with the capacities of thinking and choosing, but we are like the animals and plants in that we have bodies. We are like the angels and the three Persons in God in that we are persons, but we are unlike them in that we have bodies. We are unique: persons with bodies; bodies that express persons. God made us specifically so that there would be a visible expression of personhood in the world. The animals and plants cannot do this because they are not persons. The angels and the three Persons in God (in the divine nature) cannot do it because they do not have bodies.

The body makes visible what it means to be a person. In other words, our bodies speak a language, the language of personhood. Of course, this is nothing new. We all read body language very easily. We have all had the experience of asking a loved one: "What is wrong?" and the answer is typically, "Nothing," when the body language is literally "screaming" pain of some kind. The body reveals what we are thinking and choosing and feeling. It speaks its own language and reveals ourselves to others.

But if we are made in God's image and likeness, then the body does more than reveal ourselves. It also reveals God when we act as God acts, and express those acts outwardly in and through our bodies. In this case, the body becomes a physical image of God Himself. The body then has a dignity and value in its own right.

However, this view of the human body is not the only one found in our culture. An alternative proposal is that the body is a machine and each of us "owns" our bodies as we would own a car or a house. In this view of the human body, it becomes an object.

Some of the science fiction movies reinforce this idea of the body as a machine. In these movies, machines can be persons and persons can become machines. The subliminal message is that the human body is a collection of functioning parts, and these parts can be replaced with better parts that perform the functions even better.

Sportscasters also often refer to the bodies of athletes as machines: "He has all the tools." "He has great wheels" — as though a car or bike were running down the field or the court. "He has an arm like a rifle." And so on.

Often people will refer to their medical problems in machine-like language. Someone may say, "The old ticker isn't working so well, so I need the spark plugs changed." "The plumbing is getting old, and I need it replaced." "I need an oil change," or "I need a roto-rooter job to clean out the pipes." We may often say, "I need some fuel this morning" (referring to food), or "I want the leaded" (meaning caffeinated coffee).

There is nothing immoral about such references, but they all reinforce the idea that the human body is just a machine. **Still, it is only when we start to believe that the body is a machine that we run into difficulties.**

Things, such as machines, are bought and sold. However, none of us bought our bodies. Rather, we received them from God through the cooperation of our parents. They are part of the gift of life. The human body is the expression of the human person and not a machine. Any act that manipulates, uses or harms the human body is an attack on the human person because what we do to the body we do to the person. We should never treat any human body as something to be used. We deserve to be loved and not used. We deserve to see ourselves as ennobled, as images of God, whose bodies are sacred and holy because they speak the language of our persons and even the language of God!

NFP and the Language of the Body

Natural Family Planning reads the language of our sexuality. In other words, NFP teaches us the means to come to know ourselves and our spouses. In knowing ourselves and our spouses through our sexuality, we also touch the mystery of God because living out our sexuality reveals love, *the* most human act and *the* act of God. This knowledge leads us to an awe and wonder of ourselves and of God in creating us. Awe and wonder lead to the discovery of the mystery of ourselves, our spouses and God. This discovery of the mystery leads to authentic love, and authentic love leads to generosity. In other words, NFP can lead precisely to the knowledge that encourages us to treasure each other and God. In this way, NFP builds marriages.

Getting Started 6

Lesson 6

The Sympto-Thermal Rule: Special Situations

It is important to understand that there are some situations that require a variation of the ST Rule.

Beginners' First Cycle

Beginners should apply the ST Rule to determine the start of Phase III infertility, and then add one day. You should abstain from marital relations until Phase III for the first cycle because the rules governing the end of Phase I infertility have not yet been taught. Unmarried couples should continue to refrain from sexual intimacy until marriage so that you will become true lovers — and not users — of one another.

> ### Beginners' First Cycle
>
> - To determine the beginning of Phase III, apply the Sympto-Thermal Rule and **add one day**
>
> - Abstain until Phase III for one cycle

Hormonal Contraception: Non-Injectable and Injectable

Hormonal contraception is classified in two ways: non-injectable and injectable. Both of these can interfere with the natural interactions of a woman's hormones during her cycle. For this reason, women who are currently using either form of hormonal contraceptives cannot accurately chart their fertility signs. Once a woman stops using these hormones, however, she may be able to apply a variation of the ST Rule within a short period of time.

Non-injectable hormonal contraceptives introduce artificial hormones into a woman's body in ways other than injection. Examples include the Pill, which is ingested; the patch, which is attached to the body, the vaginal ring, and hormone-containing IUDs.

Women discontinuing non-injectable hormones will need to apply the following rule:

Post-Hormonal Rule

For the first cycle after stopping the hormones, Phase III begins on the evening of:

  1. The fourth day of drying-up after Peak Day, combined with

  2. Four normal post-peak temperatures above the LTL.

If discontinuing injectable hormones, discuss with your Teaching Couple and see the Reference Guide, pages 223–227.

The fourth temperature does not need to reach the HTL. In addition to the preceding rule, it is very important to abstain from marital relations from the time of the **withdrawal bleed** (the bleed that occurs monthly while using non-injectable hormonal contraception) until a clear determination of the beginning of Phase III infertility for the first cycle after stopping the hormones. Thus, women in this situation should refrain from marital relations in Phase I and Phase II until the end of Phase I rules are learned.

Injectable hormones are difficult to predict. They are liquid artificial hormones that are injected into a woman's body with a needle (a shot). Examples include Depo-Provera and Lunelle. The return of fertility in these situations is more complicated and beyond the level of discussion in this lesson. Women who have discontinued injectable hormones and are learning NFP should contact a local CCL teaching couple, or the CCL central office, for assistance. In addition, they should carefully read the information on this topic in the Reference Guide, pages 223–227.

Abnormal/Missed Temperatures

You should be conscientious about taking and recording your temperatures throughout your cycles when you are first learning NFP. It is especially important to be diligent in taking your temperatures throughout Phase II, and until Phase III begins. This class has only discussed situations in which all of the temperatures before and immediately after the thermal shift are recorded. Class 2 explains how to handle days when one or two temperatures appear to be abnormally out of the range of the surrounding temperatures, and/or when temperature readings are omitted.

If you have one or two temperatures in the pre-shift six or in the thermal shift that are clearly out of the range of the surrounding temperatures, or if you forget to take your temperature, refer to Class 2 for an explanation on how to apply the ST Rule in such cases.

Starting tomorrow

At this point, you should have enough information to begin observing, recording and interpreting your signs of fertility and infertility. Be sure to fill in all necessary information on your first chart. Estimate how many days it has been since your last menstrual period started, and mark that as the first day of the cycle. Each woman should begin taking her basal body temperature at the same time each day, and begin to observe mucus sensations, characteristics and cervical changes. At the appropriate time, apply the ST Rule and determine the start of Phase III infertility. When menstruation begins, start a new chart because the first day of menstruation begins a new cycle.

Supplemental Classes

If you are pregnant or have recently given birth and would like to take the postpartum class, or are interested in the premenopause class, contact a CCL teaching couple in your area, check *www.ccli.org*, or call the CCL central office directly for further information.

Love and Intimacy

The material you have just learned is very personal. Hopefully, you will be able to appreciate that this is much more than just a "biology" class; rather, NFP is knowledge that exalts our innate dignity as human persons, and can lead us to a much deeper understanding of what it means to love one another as husband and wife — to give for the good of the other and never to use one another for personal gain.

In fact, the marital act is profound, holy and good. Integrating this spiritual reality with the awareness that you are fertile during certain periods of time can be a very deep experience.

This knowledge will enhance your appreciation as a participant in a potential act of creation. And yet, as profound as this may be, there can be times when it is necessary to postpone a pregnancy by refraining from sexual intimacy during the fertile time.

The beauty of fertility awareness is that there are no barriers between you and your spouse when you engage in the marital act. Together, you learn your signs of fertility, and together you decide when to anticipate a child and when to postpone a pregnancy. The intervals of abstinence can provide opportunities for deeper romance and affection as you remain intimate in non-genital ways.

Check and record your signs of fertility

Abstinence during the fertile time helps couples appreciate each other more and become other-centered. This sacrificial gift of self-control between spouses communicates a desire to love as God loves, rather than to use the spouse selfishly. There are many times in marriage when it is not appropriate for a couple to engage in the marital act. Couples would think nothing of refraining from sexual relations when one of the spouses is sick or when one is away on a trip. During such times, love isn't missing; it is just expressed in non-genital ways — a bowl of hot soup to a spouse in bed with a cold and fever can have an enduring life-giving effect. The phone call before retiring when a couple is separated by distance — perhaps a business trip, or visiting a sick relative — becomes an opportunity to share love in verbal ways. Each separation becomes an opportunity to say, "I love you!" without engaging in the physical act of sexual intercourse. Each day of abstinence enhances the joy that lies ahead.

This is easy to understand for a sick spouse or one separated by distance, but what about when you decide to postpone a pregnancy? The same thought process applies. Whatever the reason, when a couple prayerfully chooses to refrain from the marital act, the power of love is prevalent because the decision to love is all-enduring.

Homework

Whether you are attending the classes or using this Student Guide as a *Home Study Course*, you should interpret Homework Charts 1–4 that are located in Appendix A on pages 169–170. Apply the ST Rule on each of the four charts and determine the beginning of Phase III. In class, these will be reviewed at the beginning of Class 2.

Class 2

1 Introduction

This class is divided into seven lessons: *Introduction, Review, The Sympto-Thermal Rule: Abnormal/Missed Temperatures, The Transition from Phase I to Phase II, The Effectiveness of NFP, Using NFP to Achieve a Pregnancy* and *Authentic Love and Responsible Parenthood.*

This Introduction will summarize the Class 2 lessons.

Summary: Class 2 Lessons

Lesson 2, *Review*, uses a practice exercise to review the concepts taught in Class 1 to include: the observation, recording and interpretation of the signs of fertility and the Sympto-Thermal Rule (ST Rule). You will also review the four homework charts assigned at the end of the previous class. (You should complete these charts prior to attending Class 2.)

In the previous class, the ST Rule was applied with normal temperatures within the pre-shift six and the thermal shift. There are times when one or two of these temperatures are clearly out of the range of the surrounding temperatures, taken early or late, or not taken or recorded on a given day. Lesson 3, *The Sympto-Thermal Rule: Abnormal/Missed Temperatures*, explains how to apply the ST Rule in these situations.

One of the principal objectives of Class 1 was to identify the transition from Phase II to Phase III; in this class, you will now learn to identify the transition from Phase I to Phase II. Phase I consists of the infertile time beginning with menstruation until the start of the fertile time in Phase II. The two key elements of Lesson 4, *The Transition from Phase I to Phase II*, are to help you transfer information from one chart to another, and to help you learn to identify how to determine Phase I infertile days. There will be several practice exercises in this lesson to help you understand these concepts.

Lesson 5, *The Effectiveness of NFP*, contains a short primer on defining effectiveness. This lesson also establishes the credibility of the method of NFP that you are learning by showing that the effectiveness of the Sympto-Thermal Method of NFP presented in this course is nearly the same or higher than that of contraceptives.

Lesson 6, *Using NFP to Achieve a Pregnancy*, teaches how NFP can be used to help a couple conceive a child. The lesson begins with some further discussion on anatomy and physiology by showing ovulation, conception and the growth and development of a baby in utero. Next, using concepts already developed in Class 1, you will learn how to interpret the signs of fertility to determine the optimal time to try to conceive. There is also a discussion on fertility monitors that can be of additional help. As this lesson concludes, you will learn how to determine the estimated date of childbirth using NFP.

Lesson 7, *Authentic Love and Responsible Parenthood*, continues the integration of the moral teachings of the Catholic Church. The Theology of the Body is based on the central concept that the human body is the expression of the human person and speaks a language that can be read and understood. This language can be expressed through the signs of fertility, and understanding the signs of fertility can allow couples to make virtuous decisions on trying to bring children into the world or on postponing a pregnancy. In determining how a human person ought to act, one can turn to Christ, the son of God. The principal act of God is to love, thus married love should be modeled after the five characteristics of divine love. This, in turn, leads couples to generosity and responsible parenthood.

Notes

The lessons are interspersed with practical exercises intended to reinforce the information taught. These exercises will help you to properly record and interpret the observable signs. This information is useful as you apply your knowledge of NFP to your marriage and decide to hope for a child, or to postpone a pregnancy.

Those who are attending the classes will complete certain exercises in class, as well as some homework between classes. Those using the *Home Study Course* will use additional data and directions in the Appendix to complete the exercises, and check their work against the provided answers.

Teaching couples are generally available before and after classes to review personal charts, answer questions, or discuss concerns that may arise. For those using the *Home Study Course*, CCL's central office is available to assist you. They can be contacted by phone, e-mail or through the CCL website (see page iv).

Notes

Review 2

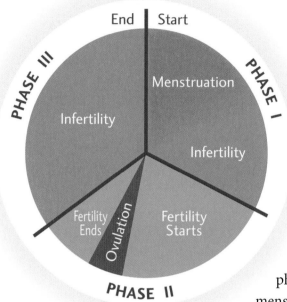

End | Start

PHASE III

PHASE I

Menstruation

Infertility

Infertility

Fertility Ends

Ovulation

Fertility Starts

PHASE II

Lesson 2

This lesson will review some of the most important concepts you have learned thus far. The female reproductive cycle can be divided into three phases. Phase I infertility begins on the first day of menstrual blood flow, and usually ends when a woman's daily observations detect the onset of the signs of fertility. Phase II is the fertile time. It is during this time that a woman ovulates. Phase II will typically last approximately eight to 12 days, sometimes longer. Phase III is a time of infertility beginning several days after ovulation and continuing until the next menstruation.

Observing and Recording the Signs of Fertility

The key observable signs of fertility are cervical mucus, temperature and cervix.

Cervical Mucus

Cervical mucus is an important fertility sign. The absence of cervical mucus usually is a sign of infertility, and the presence of cervical mucus usually indicates fertility. Cervical mucus is an aid to fertility by providing both a swimming medium for sperm and nutrients that prolong sperm life. It also helps filter out abnormal sperm so that they do not reach the egg.

You make cervical mucus observations throughout the day by identifying:

1) *sensations*, what you can feel and sense; and

2) *characteristics*, what you can see and touch

You can detect feelings of dryness or wetness as you go about your normal activities throughout the day. These *sensations* occur outside the vagina, as a noticeable feeling of dryness, a feeling of being moist, sticky or damp, or as a feeling of wetness similar to what occurs prior to the start of a menstrual period. Additionally, you can detect mucus sensations through an awareness of what you feel and sense when you wipe with toilet paper each time you use the bathroom. Be attentive to the sensations of mucus as soon as your period lessons, or by Cycle Day 5, whichever comes first.

You should record mucus sensations on the chart at the end of each day. Record "d" when you have an awareness of dryness or when you have a sensation of dryness when wiping every time you use the bathroom. Record "m" when you have an awareness of moistness, stickiness, or dampness, and record "w" when you have an awareness of wetness at any time during the day. Record "sl" when you detect slipperiness when wiping at any time when using the bathroom.

Mucus *characteristics* can be identified visually and/or by checking their quality on the toilet paper after wiping during a bathroom visit. Like mucus sensations, begin checking for mucus characteristics as soon as your period lessens, or by Cycle Day 5, whichever comes first. Record "n" if there is no mucus observed. Record "t" if the mucus is tacky — sticky, thick, pasty, creamy, or clumpy. Record "s" if the mucus is stretchy — very elastic, thin, stringy, or resembling raw egg white. Be sure to record the most fertile observation of the day even if later observations are less-fertile.

Temperature

The second fertility sign that you can observe is your temperature. Recall that the basal body temperature is the temperature of the human body at rest or upon awakening, unaffected by food, drink or activity. During a typical fertility cycle, your basal body temperature is normally low before ovulation, and then rises approximately 0.4° F after ovulation. The temperature remains high until the next menstruation, or if you are pregnant, throughout much of the pregnancy.

You take your temperature at the same waking time each day.[1] With a digital thermometer, you can take your temperature in about a minute. To maintain accuracy, it is best to remain in bed while taking it. Be sure to record the temperature on your chart.

---

[1] Temperatures recorded more than 30 minutes before or after the designated waking time may be abnormal temperatures. You will learn more about abnormal temperatures in the next lesson.

Cervix

The third key observable sign—an optional sign—is the cervix. Like cervical mucus, the cervix changes in response to the hormones estrogen and progesterone. During Phase I of the cycle, the cervix is closed and hard. It opens and softens during Phase II, and returns to the closed and hard position during Phase III. The post-ovulation changes coincide with the dramatic changes in the mucus and the rise in the basal temperatures.

You should observe your cervix once or twice each day when visiting the bathroom, but only in the afternoon or evening. The cervix exam should not be done in the morning since the muscles that support the uterus contract during the night, making the cervix harder to reach; then the muscles stretch somewhat after you have been up and around for awhile.

You should record the cervix sign on the chart as "**h**" (hard) or "**so**" (soft) and "**•**" (closed) or "**O**" (open). You can find all of the notations used for recording the mucus and cervix signs at the bottom left side of the chart.

Descriptions & Symbols

Symbols (mucus fertility)

O	No mucus
⊖	Less-fertile
⊕	More-fertile

Cervix

h	Hard	•	Closed
so	Soft	O	Open

Sensations —— Mucus Symbol —— Characteristics

Sensation		Mucus Symbol		Characteristics
d	Dry	O	Nothing	n
m	Moist	⊖	Tacky	t
w, sl	Wet, Slippery	⊕	Stretchy	s

Interpreting the Signs of Fertility

Mucus

During Phase II of a woman's menstrual cycle, the cervical mucus is produced in response to the hormone estrogen. For many women, this begins with a slight sensation of moistness, dampness or stickiness at the vulva. As ovulation approaches, these sensations become more pronounced. Women begin to feel wetter and/or slippery and eventually feel very wet (watery/runny) and/or very slippery around ovulation. The highly wet and/or very slippery feelings are distinctly different from the dry feeling that is typical after the end of your period and are in response to higher levels of estrogen. The character-

On days of lighter menstrual flow, observe if you feel dry while walking around. Detecting mucus characteristics during days of lighter menstrual flow may be difficult, however, a feeling of dryness at the vulva can assure you that mucus is still absent.

istics of the mucus also change from tacky to stretchy as ovulation approaches. Peak Day is the last day of the more-fertile mucus before the drying-up process begins, and can only be identified in retrospect. It is not until the drying-up process has begun that Peak Day can be confirmed.

In addition, the drying-up process after Peak Day represents a distinct change in mucus sensations and/or characteristics, and signals a hormonal change in a woman's body. Peak Day is easily identified on a chart; it will be the last day with a more-fertile symbol (⊕), prior to days of less-fertile (⊖) and/or no mucus (O) symbols. Remember that the mucus symbol is placed on your chart at the end of every day, so finding the last day of (⊕) should be easy. Find the Peak Day in the example below:

Identifying Peak Day › Practice

	8	8	8	8	8	8	8	8	8	8	8	8	8	8	8	8	8	8	8	8	8	8	8	8	8	8	8	8	8	8	8	8	8
	1	2	3	4	5	6	7	8	9	10	11	12	13	14	15	16	17	18	19	20	21	22	23	24	25	26	27	28	29	30	31	32	33
Peak Day *																																	
Symbols	O	O	O	O	⊖	⊕	⊕	⊕	⊕	⊕	⊕	⊖	O	O	O	O	O	O	O	O	O	O	O	O	O	O	O						
Sensations	d	d	d	d	m	w	w	w	w	w	s	l	m	d	d	d	d	d	d	d	d	d	d	d	d	d							
Characteristics	n	n	n	n	t	t	s	t	t	s	t	t	n	n	n	n	n	n	n	n	n	n	n	n	n								
Cervix																																	

If you are attending the classes, you will complete this exercise in class. If you are using this Student Guide as a Home Study Course, place a "P" on the proper cycle day of the Peak Day row in the exercise, and then check your answer on page 183 in Appendix B.

Temperature

A sustained temperature rise after ovulation is due to an increase in progesterone. Correctly interpreting the temperature rise is an important step in confirming that ovulation has occurred. A temperature rise related to ovulation consists of three temperatures[2] above the previous six temperatures, near the Peak Day.

The six temperatures before the rise are called the pre-shift six. You should number them backwards on the chart from right to left. Find the highest of those six temperatures and draw a horizontal line through it. This is the Low Temperature Level (LTL). From this base, the amount of temperature rise can be measured. Next, place a horizontal line 0.4° F above the LTL. That temperature becomes the High Temperature Level (HTL).

The Sympto-Thermal Rule

With a mucus dry-up and a temperature rise (and the optional observation of a closed and hard cervix), you now have enough information to determine the time of Phase III, post-ovulation infertility. The rule that follows is called the Sympto-Thermal Rule.

Sympto-Thermal Rule

Phase III begins on the evening of:

RULE

1. The third day of drying-up after Peak Day, combined with

2. Three normal post-peak temperatures above the LTL, and

3. The third temperature at or above the HTL or the cervix closed and hard for three days.

If the above conditions are not met, then Phase III begins after waiting an additional post-peak day for another temperature above the LTL.

---

[2] These must be **normal** temperatures. You will learn more about abnormal or missed pre-shift six or thermal shift temperatures in the next lesson.

Review › Practice Chart

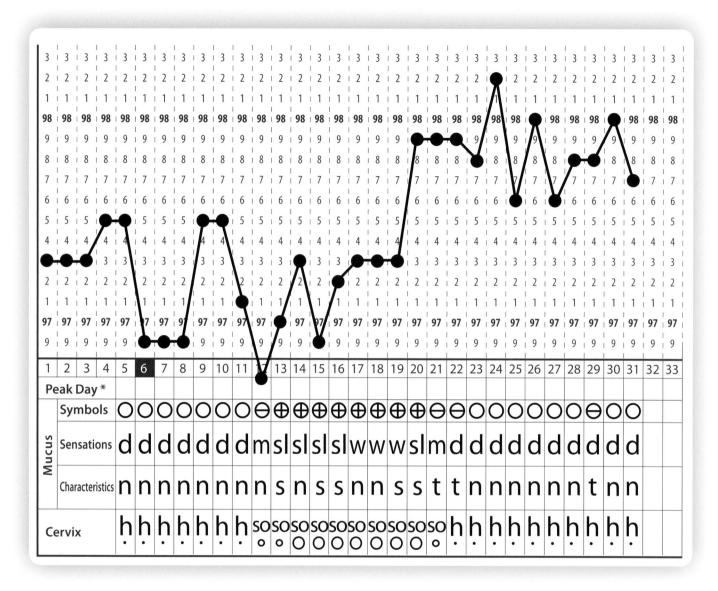

If you are attending the classes, you will complete this exercise in class. If you are using this Student Guide as a Home Study Course, follow the steps outlined on page 48 to determine the beginning of Phase III using the ST Rule, and then check your answers on page 183 in Appendix B.

Class 1 Homework

Applying the Sympto-Thermal Rule › Homework Charts 1–4

If you are attending the classes, you will review these charts in class. If you are using this Student Guide as a Home Study Course, be sure to check your answers on pages 184–187 in Appendix B.

The Sympto-Thermal Rule: Abnormal/Missed Temperatures

3

Lesson 3

The previous lesson reviewed how to apply the Sympto-Thermal Rule (ST Rule) when all the temperatures within the pre-shift six and the thermal shift appear to be within a normal range and are properly recorded on the chart. However, there may be times when a temperature is clearly out of the range of the surrounding temperatures, when it is taken early or late, when it is not recorded, or when it is not taken at all on a given day. This lesson provides the technique for handling these situations within the context of the ST Rule.

Recall from Class 1 that the basal body temperature is the temperature of the human body at rest or upon awakening, unaffected by food, drink or activity. You should take your basal body temperature at the same time each day (or at least within one-half hour of your waking time).[1] When you do not take your temperature within this time frame, you cannot be assured that it accurately reflects your basal body temperature on that particular day. Additionally, there are other situations, such as sickness, lack of sleep, travel, or other types of stress that could cause a higher or lower reading than would normally be expected on a given day of a cycle. On other occasions, the temperature may be taken at the specified time, but when recorded on the chart, it appears to be out of the range of the surrounding temperatures. When a temperature is clearly out of the range of the surrounding temperatures, it is an **abnormal temperature**. In addition, on some days you may forget to take

---

[1] See the Reference Guide for information on taking temperatures when doing shift work (page 247) or when changing time zones (page 248).

your temperature or forget to record it on the chart. These **missed temperatures** will be handled in the same manner as abnormal temperatures (explained below).

Abnormal and missed temperatures need to be identified and should be recorded and properly handled when they fall within the pre-shift six and the thermal shift. During other days of the cycle, they are not relevant when determining the start of Phase III infertility.

Recording Abnormal and Missed Temperatures

Record an abnormal temperature on the chart just as you record any other temperature. If you know the reason for the abnormality, e.g., took temperature late or woke up with a fever, then mark an "X" through the temperature dot and record that information in one of the "User Notes" sections of the chart. Be sure to indicate both the day of the cycle and the abnormality.

The absence of a recorded temperature on a given day assumes that the temperature was missed. Mark an "X" in the temperature region on the day that was missed, and make a note if appropriate.

Determining the LTL when there are Abnormal or Missed Temperatures

The LTL is set at the highest of the pre-shift six temperatures—the six temperatures prior to the thermal shift. If there are one or two abnormal or missed temperatures in the pre-shift six, use them in counting the pre-shift six, but **do not use them when setting the LTL**. The LTL should be determined from the remaining normal temperatures among the pre-shift six.

Notes

Applying the ST Rule when there are Abnormal or Missed Temperatures

Abnormal or Missed Temperature Guideline

If there are one or two abnormal or missed temperature readings in the pre-shift six, Phase III begins after waiting for four post-peak temperatures above the LTL. (While all temperatures must be above the LTL, none need reach the HTL.)

If there are one or two abnormal or missed temperature readings within the three thermal shift temperatures, the pre-shift six cannot be established until there are three normal post-peak temperatures higher than the six preceding temperatures and above the LTL. Apply the ST Rule using those normal temperatures. Remember that if the third post-peak temperature does not reach the HTL or the cervix has not been closed and hard for three days, you must wait for an additional temperature above the LTL.

If there are more than two abnormal or missed temperatures in the pre-shift six, there is insufficient data to accurately set the LTL. Thus, the ST Rule cannot be applied in this situation, but an alternative rule could be applied, which will be discussed in Class 3. Being diligent in recording temperatures accurately will help preclude this from occurring, especially throughout Phase II and for the first several days after Peak Day.

Applying the ST Rule: Abnormal/Missed Temperatures › Practice Charts 1 and 2

If you are attending the classes, you will complete these charts in class. If you are using this Student Guide as a Home Study Course, follow the steps on page 48 to apply the ST Rule to determine the start of Phase III. Be sure to follow the instructions above before applying the ST Rule. After completing the exercises, check your answers on pages 188–189 of Appendix B.

Notes

Practice 1

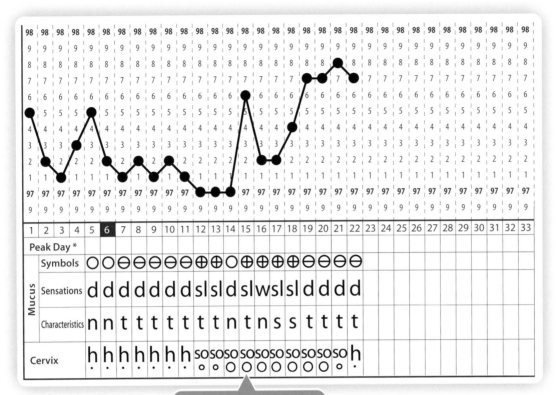

Temp 2 hours late

Practice 2

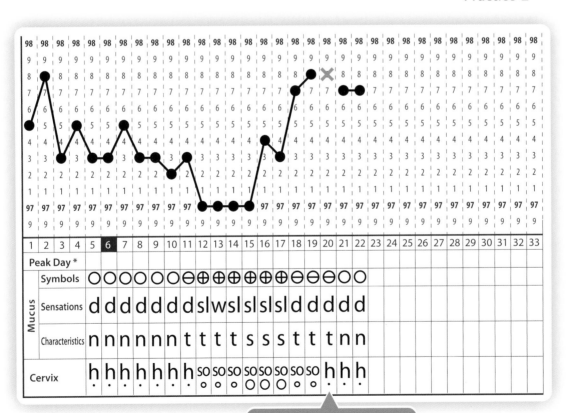

Forgot Temperature

The Transition from Phase I to Phase II

4

Lesson 4

As you learned during Class 1, the female reproductive cycle is divided into three phases. Phase I begins on the first day of menstrual blood flow, and is a time of infertility. Phase II begins with the onset of fertility signs, and continues until a few days after ovulation. This is the fertile time of the cycle. Phase III begins a few days after ovulation and continues until the next menstruation. You already know how to identify the start of Phase III infertility by applying the Sympto-Thermal Rule (ST Rule). The goal of this lesson is to understand how to determine your state of fertility during the days beginning with menstruation (Cycle Day 1, Phase I) and ending with the onset of fertility (Phase II).

Keeping Good Records

When the corpus luteum (empty follicle) ceases to function, it triggers a drop in progesterone and the beginning of menstruation. This first day of menstrual blood flow is the first day of a new cycle, and is recorded as Cycle Day 1 on a new chart. When beginning a new cycle, it is important to compare the previous cycle length with the shortest and longest cycles within the past 12 cycles, and then record the current information in the Cycle History box of the new chart.[1,2] In addition, note the first day of the thermal shift and whether or not you have a new "Earliest 'first day of temperature rise.'" This information is also recorded on the new chart, along with the new chart number and updated number of recorded cycles in which the first day of temperature rise was recorded. During this lesson, you will learn how data from previous cycles can help you identify the infertile days during, and immediately following, menstruation.

In addition to menstrual bleeding, Phase I of this new cycle is usually distinguished by the absence of cervical mucus sensations and characteristics, and by a drop in the basal body temperature (to the pre-ovulation levels of previous cycles). Phase I is an infertile time. FSH stimulates development of some immature eggs in the ovarian follicles to develop into mature eggs. (Usually, only one egg fully matures and is released.) As these follicles grow, estrogen is released which results in mucus production, the opening and softening of the cervix, the build-up of the lining of the uterus (the endometrium), and the release of a surge of luteinizing hormone (LH). A woman can tell these hormones are at work by observing her mucus sensations and characteristics. *The presence of mucus is the fundamental condition for defining the start of Phase II, the fertile time of the cycle.* Therefore, knowing whether or not cervical mucus is absent or present is essential in determining the end of Phase I and the beginning of Phase II.

Women typically have some dry days following their period. However, there may be times that women need to ascertain the absence or presence of mucus before the menstrual bleeding has ended. On days of heavier flow during Phase I, it is possible that the bleeding could mask the absence or presence of cervical mucus, making it difficult or impossible to conclude whether such a day is fertile or infertile. Still, on days of lighter bleeding, with experience you can learn how to discern whether or not cervical mucus is present.

Generally, Cycle Days 1 through 5 are infertile if no mucus is present. In a study published in 2007 by Petra Frank-Herrmann, M.D., couples who used Cycle Days 1–5 for marital relations achieved over 99% effectiveness in avoiding pregnancy when no mucus was present.[3] Professor Josef Roetzer, M. D., also found Cycle Day 6 to be infertile with no mucus present for women whose previous shortest cycles are 26 days or more.[4] In addition to these findings, G. K. Doering, M.D. discovered another technique to help women determine the infertile days prior to Phase II by using temperature information from their previous cycle history.[5]

---

[1] The length of the cycle does not include the day on which the menstruation for the next cycle begins. For example, if menstruation begins on Cycle Day 29, then the cycle that just ended was 28 days long.

[2] When recording your information on the chart for the first time, you may use data that you have gathered from your previous cycle history to record in the "Previous cycle variation" portion of the Cycle History block.

[3] P. Frank-Herrmann, et al. "The effectiveness of a fertility awareness based method to avoid pregnancy in relation to a couple's sexual behaviour during the fertile time: a prospective longitudinal study," *Human Reproduction* 22(5) (2007):1310–1319.

Doctors Frank-Herrmann, Roetzer and Doering have demonstrated the value of keeping good records of your menstrual cycle history. Their procedures for establishing days of infertility prior to ovulation have proven to be very effective in the absence of mucus. Their studies form the basis for the General Guidelines and Phase I Rules that follow.

Phase I Guidelines

Each of the Phase I Rules is based on the ability to detect the first onset of mucus. **For this reason, you should begin observing and recording mucus signs as soon as menstrual bleeding lessens, or by Cycle Day 5, whichever comes first.** CCL has two guidelines to follow once menstruation decreases that will help ensure the onset of mucus can be detected.

General Guideline – Evenings Only:

An infertile day is only determined after becoming aware of mucus sensations throughout the day and checking for mucus at each bathroom visit. For this reason, CCL recommends that once menstruation decreases, marital relations occur only in the evenings during Phase I. (You may not notice any mucus throughout the day, but then detect some mucus in the evening. If this occurs, you would consider yourself in Phase II because you detected mucus.)

General Guideline – Not on Consecutive Days:

Marital relations usually leaves seminal residue in the vaginal area. If you detect this residue during your mucus checks the following day, the seminal residue could mask the presence of mucus. You cannot assume you are infertile until you can positively assure yourself that there is no mucus present. For this reason, CCL recommends that once menstruation lessens, you should abstain on any day that follows marital relations in Phase I unless you are experienced and can positively detect the absence of mucus.

Seminal residue usually disappears within hours or by the next day after marital relations. It can look similar to stretchy mucus and/or produce a slippery sensation, but when rolled between the fingers it will

> Seminal residue looks like more-fertile mucus and can produce a slippery sensation, but, when rolled between the fingers, it dissipates and appears to be absorbed.

---

[4] Roetzer, 36. This is based on women having knowledge of at least their last 12 cycles of history. There will be more on effectiveness in a later lesson.

[5] G.K. Doering, M.D. "About the dependability of the temperature method to avoid conception," *Deutsche Medizinische Wochenschrift* 92 (1967) 1055–1196.

dissipate and appear to be absorbed. Seminal residue can be recorded on the chart as "SR." See the Reference Guide, page 240, for more on how to distinguish seminal residue from mucus.

Day 5/6 Rule

The Day 5/6 Rule is an effective way to determine the infertile days at the start of your cycle prior to having charting experience.

Day 5/6 Rule

Assume infertility on Cycle Days 1–5.

For women with cycles 26 days or longer in the last 12 cycles, assume infertility on Cycle Days 1–6.

Conditions for use:

This rule assumes the absence of mucus.

Note that at any time mucus is observed, **Phase II fertility begins**. At the start of a new cycle, record Cycle Day 5 or 6 on your chart in the Cycle History box as applicable — either circle the appropriate day or cross out the day that does not apply. Also note that women who are discontinuing hormonal contraceptives should use Cycle Day 5 until they have 12 cycles uninfluenced by artificial hormones.

This rule can be applied beginning with your second cycle. You need to have recorded one cycle to ensure that the next bleeding was preceded by ovulation and, thus, was a true menstruation.

Day 5/6 Rule › Practice

If you are attending the classes, you will complete this exercise in class. If you are using this Student Guide as a Home Study Course, follow the directions below and then check your answers on page 190 in Appendix B.

Using the information provided on the chart, complete the exercise by applying the Day 5/6 Rule to determine the infertile days prior to Phase II.

Cycle History	Shortest Cycle	Infertile Days
12 cycles	26 days	
12 cycles	24 days	
10 cycles	28 days	

Doering Rule

As mentioned earlier, by noting the earliest first day of temperature rise, a couple can assume which days will be infertile prior to ovulation in future cycles. Dr. Doering used this information to propose a rule to determine the end of Phase I.

In his study, Dr. Doering reported this rule was a 97% effective means of determining the infertile days in Phase I. Note, however, that Dr. Doering achieved 97% effectiveness for Phase I without checking for mucus. As the CCL program always gives precedence to the appearance of mucus, the effectiveness of the Doering Rule as taught by CCL may be greater than 97%.

Doering Rule

Subtract seven from the earliest first day of temperature rise in the last 12 cycles. Mark that cycle day as the last day that you can assume Phase I infertility.

Conditions for use:

This rule assumes the absence of mucus.
This rule requires six cycles of temperature history.

RULE

To begin using this rule, couples need only have six cycles of temperature history. After six cycles of temperature history, subtract seven from the earliest first day of temperature rise in those cycles. Then after seven cycles, use the last seven cycles, and so on until you reach 12 cycles of history. From that point, continue to use just the last 12 cycles of temperature history. Again, if mucus is observed at any time, Phase II fertility begins.

Doering Rule › Practice

If you are attending the classes, you will complete this exercise in class. If you are using this Student Guide as a Home Study Course, follow the directions below and then check your answers on page 190 in Appendix B.

Using the information provided on the chart, complete the exercise by applying the Doering Rule to determine the infertile days prior to Phase II. (Assume at least six cycles of experience.)

Earliest First Day of Temperature Rise	Infertile Days
Cycle Day 21 (21-7)	Cycle Days 1-14
Cycle Day 14	
Cycle Day 18	
Cycle Day 12	

Last Dry Day Rule

The clearest indication that Phase I infertility has ended is the presence of cervical mucus. As soon as you detect mucus sensations and/or characteristics, you are in Phase II fertility. Therefore, Phase I ends on the last day on which mucus was not detected.

RULE

Last Dry Day Rule

The end of Phase I is the last day without mucus sensations or characteristics.

Conditions for use:

This rule requires six cycles of experience.
Women should have at least six days of mucus from its onset through Peak Day.

You should begin making mucus observations as soon as menstrual bleeding decreases, or by Cycle Day 5, whichever occurs first. For example, if the menstrual bleeding begins to decrease on Cycle Day 4, you should start observing the mucus signs on that day.[6]

CCL requires six cycles of experience because it might take that long to become proficient in identifying the first onset of mucus. Also, a history of having at least six days of mucus up through Peak Day takes into account the possibility of long sperm life.

Last Dry Day Rule › Practice

If you are attending the classes, you will complete this exercise in class. If you are using this Student Guide as a Home Study Course, record the symbols for the days having mucus notations until you reach Phase II. As soon as you determine the last infertile day (the last day of Phase I), draw a vertical line between Phase I and Phase II. Check your answers on page 191 in Appendix B.

⌄ Practice 1

	1	2	3	4	5	6	7	8	9	10	11	12	13	14	15	16	17	18	19	20	21	22	23	24	25	26	27	28	29	30	31	32	33
Peak Day *																																	
Symbols				○	○																												
Sensations	d	d	d	m	sl	sl	sl	sl	sl	w / sl	w / sl																						
Characteristics	n	n	n	t	t	t	s	s	s	n																							
Cervix																																	

⌄ Practice 2

	1	2	3	4	5	6	7	8	9	10	11	12	13	14	15	16	17	18	19	20	21	22	23	24	25	26	27	28	29	30	31	32	33
Peak Day *																																	
Symbols	○	○	○	○	○	○																											
Sensations	d	d	d	d	d	d	w	sl	sl	sl																							
Characteristics	n	n	n	n	n	n	n	n	s	n																							
Cervix																																	

---

[6] If the bleeding extends beyond Cycle Day 6, you may want to consult *Fertility, Cycles & Nutrition* by Marilyn Shannon to see if any of its suggestions will shorten the length of the menstrual bleed.

	8		8		8		8		8		8		8		8		8		8		8		8		8		8		8		8		8		8		8		8		8		8		8		8		8		8		8		8		8		8		8		8
1	2	3	4	5	**6**	7	8	9	10	11	12	13	14	15	16	17	18	19	20	21	22	23	24	25	26	27	28	29	30	31	32	33

Peak Day *								
Symbols	◯	◯	◯	◯	◯			
Mucus Sensations	d	d	d	d	d	d	w	w	s l
Characteristics	n	n	n	n	t	t	t	t	s
Cervix									

Days of Infertility in Phase I › Practice

Complete the exercise below to help you determine days of infertility during Phase I. If you are attending the classes, you will discuss the answers in class. If you are using this Student Guide as a Home Study Course, you will find the answers on page 191 in Appendix B.

T | F   The first five days of a cycle are infertile regardless of the presence of mucus.

T | F   The Last Dry Day Rule says that the last day with no mucus (sensations or characteristics) is the last day of Phase I.

T | F   A tacky mucus characteristic is a fertile sign.

T | F   Successfully applying the Phase I rules hinges on the ability to detect the very first sign of mucus.

Notes

Phase I Rules in Practice

- The presence of mucus sensations and/or characteristics indicates the end of Phase I and the start of Phase II. If there is any mucus present, assume Phase II fertility has begun.

- For Cycle 1, assume you are fertile until you can confirm the start of Phase III infertility. Thus, there is no application of Phase I rules on the first cycle.

- For Cycles 2 through 6, you may apply the Day 5/6 Rule.

- When you have six cycles of charting experience, you may apply the Day 5/6 Rule, Doering Rule, or Last Dry Day Rule.

Notes

Date (mm-mm/yyyy)	Oct–Nov 2011	Chart No.	20

Age __26__ Weight __170__ Height __5'9"__

Temp. time __5:30 AM__

Fill-in when sending chart in for review.

Membership No. _____ Phone _____

Name __Sue Nguyen__

Address _____

City _____ State ____ Zip _____

Email _____

CYCLE HISTORY

Previous cycle variation: Short __26__ Long __33__

Cycle variation based on __12__ recorded cycles

Earliest "first day of temperature rise" __15__

based on last __12__ cycles (up to 12)

End of Phase I: Day 5/6 Rule 5 ⑥ Doering Rule __8__

ADDITIONAL USER NOTES

How many days in this cycle? _____

What was 1st day of temperature rise? _____

Day of cycle	1	2	7	8	9	10	11	12	13	14	15	16	17	18	19	20	21	22	23	24	25	26
Menstruation	✗																					✗
Coitus record																						
Day of month																						
Day of week																						

Peak Day

If you are attending the classes, you will complete this exercise in class. If you are using this Student Guide as a Home Study Course, follow the directions below and then check your answers on pages 192 in Appendix B.

This exercise will show you how to transfer pertinent data from a completed chart to the next chart and to calculate the last potential infertile day in the new cycle using both the Day 5/6 Rule and Doering Rule. Use the following process to complete these exercises:

1. Determine the cycle length of the completed cycle and answer the questions in the "Additional User Notes" box.

   - How many days in this cycle?
   - What was the first day of temperature rise in this cycle?

2. What is the significance of this new data?

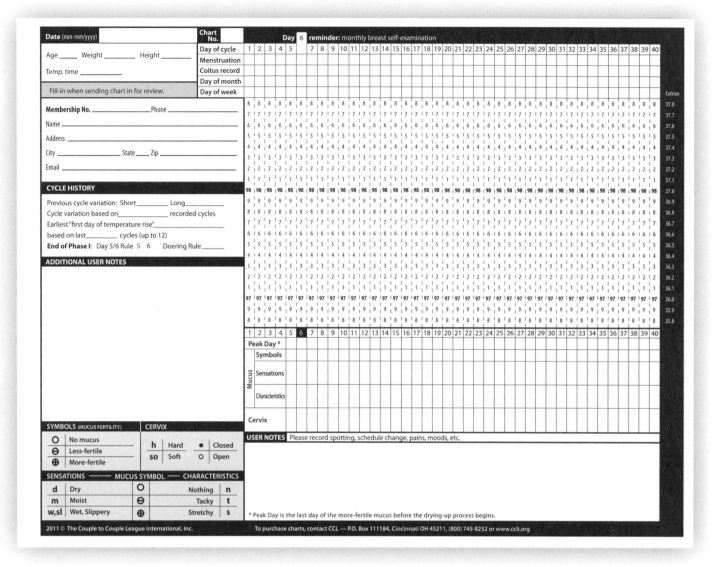

3. Transfer/update the following data onto the accompanying blank chart:

- Date, age, weight, height, temperature time
- Chart number, day of month, day of week
- Data for Cycle Day 1

4. Determine and record the following information in the Cycle History box:

- Previous cycle variation
- "Earliest first day of temperature rise"

5. Determine and circle the appropriate cycle days for the Day 5/6 Rule and Doering Rule.

Phase I Rules › Practice

Now it is time to put all this information together in order to determine days of Phase I infertility, and transition to the start of Phase II fertility. The three rules are:

- The Day 5/6 Rule
- The Doering Rule
- The Last Dry Day Rule

If you are attending the classes, you will complete this exercise in class. If you are using this Student Guide as a Home Study Course, see page 171 in Appendix A for the data to be recorded on the practice chart. Determine the end of Phase I for each rule. After completing the exercise, check your answers on page 193 in Appendix B.

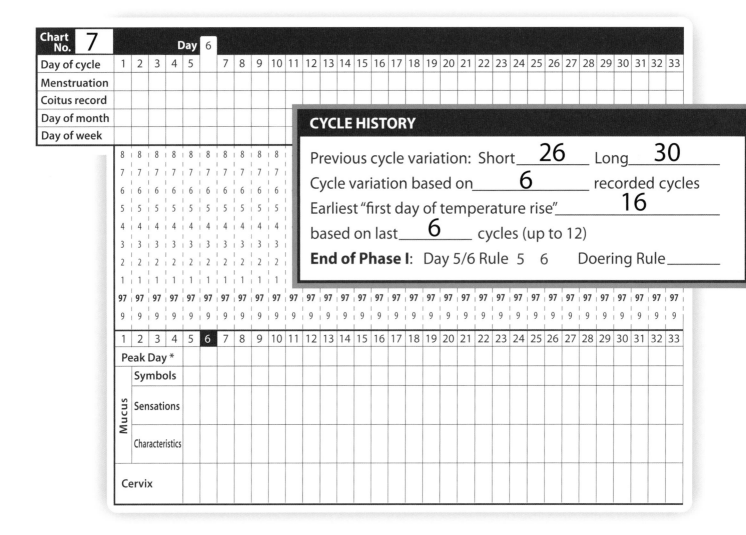

Chart No. 7					Day 6																										
Day of cycle	1	2	3	4	5		7	8	9	10	11	12	13	14	15	16	17	18	19	20	21	22	23	24	25	26	27	28	29	30	31	32	33
Menstruation																																
Coitus record																																
Day of month																																
Day of week																																

CYCLE HISTORY

Previous cycle variation: Short ___26___ Long ___30___

Cycle variation based on ___6___ recorded cycles

Earliest "first day of temperature rise" ___16___

based on last ___6___ cycles (up to 12)

End of Phase I: Day 5/6 Rule 5   6   Doering Rule _____

	1	2	3	4	5	6	7	8	9	10	11	12	13	14	15	16	17	18	19	20	21	22	23	24	25	26	27	28	29	30	31	32	33
Peak Day *																																	
Mucus – Symbols																																	
Mucus – Sensations																																	
Mucus – Characteristics																																	
Cervix																																	

Marital Intimacy during Phase II

Intimacy involves the innermost, private and personal part of each individual. It is more than physical. It can include countless acts of spoken or unspoken, physical or non-physical interchanges between spouses. Therefore, **marital intimacy** encompasses much more than the sexual embrace (marital relations). It may include silent or verbal prayer together, or simply being in the presence of your spouse at times when words cannot adequately express thoughts or feelings. Because marital intimacy is expressed and nurtured both through words and through body language, marital relations involve much more than just a physical expression. Knowing that you are fertile during certain days of the month can have a profound impact on spousal intimacy. When you know you are fertile, the decision to physically *become one* conveys the realization that you could also become *co-creators* of another unique and unrepeatable person. This, in turn, can deepen your spousal intimacy on all levels — physically, psychologically and spiritually.

As you know, your ability to conceive comes and goes. When you are aware of your fertility, Phase I can become a time of hopeful expectancy as you await Phase II fertility, or it can be an occasion to reaffirm your decision to postpone a pregnancy for the time being. If you are in the former situation, any decision regarding marital relations should be rooted in deference toward one another. If you are in the latter situation, abstinence on any days of potential fertility becomes the means to a greater good that extends beyond yourselves. Both situations can evoke a profound appreciation for your sexual powers and for the gift of new life. Both provide opportunities to give and to receive authentic love and to experience marital intimacy on its deepest level.

The next lesson will discuss in detail the effectiveness of NFP.

Notes

5 The Effectiveness of NFP

Lesson 5

Natural Family Planning has no harmful side effects. It involves knowledge of one's fertility, and it enriches the mutual respect for the dignity of each spouse. But, does it actually provide reliable information regarding a woman's fertility on a daily basis, and is it really effective in helping a couple to plan or postpone a pregnancy?

Effectiveness is a percentage normally derived from studies that have determined *unintended pregnancy* rates. An **unintended pregnancy rate** is measured in terms of the number of women out of 100 who become pregnant in one year using a method intended to delay/postpone pregnancy. Therefore, an unintended pregnancy rate of 15% or 0.15 means 15 couples out of 100 conceived during one year of using that method. A 99% effective rule or method, therefore, means that 99 couples out of 100 did not conceive during one year of using that method. There are also two types of effectiveness: **method effectiveness** and **user effectiveness.**

Method Effectiveness

This is the effectiveness of a particular method intended to delay/postpone pregnancy that assumes *perfect use*, and is calculated using *only* those unintended pregnancies that resulted from correctly following the rules of the method and the cycles in which the method was correctly and consistently used.

For NFP users of a particular rule or method, this would include any pregnancy that occurs even when the couple correctly follows and applies all of the rules without exception. A parallel example involving the hormonal contraceptive pill would be including pregnancies that occur when the pill is taken exactly as prescribed without exception. A high method effectiveness implies that, when used correctly, the user can have a very high confidence level that the rules will identify days of fertility and infertility.

User Effectiveness

This is the effectiveness of a particular method intended to postpone/delay pregnancy based on the *actual practices* of the couples using the method. It is calculated using all unintended pregnancies occurring during a study and *all* months or cycles, which includes incorrect and correct application of a method and its rules.

For example, the calculation of user effectiveness of the Sympto-Thermal Method of NFP would include an unintended pregnancy that resulted from a couple who engaged in the marital embrace during days when mucus was present prior to ovulation. User effectiveness also accounts for a couple's understanding and application of the rules. Reliability is reduced through poor instruction or inaccurate recordings. For all methods, user effectiveness will always be less than, or equal to, method effectiveness.

STM Effectiveness

German Study

A study of the effectiveness of the sympto-thermal rules associated with NFP was published in 2007.[1] The study used rules that were comparable to CCL's Day 5/6 Rule and Sympto-Thermal Rule, and found a method effectiveness of 99.6% and a user effectiveness of 98.2%. (See Reference Guide, page 218, for a more-detailed discussion of this study.)

Other Data

As previously indicated, many of the rules presented in the NFP classes taught by CCL are based on the early work of Dr. Josef Roetzer. Since his early pioneering work, others have confirmed the effectiveness of the Sympto-Thermal Method. For example, a large study

---

[1] P. Frank-Herrmann, J. Heil, C. Gnoth, et al. "The effectiveness of a fertility awareness based method to avoid pregnancy in relation to a couple's sexual behaviour during the fertile time: a prospective longitudinal study," *Human Reproduction* 22(5) (2007):1310–1319.

conducted in nine countries in Europe found a user effectiveness of over 97%.[2] Another study conducted in the 1990s found a method effectiveness of 99.4% and a user effectiveness of 97.8%.[3] (See Reference Guide, page 219–222 for a more detailed discussion of the data supporting CCL's rules.)

Comparative Effectiveness of Methods

While NFP's effectiveness can be compared to that of contraceptives, there are differences between the two. Natural Family Planning effectiveness pertains to a couple's ability to determine fertile and infertile times of a woman's cycle. The effectiveness of various contraceptives relates to the ability of pills or devices to prevent a pregnancy from occurring or from continuing. The user effectiveness of NFP also involves the ability of a couple to refrain from sexual intercourse on days that the method indicates are fertile if they intend to postpone a pregnancy. The user effectiveness of contraceptives relates to a woman/couple

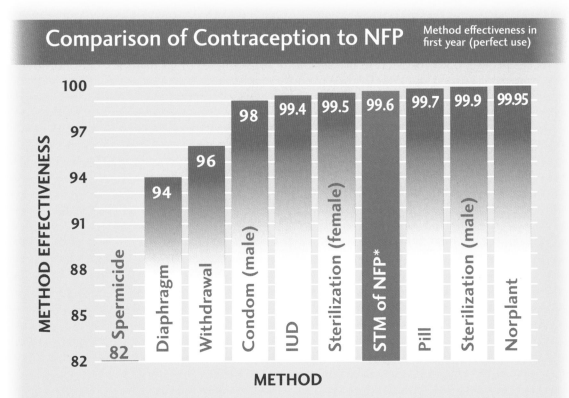

R. Hatcher, et al., *Contraceptive Technology*, 18th revised edition (New York, NY: Ardent Media, 2004), see Table 31–1, 792–847.

* P. Frank-Herrmann, J. Heil, C. Gnoth, et al. "The effectiveness of a fertility awareness based method to avoid pregnancy in relation to a couple's sexual behavior during the fertile time: a prospective longitudinal study," *Human Reproduction*, 22(5) (2007): 1310–1319.

---

[2] European Natural Family Planning study groups. "Prospective European multi-center study of natural family planning (1989–1992): interim results," *Advances in Contraception* 9 (1993):269–283.

[3] P. Frank-Herrmann et al. "Natural family planning with and without barrier method use in the fertile phase: efficacy in relation to sexual behavior: a German prospective long-term study," *Advances in Contraception* 13 (1997)179–189.

using the devices or taking the pills as specified if they intend to postpone a pregnancy.

The graph on the previous page compares the *method effectiveness* of various forms of contraception with NFP. It should be noted that no method is 100% effective; unplanned pregnancies occur in all methods.

In summary, the Sympto-Thermal Method of NFP (green bar on the graph) taught in this course is extremely effective in determining the fertile and infertile times of a woman's cycle. The 2007 German study also showed that couples who have a desire to postpone a pregnancy during a given cycle can do so using NFP with the same accuracy as contraceptives.

Notes

6 Using NFP to Achieve a Pregnancy

Lesson 6

Now that you have learned how to read the language of the body regarding fertility and infertility effectively, you can use this knowledge to make virtuous decisions regarding responsible parenthood. In other words, you have enough information to plan or to postpone a pregnancy, while maintaining an attitude of respect for your spouse and generosity toward life.

The Church has long called children the "supreme gift of marriage" because they contribute to the welfare of the spouses (i.e., children help their parents become less self-focused) and they help build up God's kingdom ("Be fruitful and multiply," Gen. 1:28). In each child, couples should recognize a gift coming to them from the Creator, a precious gift to be loved and welcomed with joy.

The cyclical nature of NFP provides couples a unique opportunity to routinely revisit the decision to hope for a child or to postpone conception. While one month you may need to sacrifice the desire for a child for the greater good of the family, the next month a possible conception would be welcomed.

In this lesson, you will learn how to use NFP to help achieve a pregnancy, how nutrition affects conception, and how to accurately estimate the date of childbirth (EDC) using data found on your own charts.

Male Fertility

In Class 1, you learned that during marital relations, approximately 200–500 million sperm enter a woman's vagina. Individual sperm life depends on both its own viability and the presence of mucus in the vagina. In the absence of mucus, sperm normally live no more than a few hours; but, in the presence of mucus, they can live up to five days. It is mucus that enables sperm to stay alive for extended periods of time. It also capacitates the sperm (i.e., makes it capable of fertilizing the egg), which is critical for achieving a pregnancy.

Female Fertility

As ovulation approaches, a woman's level of estrogen increases and signals the brain to release higher doses of luteinizing hormone (LH). This surge in LH around mid-cycle triggers the release of an egg from the ovarian follicle (see graph, page 12). The follicle then becomes the corpus luteum and produces progesterone. The egg enters the Fallopian tube and is capable of being fertilized only within the next 24 hours. (Occasionally, there is a second ovulation, and this occurs within 24 hours after the first one.)

The graph below depicts the limited time each month that a viable male sperm can fertilize a female egg, thus creating a new human life. This is reflected by the ability of an individual

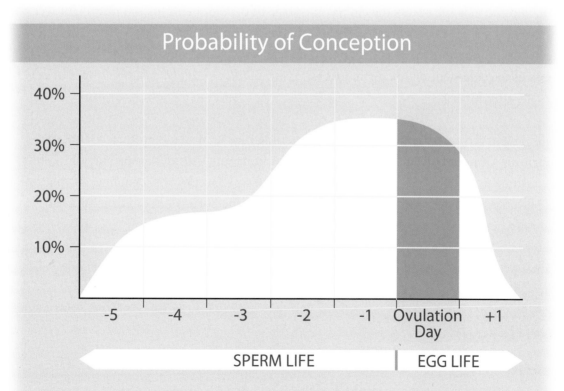

Allen J. Wilcox, M.D., Clarice R. Weinberg, Ph.D., and Donna D. Baird, Ph.D., "Timing of Sexual Intercourse in Relation to Ovulation," *New England Journal of Medicine* 333:23 (December 7, 1995): 1517–1521.

sperm to live a maximum of five days in the presence of mucus, and the ability of one egg to live a maximum of 24 hours. The graph also includes the possibility of a second egg being released and living for a maximum of 24 hours. One aspect of "the art of natural family planning" to achieve a pregnancy is to maximize the timing and ability of a viable sperm to fertilize an egg.

Conception

Conception or fertilization occurs when one sperm penetrates one egg — providing a complete set of genetic material (one-half from the mother and one-half from the father) to the newly conceived life. At this stage, the new life is called a **blastocyst** as it begins to divide and grow. During this early division process the blastocyst travels down the Fallopian tube, and in approximately six to nine days, it develops some threadlike projections on its surface that enable it to attach to the lining of the uterus. This attachment process is called **implantation**, and the new life enters the embryonic stage of development for the next eight weeks. (After eight weeks, the **embryo** enters another stage and is called a **fetus**. Remember that life begins at the moment of conception. The terms *blastocyst, embryo* and *fetus* describe stages of development before birth, just as *infant, toddler* and *teen* describe stages of development after birth.)

Within eight days after conception, the developing placental tissue produces **Human Chorionic Gonadotropin (hCG) hormone**. This hormone stimulates the corpus luteum to continue producing progesterone for the first 10 to 12 weeks of pregnancy. At that time, the placenta takes over progesterone production and the corpus luteum degenerates.[1]

---

[1] Thomas W. Hilgers, M.D., *Reproductive Anatomy and Physiology, Second Edition* (Omaha: Pope Paul VI Institute Press, 2002), 38–39.

Notes

Developing Baby

At conception, a person's sex is determined. Soon thereafter, blood vessels and lungs begin to form. By three weeks, his heart is beating. During the second month, his skeleton changes from cartilage to bone; fingers, toes and facial muscles develop; eyelids begin to form; internal organs are present; and muscles begin to exercise. By eight weeks, all body systems are present; teeth form; ears, nose, lips, and tongue can be seen; and brain waves are recorded. He can touch, yawn and hiccup. By 12 weeks, the baby's fingernails and toenails form, and he has his own fingerprints. He can squint, swallow, move his tongue, sleep, awaken, and he is sensitive to touch. When he is about four months in utero, fine hair begins to grow on his head, eyebrows and eyelashes; and he has facial expressions similar to his parents. In addition, he can dream because rapid eye movement has been recorded at this stage of development. At five months, the baby's mother can feel him move, stretch and kick. By six months, he sleeps, wakes and can respond to sound. He has a good chance of survival if born. By seven months, the eyelids open and close, and the baby can look around. He can taste; he recognizes his mother's voice and has a strong grip. By eight months, the lungs are fully developed and ready to breathe air.[2] Only time, nutrition and protection are needed to prepare the baby for birth.

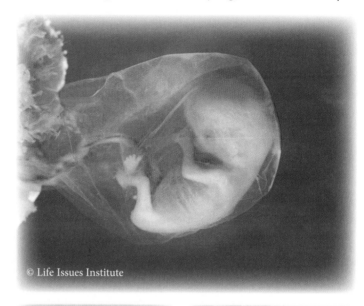

© Life Issues Institute

© Life Issues Institute

© Life Issues Institute

---

[2] Developmental milestones of an unborn baby taken from "Milestones of Early Life," Life Issues Institute, (2006 Heritage House '76, Inc.) and "What They Never Told You About the Facts of Life," Human Development Resource Council, Inc., (Revised 2005).

Key Observable Signs for Achieving a Pregnancy

Mucus

As you learned in the first class, more-fertile mucus is present in the days nearest to and including the day of ovulation, which is often Peak Day. Mucus provides nutrition and aids in transport of the sperm. Its presence allows the sperm to reside in the cervical area for as long as five days after ejaculation, periodically releasing sperm into the Fallopian tube in search of an egg. The mucus dries up after ovulation due to the increase of progesterone.

Temperature and Luteal Phase

Under the influence of progesterone, the basal body temperature rises approximately 0.4° F after ovulation. If conception does not occur, the temperature remains at a higher level for about two weeks until the next menstruation. For each woman, the time between the first day of temperature rise and the next menstruation is generally a consistent number of days. This time is called the **luteal phase** because it corresponds with the life of the corpus luteum (discussed earlier in this lesson).

The length of the luteal phase is important because it can indicate the probable first day of the next menstruation, the potential for implantation of a new life, and achievement of a pregnancy. After a woman identifies the first day of the luteal phase in a cycle, she can predict (within one or two days) when the next menstruation will begin. There are many advantages in knowing when to anticipate the next menstrual bleeding. Women who experience physical and/or emotional difficulties from monthly hormonal changes may be able to minimize their symptoms by preparing for them in advance.[3]

---

[3] Marilyn M. Shannon, *Fertility, Cycles & Nutrition,* 4th edition (Cincinnati: The Couple to Couple League, 2009) 67–78.

Notes

The luteal phase can be useful in providing early information to a woman that she is pregnant. If conception does occur, the temperature remains at a higher level during much of the pregnancy. An early sign of pregnancy is a sustained higher temperature level beyond the luteal phase. For example, if a woman normally has a luteal phase of 11–13 days and her temperatures remain high for 21 days, these temperatures provide a very early indicator that she is probably pregnant.

Earlier in this lesson you learned that it takes approximately six to nine days for the blastocyst (new life) to travel through the Fallopian tube and implant in the uterus. Therefore, a luteal phase less than 10 days may be insufficient to sustain a pregnancy. The progesterone will drop and the lining of the uterus will shed as the period occurs. A short luteal phase may cause infertility in a couple who is otherwise fully capable of conceiving and carrying a child. A couple who identifies a luteal phase inadequacy can work to remedy this situation by following nutritional suggestions in *Fertility, Cycles & Nutrition* and/or by consulting with a physician who is knowledgeable in fertility awareness/NFP methods. (See Reference Guide for further information.)

Cervix

The cervix is relevant because it opens and softens as ovulation approaches. This allows sperm to move into the uterus and Fallopian tube and enhances the possibility of conception. After ovulation, the cervix closes and hardens, and will protect a newly conceived life from the outside world.

Interpreting the Signs of Fertility to Achieve a Pregnancy

Observing and recording the three signs — cervical mucus, temperature and cervix — usually provides enough information for a couple to know when they are experiencing Phase II (fertility) in any given cycle. In this way, NFP can assist them in achieving a pregnancy. In most cycles, a changing pattern of mucus that progresses to the highly slippery and/or very wet sensations indicates the approach of ovulation. The more-fertile mucus is usually present in the days close to ovulation; then it becomes less-fertile and/or dries up after ovulation. The cervix is open and soft prior to ovulation and closed and hard after ovulation. Using the Sympto-Thermal Method of NFP, it is the temperature sign that can actually confirm ovulation. The thermal shift is a positive indication that ovulation *has already occurred*, and extended days of higher temperatures can be an early sign of pregnancy.

A 2003 study of "truly fertile couples" reported that 88% of the couples were able to achieve a pregnancy within six months through fertility awareness. By 12 months, 98% of these couples successfully achieved a pregnancy when timing marital relations to the most fertile times of a woman's cycle.[4] For couples desiring to maximize their ability to achieve a pregnancy, the application of the information provided in this course can help them pursue this goal. Planning marital relations around the time of maximum fertility will increase the probability of conception.

Helps for Achieving a Pregnancy

1. Focused Fertility Awareness

a. **Mucus** — Remember that the term "Peak" associated with the Peak Day implies that this might be the day of highest fertility because research has shown it to be most frequently the day of ovulation. The days of highest probability to achieve a pregnancy are Peak Day and the two preceding days.[5] As you have already learned, Peak Day can only be determined in retrospect. However, you also know that the days prior to and including Peak Day are typically days with slippery sensations, a very wet (runny, watery) feeling, and/or the presence of the stretchy, elastic, stringy or thready mucus. Marital relations on these days can maximize the chances of conception.

b. **Temperature** — The basal body temperature can also be of assistance when trying to conceive. The first day that the temperature begins to rise is closely associated with the day of ovulation. In addition, often when estrogen reaches its highest level prior to ovulation, the basal temperatures may be somewhat depressed. This is sometimes signaled by a dip in the temperature prior to the thermal shift. If you detect a dip in temperatures, consider the days immediately following as possible days of high fertility.

2. Maximize Sperm Count

During marital relations, a healthy male ejaculates between 200 and 500 million sperm. Although it takes only one sperm to achieve a pregnancy, the probability of conception is enhanced with an increased sperm count. Sperm count is also maximized with five days of abstinence. Thus, abstaining for a few days before Phase II could result in a higher sperm count and an increased probability of achieving a pregnancy.

---

[4] Gnoth, C., Dodehardt, D. et al., "Time to pregnancy: results of the German prospective study and impact on the management of infertility," *Human Reproduction* 18:9 (September 2003): 1959–1966.

[5] Colombo, B., Mion, A., Passarin, K., and Scarpa, B. "Cervical mucus symptom and daily fecundability: first results from a new database," *Statistical Methods in Medical Research* 15 (2006): 161–180.

3. Good Nutrition/Lifestyle Habits

Perhaps the most immediate and basic action husbands and wives can take in preparation for pregnancy is to adopt a healthy lifestyle. Good eating habits, moderate exercise, regular sleep, and spiritual development can provide the right balance for maintaining optimal health. Some basic nutritional strategies that can enhance fertility for both women and men include, but are not limited to, the following:[6]

a. Eat nutritionally well-balanced meals, and consider taking multivitamin/mineral supplements. Vitamins and minerals affect the interplay of the reproductive hormones. (Women attempting to achieve pregnancy should talk to their physician about taking folic acid to lessen the risk of certain birth defects.)

b. Decrease caffeine and foods with additives.

c. Eliminate alcohol.

d. Don't smoke. Nicotine may impair sexual function in men, and women who smoke are estimated to have decreased fertility when compared with non-smokers.

e. Women should try to maintain a healthy weight. Being underweight or having too little body fat can cause scant cervical mucus, long menstrual cycles, anovulatory cycles (cycles without ovulation), and possibly infertility. Being overweight can cause cycle irregularity and infertility with or without regular cycles.[7]

Be sure to keep good records of your monthly fertility. Inadequate functioning of your fertility hormones can cause a short luteal phase, premenstrual spotting, postmenstrual brown spotting, poor thermal shift, extended mucus, scant mucus, **amenorrhea** (absence of menstrual periods), or unexplained infertility.[8] (See Class 3 for additional information.)

---

[6] The Couple to Couple League advises you to speak with your physician about any self-help measures you would like to try, especially with regard to dietary changes and vitamin/mineral supplements.

[7] Shannon, 106–109, 118–120.

[8] Shannon, 95–99.

Suggestions for minimizing these problems can be found in Marilyn Shannon's book, *Fertility, Cycles & Nutrition*. It includes information on cycle irregularities, pregnancy-related problems, repeated miscarriages, birth defects, female and male infertility, specific nutritional needs when coming off hormonal contraceptives, and much more. Most importantly, it offers potential solutions to alleviate these and many other problems as well.

Fertility Monitors & CycleProGo®

In addition to the preceding hints for achieving pregnancy, women may find it helpful to use a **fertility monitor**. Fertility monitors measure hormone levels, such as estrogen or luteinizing hormone (LH), because these hormones peak immediately prior to ovulation.[9] Some also detect **electrolytes** (substances that form ions in solution and are capable of conducting electricity) in saliva, urine, or cervical mucus. All monitors in use in the United States require the approval of the Food and Drug Administration (FDA). As of this writing, they are approved only as a means of achieving a pregnancy. Probably the most affordable high quality monitor available in the United States is the Clearblue Easy Fertility Monitor. Most home fertility monitors identify the surge in LH that triggers ovulation; however, the Clearblue Easy Fertility Monitor also shows additional fertile days by detecting a rise in estrogen. Therefore, this monitor can inform most women of an extra one to five days of higher fertility prior to their peak fertility or LH surge. Such a monitor can be a useful tool in identifying the fertile window of time for achieving a pregnancy.

Some couples find charting software to be helpful as well. The Couple to Couple League offers a mobile charting app (CyclePro*Go*®) that identifies the fertile and infertile times of the cycle. Couples can also allow their NFP Teaching Couple view access to their chart to provide comments and assistance. For more information, visit ***www.ccli.org***.

---

[9] There are a wide range of fertility monitors on the market today. This paragraph is designed to introduce you to the presence of such monitors as a possible aid to detecting fertile times of a woman's cycle. An internet search will reveal a variety of models and prices. In addition to ongoing costs for test strips, expect to pay about $200 or more for a high quality monitor. This is by no means a complete discussion of the subject.

Notes

Calculating Due Dates › Naegele Rule

Today, while imaging technology can help a physician determine the size and physical attributes of a developing baby, the "due date" is a key factor in determining the preparedness of the baby for delivery. Miscalculated due dates may lead to women delivering babies before they are truly due, or to mothers undergoing cesarean sections to deliver babies prematurely. The most common method used by physicians to determine the due date is the Naegele Rule, named after the physician who developed it. It depends on an accurate determination of the first day of the last menstruation, and assumes that women do not know the date they ovulated.

Naegele Rule:

The Estimated Date of Childbirth (EDC) is calculated by adding seven days to the first day of the last menstrual period, and then adding nine months.

First day of last menstrual period

+ 7 days

+ 9 months

Equals Estimated Date of Childbirth (EDC)

For women who ovulate around Cycle Day 14, the Naegele Rule is very precise. Unfortunately, its precision decreases if the length of a woman's cycle is greater than, or less than, 28 days.

Calculating Due Dates › Prem Rule

Dr. Konald Prem, former chairman of the Obstetrics and Gynecology Department of the University of Minnesota, refined the calculation of the due date based on the date of ovulation by using the first day of elevated temperatures as the baseline —a known time close to the actual day of ovulation. Since the Prem Rule is based much closer to the actual day of ovulation, it is a better predictor of the date of childbirth than the Naegele Rule.

Prem Rule:

The Estimated Date of Childbirth (EDC) is calculated by subtracting seven days from the first day of thermal shift, and then adding nine months.

First day of thermal shift

− 7 days

+ 9 months

Equals Estimated Date of Childbirth (EDC)

Comparing Estimated Date of Childbirth

1st Day of Menstrual Period	1st Day of Temperature Rise	Due Date using the Naegele Rule	Due Date using the Prem Rule
February 3	February 12	November 10	November 5
February 3	February 17	November 10	November 10
February 3	February 24	November 10	November 17

As you can see, the due dates differ when a woman has a cycle in which she does not ovulate on Cycle Day 14. The Prem Rule reflects due dates more closely tied to the day of ovulation (and thus conception). Thus, it is more accurate than the Naegele Rule, which is calculated from menstruation rather than ovulation.

Notes

Achieving a Pregnancy › Practice Chart

The following exercise will summarize several lessons presented in this class.

If you are attending the classes, you will complete this exercise in class. If you are using this Student Guide as a Home Study Course, analyze the chart as follows:

1. Determine the end of Phase I by the Last Dry Day Rule and draw a vertical line between the last day of Phase I and the first day of Phase II.

2. Determine the start of Phase III by applying the ST Rule, and draw a vertical line through that cycle day and temperature on the chart.

3. Calculate the Estimated Date of Childbirth (EDC) using the Prem Rule on page 103.

Check your answers on page 194 in Appendix B.

7 Authentic Love and Responsible Parenthood

Lesson 7

In the last class, you learned that NFP is the knowledge of the body's rhythms of fertility. Natural Family Planning reads the language of the sexual powers and teaches us a means to come to know ourselves and our spouses. This requires an understanding of who we are and how we express ourselves. We are human persons. We have a mind, a free will and a body, and as human persons, we are capable of loving as God loves.

In an earlier lesson of this class, you were taught how to calculate which days fall within Phase I infertility, and how to discern the transition to Phase II fertility. During these phases, you will be making some significant decisions regarding sexual intimacy: Will you prayerfully hope for a child and have marital relations during the fertile time; or will you prayerfully decide to postpone pregnancy for the time being, thus abstaining each day after intercourse in Phase I and throughout Phase II?

In his essay, "The Human Body...a sign of dignity and a gift,"[1] Reverend Richard M. Hogan explains the unique love between a husband and a wife, and how fertility awareness can actually lead them to **responsible parenthood** (which is defined as the virtuous decision to plan or to postpone conception). His explanation includes a discussion of the five characteristics of divine love, and why it is crucial for married couples to embrace these same characteristics as much as they possibly can.

---

[1] Rev. Richard M. Hogan, *The Human Body...a sign of dignity and a gift* (Cincinnati: The Couple to Couple League, 2005).

Love is a decision — giving for the good of the other. Each spouse must *choose* to give himself or herself as a *permanent* gift to the other. This choice to become a *self-gift* involves *knowledge* of the value and dignity of the spouse. In addition, God created man and woman so that the intimate physical gift of love between husband and wife can be *life-giving*. When properly understood, this ability to participate in the power of creation is itself a great gift to the couple, because only human beings can give life to new unique persons of equal value to themselves. Each child is another expression of God in this world and will live for all eternity.

Characteristics of Love

- Choice
- Based on knowledge
- Self-gift
- Permanent
- Life-giving

In addition, God gave us a mind and a will so that we could make decisions regarding the creation of a new human person (called **procreation**). The choice to postpone a pregnancy by abstaining from marital relations during the fertile phase is very different from the choice to alter the husband's or the wife's body (either chemically or physically) in order to attain the same goal. Father Hogan explains the reasoning behind this important distinction.

"Some people think that a decision by a couple to time their acts of love in order to space children using NFP is the same as the decision by a couple to avoid pregnancy through contraception. This is a confusion of purposes and means. The purpose may be the same, but the means are different. The NFP couple delaying another pregnancy and the contraceptive couple delaying a pregnancy are engaging in two radically different acts… The NFP couple, while engaging in non-procreative intercourse by making use of the infertile times, give themselves to each other totally and completely as they are at that moment. The contracepting couple withholds their fertility from each other in an anti-procreative act and do not give themselves totally. Remember, love is defined as a total self-gift… Further, the contracepting couple alters either both their bodies or one of them and in so doing they violate the integrity of their own bodies."[2]

There are many misconceptions regarding responsible parenthood. Many believe that the church says couples must have as many children as possible, and the purpose of sex is solely to have children. This is simply not true. For instance, *Humanae Vitae* teaches that responsible parenthood is lived out by couples who prudently and generously decided to have more children, but also by those who "for serious reasons and with due respect to moral precepts, decide not to have additional children for either a certain or an indefinite period of time" (*Humanae Vitae*, 10). Couples are to be open to the Lord's call and to be faithful interpreters of his plan. This happens both in generously opening their hearts to more children, and when "for serious reasons and in respect for the moral law, they choose to avoid a new birth for the time being or indefinitely" (*Evangelium Vitae*, 97).

---

[2] Hogan, 9.

So while married couples are called to generosity in the service of life, they are also called to prayerfully discern how many children are appropriate for them at the present time. It is important, therefore, for couples to prayerfully discern together the number of children that is right for them based on their physical, economic, psychological, and social conditions. These broad guidelines constitute "just reasons," and the Church does not specifically define what these conditions are, or how many children are right for one couple or another.

These ideas are actually captured in the vows of marriage. To be a true marriage in the Church you must promise an openness to God's will with children. That means trusting God through prayer for having children and caring for the ones that come. Then when you follow God's design for husband and wife each marital act will be life giving. At times that will result in a flesh and blood baby, but every time it will enliven the unity you share. The key is following God's design as you promise on the wedding day.

Talk to each other, pray together, and listen to God's calling for you and your family.

Homework

Whether you are attending the classes or using this Student Guide as a Home Study Course, you should interpret Homework Charts 5–7 that are located in Appendix A on pages 172–175. Determine the end of Phase I with each Phase I rule and apply the ST Rule to determine the beginning of Phase III on each of the three charts. In class, these will be reviewed at the beginning of Class 3.

Class 3

Introduction • Review • Other Methods of NFP • Applying NFP in Special Situations
Behaviors that Attack Human Dignity and Marital Love • Contraception
Benefits of Breastfeeding and Its Effect on Fertility
NFP During Premenopause • Benefits of NFP

1 Introduction

This third class is divided into nine lessons: *Introduction, Review, Other Methods of NFP, Applying NFP in Special Situations, Behaviors that Attack Human Dignity and Marital Love, Contraception, Benefits of Breastfeeding and Its Effect on Fertility, NFP During Premenopause,* and *Benefits of NFP.* This *Introduction* will summarize the Class 3 lessons.

Summary: Class 3 Lessons

Lesson 2, *Review*, uses a practice exercise to discuss the concepts taught in Class 2, including:

- how to handle abnormal/missed temperature information
- how to identify the transition from Phase I to Phase II, and
- how to calculate the Estimated Date of Childbirth (EDC)

In addition, you will review the three homework charts assigned at the end of the previous class. (You should complete these charts prior to attending Class 3.)

Lesson 3, *Other Methods of NFP*, has a two-fold purpose. First, it will introduce you to some of the other popular methods of NFP found in the United States today. Second, it will explain how the CCL Mucus-Only and Temperature-Only Rules have been derived from those methods, and how you can use these rules when one or more of the measurable signs of fertility are not present or are confusing in a given menstrual cycle. Lesson 3 also explains how modern NFP differs from the Calendar Rhythm Method. This lesson is not intended to be an instructional guide for any of the other methods, but merely an introduction to them.

In Lesson 4, *Applying NFP in Special Situations*, you will learn how to interpret your signs of fertility during various situations that are less common, to include: having cycles with unusual mucus patterns or breakthrough bleeding, stress, illness, and while taking medications. At the end of this lesson, you will know how to identify these conditions and how to interpret your fertility while experiencing them.

Lesson 5, *Behaviors that Attack Human Dignity and Marital Love*, explains how the characteristics of true love are violated by each type of contraception but not by the use of NFP. The following lesson, *Contraception*, shows the actions of the various methods and some of the medical and moral side effects of them.

The next two lessons are brief because they generally are not of immediate concern for most of the attendees of this course, although they do provide valuable information for the future. Based on studies from major health organizations, the benefits of breastfeeding extend even beyond baby and mother. Lesson 7, *Benefits of Breastfeeding and Its Effect on Fertility*, clarifies some of the major advantages and reveals how baby feeding affects fertility. Lesson 8, *NFP During Premenopause*, provides a preview of how fertility awareness can help a woman determine when she enters the time of premenopause and menopause, as well as some of the changes she will observe during that time. (Note that the Couple to Couple League offers supplemental classes on the postpartum and premenopause transitions in addition to this course.)

The class and the course conclude with Lesson 9, *Benefits of NFP*, which reviews not only the physical benefits, but the psychological and spiritual benefits of NFP as well.

Notes

2 Review

Lesson 2

This *Review* primarily focuses on the rules presented during Class 2. These include rules associated with proper application of abnormal/missed temperature information, identifying the transition from Phase I to Phase II, and calculating the Estimated Date of Childbirth (EDC).

Applying the Sympto-Thermal Rule: Abnormal/Missed Temperatures

An **abnormal temperature** is one that appears to be out of the range of the surrounding temperatures when it is recorded on the chart. A **missed temperature** is one that either was not taken or was not recorded on the chart.

If there are one or two abnormal or missed temperatures in the pre-shift six, use them in counting the pre-shift six, but do not use them when setting the LTL. The LTL should be determined from the remaining normal temperatures among the pre-shift six.[1] When applying the Sympto-Thermal Rule, Phase III begins after *waiting for four post-peak temperatures above the LTL*. (While all temperatures must be above the LTL, none need reach the HTL.)

---

[1] This discussion of abnormal/missed temperatures only pertains to their application when using the ST Rule. When applying abnormal or missed temperatures for CCL's Temperature-Only Rule, see footnote 4 on page 124.

If there are abnormal or missed temperature readings within the three thermal shift temperatures, *the pre-shift six cannot be established until there are three normal post-peak temperatures above the LTL.* Apply the ST Rule using those normal temperatures. In this case, if the third post-peak temperature does not reach the HTL or the cervix has not been closed and hard for three days, you must wait for an additional temperature above the LTL.

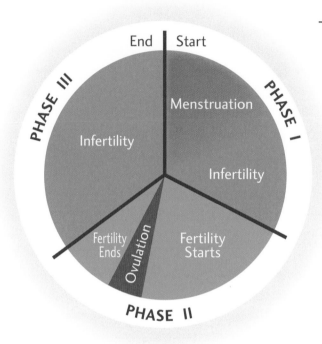

Identify the Transition from Phase I to Phase II

Phase I begins on the first day of menstruation, and Phase II begins with the onset of mucus sensations and/or characteristics. *The presence of mucus is the fundamental condition for defining the start of Phase II.*

Ending Phase I

General guidelines to eliminate confusion regarding the mucus sign:

- **Evenings Only** — CCL recommends that once menstruation lessens, marital relations occur only in the evenings during Phase I.
- **Not on Consecutive Days** — CCL recommends that once menstruation lessens, you should abstain on any day that follows marital relations in Phase I unless you are experienced and can positively detect the absence of mucus.

Rules to determine the limits of Phase I infertility:

Day 5/6 Rule

Assume infertility on Cycle Days 1–5.

For women with cycles 26 days or longer in the last 12 cycles, assume infertility on Cycle Days 1–6.

Conditions for use:

This rule assumes the absence of mucus.

Doering Rule

Subtract seven from the earliest first day of temperature rise in the last 12 cycles. Mark that cycle day as the last day that you can assume Phase I infertility.

Conditions for use:

The rule assumes the absence of mucus.
This rule requires six cycles of temperature history.

Last Dry Day Rule

The end of Phase I is the last day without mucus sensations or characteristics.

Conditions for use:

This rule requires six cycles of experience.
Woman should have at least six days of mucus from its onset through Peak Day.

Estimated Date of Childbirth (EDC)

Naegele Rule:

The EDC is calculated by adding seven days to the first day of the last menstrual period, and then adding nine months.

Prem Rule:

The EDC is calculated by subtracting seven days from the first day of thermal shift, and then adding nine months.

Rule to determine Phase III infertility:

Sympto-Thermal Rule

Phase III begins on the evening of:

1. The third day of drying-up after Peak Day, combined with

2. Three normal post-peak temperatures above the LTL, and

3. The third temperature at or above the HTL or the cervix closed and hard for three days.

If the above conditions are not met, then Phase III begins after waiting an additional post-peak day for another temperature above the LTL.

RULE

Steps for Applying the Sympto-Thermal Rule

1. Find Peak Day and number the three days of drying-up after it from left to right.

2. Close to Peak Day, find three temperatures that are higher than the six preceding temperatures.

3. Number the pre-shift six from right to left.

4. Draw the Low Temperature Level (LTL) on the highest of the pre-shift six temperatures.

5. Draw the High Temperature Level (HTL) at 0.4° F above the LTL.

6. Find the third of three normal post-peak temperatures that are all above the LTL ("post-peak" means occurring after Peak Day). If this third temperature is at or above the HTL, Phase III begins on the evening of that day.

7. If the third normal post-peak temperature does not reach the HTL, check the cervix sign (if recorded). If there are three days of a closed, hard cervix, then it is not necessary for the third normal post-peak temperature to reach the HTL. Phase III begins on the evening of that day.

8. If the requirements in steps #6 and #7 are not met, wait for an additional normal post-peak temperature above the LTL; Phase III begins that evening.

9. After you apply the ST Rule and determine the start of Phase III, draw a vertical phase division line through the temperature dot on the first day of Phase III.

Notes

Review › Practice Chart

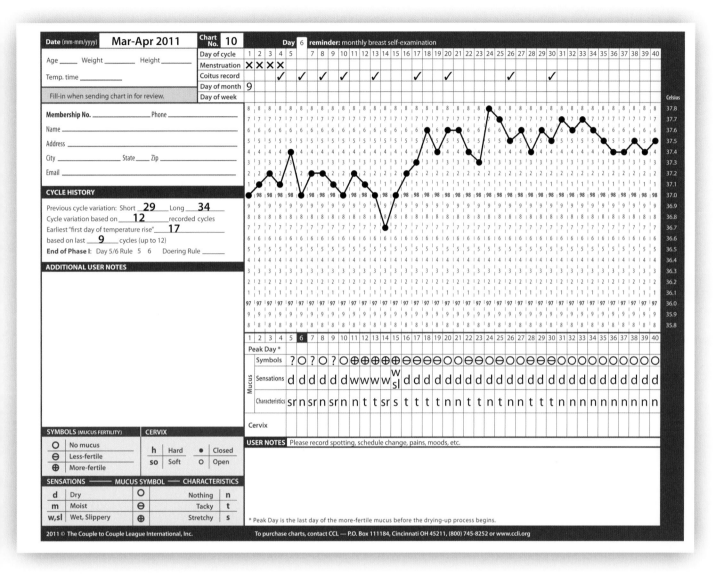

If you are attending the classes, you will complete this exercise in class. If you are using this Student Guide as a Home Study Course, be sure to check your answers on page 195–196 of Appendix B.

Determine the end of Phase I by calculating:

- Day 5/6 Rule (circle the appropriate day)
- Doering Rule (circle the appropriate day)
- Last Dry Day Rule

Draw a line between Phase I and Phase II indicating the latest possible end of Phase I.

Next, follow the steps preceding this exercise and apply the ST Rule to determine the start of Phase III.

Considering the number of consecutive temperatures at the higher temperature level, could this chart indicate pregnancy? If so, determine the Estimated Date of Childbirth (EDC) using the Prem Rule.

Homework Charts 5–7

If you are attending the classes, you will review these charts in class. If you are using this Student Guide as a Home Study Course, be sure to check your answers on pages 197–199 of Appendix B.

Notes

Other Methods of NFP 3

Lesson 3

This lesson will introduce you to Calendar Rhythm and explain how it differs from modern NFP. It will also introduce you to some of the other methods of NFP taught in the United States today. These methods are the sources for CCL's Mucus-Only and Temperature-Only Rules that are used when either the mucus sign or the temperature sign of fertility is not present or reliable in a menstrual cycle. This lesson is not intended to be an instructional guide for any of the other methods, but merely an introduction to them.

Calendar Rhythm

The basis for Calendar Rhythm is the research of two physicians — Dr. Kyusaku Ogino, a Japanese gynecologist, and Dr. Hermann Knaus, an Austrian obstetrician and gynecologist — whose work in the 1920s formed the foundation for determining fertile and infertile days in a woman's cycle. Key to this system was a discovery that ovulation occurred about two weeks before the next menstruation. This research was first presented as a system in 1930 by Dr. Jan N. J. Smulders, a Dutch obstetrician and gynecologist, using Ogino's original data.[1] Calendar Rhythm, the forerunner of modern NFP, relied solely on cycle history and did not take into account any activity or signs of fertility occurring during the current cycle.

---

[1] Ogino, K: Ovulationstermin and Konceptionstermin. *Zbl. Gynaek.* 54: 464, 1930.

The Calendar Rhythm Rules:

1. The last cycle day of pre-ovulation infertility (Phase I) is the shortest previous cycle minus 19, and

2. The first cycle day of post-ovulation infertility (Phase III) is the longest previous cycle minus 10.

For example, if your shortest previous cycle is 27 days, since 27–19 = 8, the first eight cycle days would be considered infertile, and Phase II would begin on Cycle Day 9. If your longest previous cycle was 36 days, since 36–10 = 26, Phase III infertility would begin on Cycle Day 26.

This formula worked reasonably well (method effectiveness around 91%)[2] for women with relatively regular cycles (assuming a difference in cycle lengths between the previous shortest and longest cycles of seven days or less). If a woman experienced moderately irregular cycles (an eight to 20 day difference in length between her shortest and longest previous cycles) or highly irregular cycles (a cycle length difference of greater than 20 days), then a large number of days of the cycle were considered to be part of Phase II fertility. This was especially inconvenient if a woman experienced an uncharacteristically long cycle for some reason, possibly due to stress or illness. That "odd" long cycle then caused several days to be artificially built into the fertile time for subsequent cycles.

Besides affecting future cycles, an unexpected delayed ovulation in the current cycle could not be accounted for using Calendar Rhythm. The method could indicate a premature start of Phase III, as you will see illustrated in the following exercise.

Notes

---

[2] See discussion of method effectiveness on pages 90–93.

Calendar Rhythm › Practice Chart

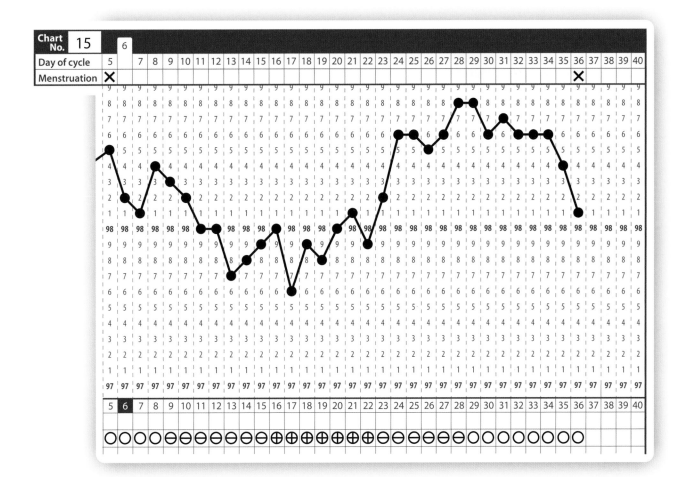

Application of Calendar Rhythm:

       Shortest Cycle (26) – ___ = ___ as Last Cycle Day of Phase I

       Longest Cycle (30) – ___ = ___ as First Cycle Day of Phase III

If you are attending the classes, you will complete this exercise in class. If you are using this Student Guide as a Home Study Course, be sure to check your answers on page 200 of Appendix B.

Apply the Calendar Rhythm rules to this chart.

Then, interpret the chart according to CCL's Phase I rules and the Sympto-Thermal Rule.

The **Standard Days Method** is another calendar-based method.[3] However, it does not allow for much cycle variation (you must have cycles between 26 and 32 days) and, like Calendar Rhythm, does not take into account a woman's daily observations which provide the best indicator of her present fertility status.

Mucus-Only Methods

Worldwide, the most common NFP method is taught by the World Organization of Ovulation Method Billings (WOOMB, also known as the *Billings Ovulation Method*, BOM). WOOMB got its start in 1953, when **Drs. John and Evelyn Billings** pioneered a revolutionary method for assisting couples to achieve or postpone a pregnancy. As a physician working in Melbourne, Australia, John Billings discovered that couples could learn how to read and interpret the cervical mucus of a woman's menstrual cycle, and thus determine the time of ovulation. Much of the Billings' instruction is woman-to-woman, although couples sometimes are involved. In the United States, its affiliate is referred to as BOMA-USA, Billings Ovulation Method Association, USA.

Another mucus-only approach in the United States with significant impact is the *Creighton Model*, also commonly referred to as CrMS. It was founded by **Dr. Thomas Hilgers**, an Ob-Gyn at Creighton University, Omaha, NE. The CrMS is also the basis for the women's health science, NaProTECHNOLOGY (natural procreative technology), which helps identify and treat the root causes of reproductive and fertility problems. There are substantial differences in the categorization of mucus types and method guidelines used by the Creighton and Billings Methods.

There are other mucus-only methods throughout the country, to include Family of the Americas, and some diocesan-based programs. Mucus-only methods provide the underpinning for CCL's Mucus-Only Rule for those situations where a couple may not have a reliable temperature sign in a particular cycle.

This illustrates one of the strengths of the STM taught by CCL — when one of the fertility signs is unavailable, there may be two other unaffected signs that can provide you with sufficient knowledge to determine the phase of the cycle. For example, suppose the temperature sign is missing or somehow compromised. In those cases, you can use the following Mucus-Only Rule to determine Phase III infertility. Note: The Mucus-Only Rule should not be used to get an earlier start of Phase III in the presence of valid temperature data.

---

[3] See *http://www.irh.org/index.htm*, Institute for Reproductive Health, Georgetown University School of Medicine.

CCL Mucus-Only Rule

CCL Mucus-Only Rule › Practice Chart

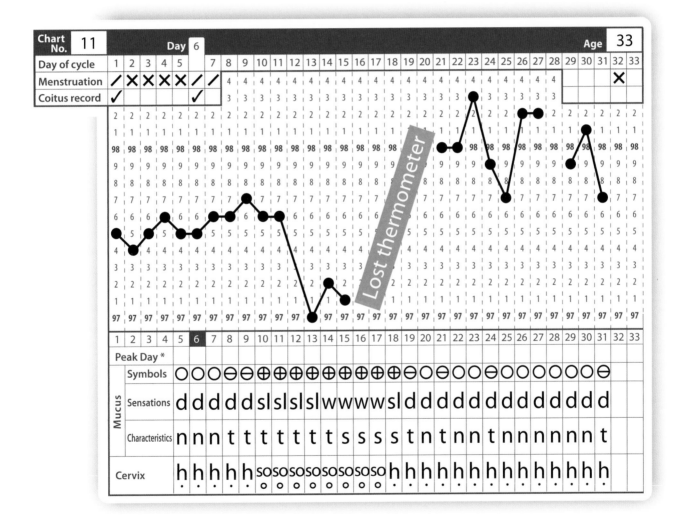

If you are attending the classes, you will complete this exercise in class. If you are using this Student Guide as a Home Study Course, determine the start of Phase III using the CCL Mucus-Only Rule. Be sure to check your answers on page 201 of Appendix B.

There is one important difference between the Sympto-Thermal Rule and the Mucus-Only Rule. When using the Sympto-Thermal Rule, you can generally treat days of *bleeding that follow a thermal shift as infertile days because bleeding preceded by a thermal shift indicates the beginning of menstruation.* However, if the Mucus-Only Rule is applied because the temperature sign was not present or could not be interpreted, the next bleeding may not be menstruation because you cannot confirm that it follows an ovulation. It could be a cycle irregularity called "breakthrough bleeding," which is described on pages 131–132 of the next lesson. Without a preceding sustained thermal shift, you cannot be sure that the bleeding is a true menstruation; it might be breakthrough bleeding, a potentially fertile time. So if you have applied the Mucus-Only Rule and cannot confirm that a change in temperatures took place, you should assume the next bleeding episode is fertile, and if you are postponing or avoiding pregnancy, you should abstain until you can confirm the start of Phase III with the Sympto-Thermal Rule.

Temperature-Only Methods

In Class 2 you learned that Dr. G. K. Doering developed a rule for determining the end of Phase I based on the past history of the earliest first day of temperature rise. He also developed a rule for determining Phase III based on basal body temperature. CCL has based its Temperature-Only Rule on Doering's work. Just as with the CCL Mucus-Only Rule, this rule for determining the start of Phase III should normally be used in situations that prevent the adequate interpretation of, in this case, mucus. For instance, this rule could be used for a woman learning NFP who does not yet fully understand the various types of mucus sensations and/or characteristics. This rule may also be useful for women experienced with NFP when their observation of mucus is compromised (e.g. by medications or infections).

CCL Temperature-Only Rule

CCL Temperature-Only Rule

Phase III begins on the evening of the fourth day of normal temperatures above the LTL. The last three temperatures must be on consecutive days, and at or above the HTL.[4]

---

[4] The pre-shift six, LTL and HTL are determined the same as with the ST Rule. The Temperature-Only Rule is over 99% (user and method) effective based upon Dr. G.K. Doering's original work. However, efficacy is unknown when the rule is applied with abnormal or missed temperatures in the pre-shift six, since Dr. Doering did not include abnormal or missed temperatures in his procedure. See pages 213–222 of the Reference Guide for more on effectiveness.

CCL Temperature-Only Rule › Practice Chart

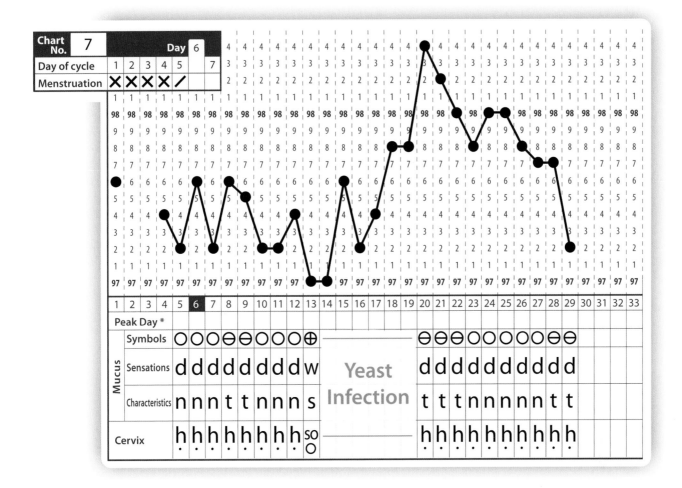

If you are attending the classes, you will complete this exercise in class. If you are using this Student Guide as a Home Study Course, use the CCL Temperature-Only Rule to determine the start of Phase III. Be sure to check your answers on page 202 of Appendix B.

Notes

Applying NFP in Special Situations

Lesson 4

Up to this point in the course, you have generally been provided situations that are typical for most healthy women who are observing their fertility signs. In this lesson, you will learn how to interpret your signs of fertility during various situations that are less common, to include: unusual mucus patterns, breakthrough bleeding, stress or illness, and during times you need to take medications. At the end of this lesson, you will know how to identify these conditions and how to interpret your fertility signs while experiencing them.

Notes

Healthy Mucus Pattern

First, it is important to recognize a healthy mucus pattern. An example of typical mucus observations within a normal menstrual cycle is shown here. It is characterized by days of no mucus after menstruation, followed by a patch of five to seven days of mucus, which begins with less-fertile mucus followed by several days of more-fertile mucus. Peak Day is followed by days of drying up with less-fertile mucus or no mucus to the end of the cycle.

Healthy Mucus Pattern

- Day(s) of no mucus after menstruation
- Day(s) of less-fertile mucus
- Several days of more-fertile mucus through Peak Day
- Days of drying-up with less-fertile or no mucus after Peak Day until next menstruation

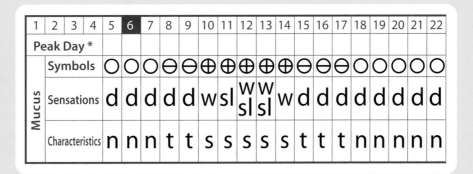

Special Situations › Unusual Mucus Patterns

There are three types of unusual mucus patterns you may encounter as you go through your fertile years: scant mucus, patches of mucus and continuous discharges.

Scant Mucus Pattern

A **scant mucus pattern** is characterized by the lack of definition and quantity. When first learning NFP, some women can be confused trying to identify the mucus sign, and the result is fewer observations of mucus.[1] Some women can also have a scant mucus pattern when they take medication that has the capability of drying up mucus, e.g., antihistamines. In situations where you experience or record scant mucus, try to apply the Sympto-Thermal Rule. With a scant mucus pattern, Peak Day could be the last day of the best sensation/characteristic you have. Ask your Teaching Couple for assistance. If the mucus pattern cannot be interpreted, the Temperature-Only Rule may be helpful. Below is an example of a scant mucus pattern.

Scant Mucus Pattern

- **Mucus sensations or characteristics lacking in definition and quantity**
- **Last day of best sensation/characteristic could be Peak Day**
- **Try to apply ST Rule; use Temperature-Only Rule as backup**

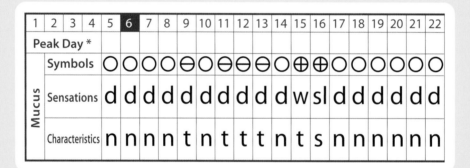

Notes

---

[1] Most women are capable of observing their mucus sign and writing down their observations. If you are unsure about what letter to assign your observations at the end of the day, you are encouraged to record them in your own words in the Notes section of your chart. Your teaching couple can help explain what type of mucus you have observed.

Patches of Mucus

Another example of an unusual mucus pattern can be described as **patches of mucus** — one or more days of mucus followed by days of no mucus. Mucus patches often occur during the return of fertility after childbirth, premenopause, after discontinuing injectable hormonal contraceptives, and in some long cycles (such as occur with Polycystic Ovary Syndrome, or PCOS). The patch rule to use after discontinuing injectable hormonal contraceptives can be found in the Reference Guide on page 225. If you are in the postpartum or premenopausal transition, you can learn more about the Mucus Patch Rule in the appropriate CCL supplemental class or by ordering a *Transitions Student Guide*. If you experience patches of mucus at other times, contact your Teaching Couple. Below is an example of mucus patches.

Patches of Mucus

- One or more days of mucus followed by dry/nothing days
- Often occur after childbirth, premenopause, or discontinuing injectable hormonal contraceptives
- Contact Teaching Couple

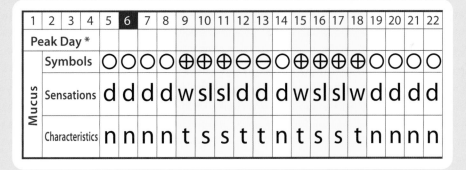

Continuous discharge

Sometimes a woman may observe a continuous discharge (also known as vaginal discharge); it could even occur day after day from Phase I through Phase III. A variety of factors can produce a continuous discharge. In some cases, it may be due to irritation caused by a particular hygiene or personal care product, or even specific types of clothing. A continuous discharge could also be the result of a medical condition like an infection, especially if it is accompanied by irritation, has a different appearance from normal mucus, or produces a wet sensation every day, even when the other fertility signs indicate Phase III. (See pages 248–250 of the Reference Guide for information on vaginal discharges.) With continuous discharges, it may be possible to apply the Temperature-Only Rule.

Continuous Discharge

- Discharges present throughout the cycle

- May be able to apply the Temperature-Only Rule

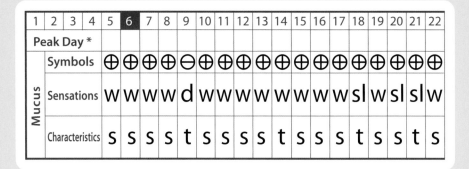

General Suggestions for Special Situations

One advantage of the Sympto-Thermal Method of NFP is that you normally have more than one sign that can assist you in determining the status of your fertility. When you cannot adequately interpret your mucus sign, you can rely on the temperature sign with corroborating information from the cervix to determine the times of fertility and infertility. While also taking steps to try and improve the mucus sign, you can use the Temperature-Only Rule. This is a good time to speak to a CCL Teaching Couple, who may be able to help you deal with unusual or confusing mucus signs. In addition, several of these conditions may be improved by following suggestions in *Fertility, Cycles & Nutrition*. If these recommendations do not help improve the mucus pattern, and especially if you experience irritation or any kind of peculiar discharge, you should consult a physician for assistance.

Special Situations › Breakthrough Bleeding

During a woman's fertile years, she may experience bleeding episodes that are not part of menstruation. Such occurrences are more likely to develop in the following situations: cycles of young women during the puberty years, long cycles, or the postpartum and premenopause times. In the previous lesson, breakthrough bleeding was introduced as a potential problem related to the use of CCL's Mucus-Only Rule. Additionally, "breakthrough bleeding" can mask the presence of mucus, and it can be a potentially fertile time because it could occur just before ovulation. Physiologically, breakthrough bleeding develops when the endometrium builds up so much that the top layer cannot be sustained. Thus, the endometrium breaks down. It may appear as spotting, or it may resemble a normal menstrual flow. It is important to be aware that mucus can be present during this bleeding episode.

If you experience breakthrough bleeding, you should assume Phase II fertility on all days with a bloody discharge that are not preceded by a thermal shift.

The chart on the next page is an example of breakthrough bleeding occurring near ovulation.

Notes

Breakthrough Bleeding › Practice Chart

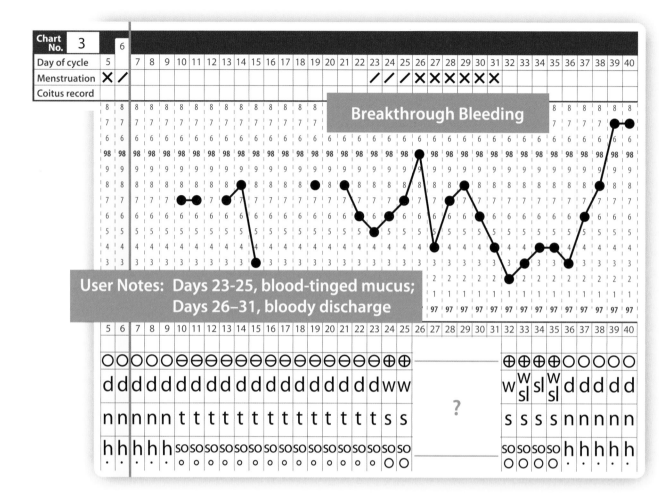

If you are attending the classes, you will complete this exercise in class. If you are using this Student Guide as a Home Study Course, determine the start of Phase III. Be sure to check your answers on page 203 of Appendix B.

If you experience one of these bleeding patterns at approximately the same time that a menstrual period would occur, this "cycle" may be anovulatory (a "cycle" where ovulation did not occur). Anovulatory cycles have a higher chance of occurring when your cycles begin to return while breastfeeding, during the premenopause years, or after discontinuing hormonal contraceptives. If you experience anovulatory cycles at times other than postpartum or premenopause, you should consult a physician.

Special Situations › Stress and Illness

Any significant physical or mental stress or illness can affect a woman's fertility. Physiologically, a woman's reproductive system can be disrupted and can even temporarily shut down during times of stress or illness. CCL has reviewed many charts showing delayed ovulation following such events as an illness, a death in the family, a move, intense exercise, or an upcoming wedding. Look at the following chart from a woman under stress in the month before her wedding.

Stress › Chart

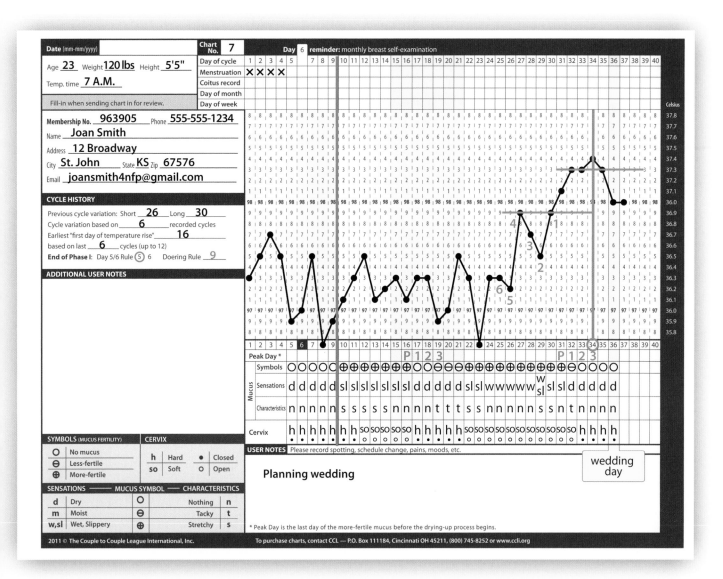

The chart above shows the fertility signs appearing at the normal time (Cycle Days 10–16) according to her previous cycle history, but then they disappear at a time when she would have expected a thermal shift (Cycle Days 17–18). In analyzing this portion of the chart, you may want to consider Peak Day to be Cycle Day 16, but notice there is no accompanying thermal shift. This appearance and then disappearance of fertility signs points to an interruption in the ovulatory process most likely caused by the stress of planning a wedding. Even though the mucus has disappeared and the cervix is closed and hard on Cycle Days 17 and 18, this woman should still consider herself in Phase II. She should expect a return of mucus and eventual ovulation. In this case less-fertile mucus returned on Cycle Day 19, and changed to more-fertile mucus beginning on Cycle Day 22. These more-fertile signs continue until Peak Day occurs on Cycle Day 31, accompanied by a drying-up pattern and a thermal shift. The significance of this chart is that stress can cause women to have one (or more) mucus patches before the mucus patch that finally results in ovulation. (Additional analysis is on page 204 of Appendix B.)

Illness › Practice Chart

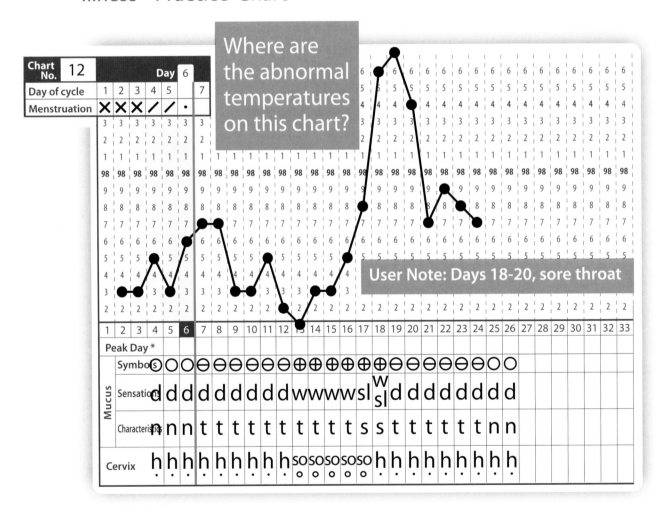

If you are attending the classes, you will complete this exercise in class. If you are using this Student Guide as a Home Study Course, determine the start of Phase III. Be sure to check your answer on page 205 of Appendix B.

What to do

In some cases you may be able to make lifestyle changes to help reduce the stress or illness that is impacting your cycle. In other cases, it is not possible to reduce the stress because it may be caused by an external force. However, you may be able to reduce the impact of the stress through the following behaviors:

- good eating habits

- moderate exercise

- regular sleep

- spiritual development

For example, in a stressful work situation, be sure to have a well-balanced breakfast and lunch — even if it means carrying lunch to your workplace. Poor nutrition causes physiological changes that can induce stress.

Moderate exercise and regular sleep are further ways of reducing stress. Taking time out to stretch, walk or relax through prayer and spiritual reflection often have profound effects on a person's stress level.

Properly learning to read your body language regarding your sexuality is very empowering. This knowledge allows you to practice NFP successfully even during times of stress or illness by relying on all unaffected signs of fertility.

Notes

Special Situations — Medications

Medications can sometimes affect fertility signs. They may disrupt mucus, temperature and/or cervix signs, or they may delay ovulation or shorten the luteal phase. The chart below illustrates a short luteal phase while the woman is taking an antidepressant. For further information on medications and their possible effects on fertility signs, consult pages 227–235 of the Reference Guide.

Medications › Practice Chart

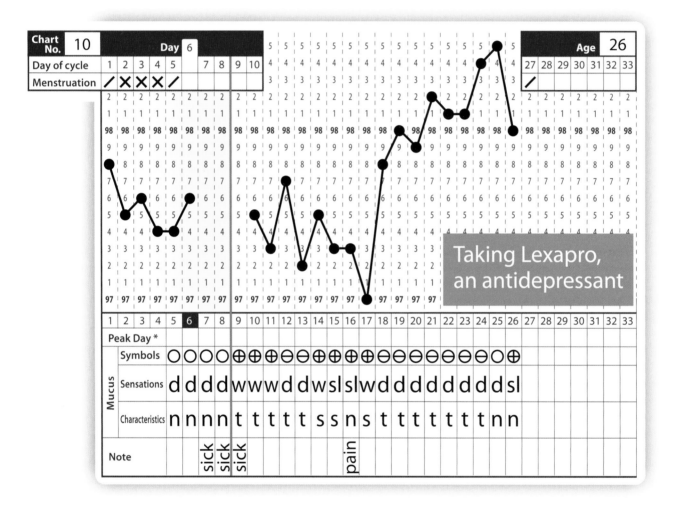

If you are attending the classes, you will complete this exercise in class. If you are using this Student Guide as a Home Study Course, determine the start of Phase III. Be sure to check your answer on page 206 of Appendix B.

Behaviors that Attack Human Dignity and Marital Love

5

Lesson 5

One basic principle of the writings of Pope John Paul II in his Theology of the Body is that the human body is the outward expression of the person. The body speaks the language of being a person, and it reveals who we are and how we should act. When we act as an image of God, the human body reveals not only our own person, but also the mystery of God. Natural Family Planning reads this language of the body in a very particular way.

In Class 2 you learned the five characteristics of love by analyzing Christ's passion. Christ's love and sacrifice was **His own choice**, **based on knowledge**. It was also a **self-gift**, it was **permanent**, and it was **life-giving**. In marriage, we are called to love our spouse as Christ loves. Regarding our sexuality, this means we are called to bring all five characteristics of God's love into our marital relations. If we do not have all five characteristics present, we are not loving as God loves. In fact, we are "using" our spouse. This idea is key for evaluating sexual behaviors to determine if they are genuinely loving.

Violations of the human body are violations of the individual human person and violations of love. This is why we should never alter a healthy, major functioning part of the body, because to do so is to treat the body as a thing or a machine and to claim ownership.

Who would want to violate his own body? Sometimes we do this without realizing it. For example, **contraception** — the use of mechanical, chemical or medical procedures to prevent conception from taking place as a result of sexual intercourse — involves the alteration of a healthy, major functioning part of the body. Therefore, it is a use of oneself and is unworthy of our dignity and value. Similarly, pornography, lust and masturbation (solitary or mutual) involve the use of oneself and sometimes another, and also violate the dignity of the person.

Sometimes people say that the Catholic Church's teaching on sexuality and morality is not consistent with the modern world. It may seem like the Church is always saying no. In reality, the Church is saying yes to the true vision of the human person, and yes to the wonderful mystery that we are called to love as God loves. When the Church says no, it is to protect us from using ourselves or others as objects. We are worth more than that. Such behaviors are unworthy of the human person and unworthy of our calling as images of God.

In vitro fertilization, for example, violates the dignity of husband, wife and child. They are each manipulated because "they treat their bodies as things or sources of biological material and not as the expression of their persons."[1] With in vitro fertilization, there is more at stake in the conception of a child than two cells coming together, and more than just biology. So in vitro fertilization is a use of the mother, of the father, and even of the baby, because the procedure involves taking sperm from the man (regardless of his personhood), an egg from the woman (regardless of her personhood), and using these biological parts to manipulate a child into existence. A child has a right to be conceived, carried and born in the body of his mother because he is the result of a love relationship between father and mother.

Engaging in the marital embrace outside of marriage also violates marital love. The act of **fornication** (sexual relations outside of marriage) not only violates permanence since the couple is not yet married, it usually violates the life-giving aspect of love as well (because an unmarried couple usually is not ready, prepared or willing to have a child, and thus they contracept). Both contraception and **abortion** (termination of a newly conceived life) also violate the mystery of marital love because they are neither a total self-gift nor life-giving.

Again, without all five characteristics, we are not loving as God loves. For example, if you take permanence out, it is not authentic marital love. People may believe that it is love. They may even feel emotionally that it is love. But when considering how God loves, it is not love. And if it is not love, then it must be use.

But what if you have done some of these things? That is why Christ went to the cross, and died and rose from the dead, so you are able to stand under the cross and be washed by his blood. In the Catholic tradition, this occurs through the Sacrament of Reconciliation. Anything can be forgiven because of the infinite suffering of Christ on the cross and his resurrection. Everyone sins, and everyone needs forgiveness. Certainly these sins can be serious, but do not despair if at some time in your life you have done something that the Church asks you not to do. The important thing is to now understand that these behaviors are violations of human dignity and human love. You can ask for forgiveness, pick yourself up and try again.

---

[1] Rev. Richard M. Hogan, *The Human Body…a sign of dignity and a gift* (Cincinnati: The Couple to Couple League, 2005), 22.

Contraception 6

Lesson 6

All forms of contraception violate at least one of the characteristics of love, and thus are immoral. They also have negative or harmful side effects. This lesson will review the most common methods of contraception.

Hormonal Contraceptives

Hormonal contraceptives are both contraceptive and abortifacient (capable of causing an early abortion). The estrogen and progestins present in these types of contraceptives "fool" the pituitary gland into believing that there is sufficient stimulation of the ovaries, so it produces less FSH and LH. This in turn leads to the suppression of ovulation in most cycles. But these contraceptives also have other modes of action. The hormones may cause the mucus to thicken, making it more difficult for sperm to travel up through the cervix, or they slow tubal motility, which affects sperm and egg movement through the Fallopian tube. Additionally, the final action of hormonal contraceptives is to thin the endometrium (inner lining of the uterus), thus reducing its blood supply. This latter action prevents any newly conceived human life from implanting in the uterus. If the new life cannot implant, it does not receive oxygen or nutrition and dies at a very early point in its life, thus causing an early abortion, usually unknown by the couple. We know that this happens because breakthrough ovulation is known to occur up to 28% of the time with the most commonly prescribed combined oral contraceptives, and from 33%–65% of the time for progestin-only pills.[1]

The chart below lists just some (not all) of the common types of hormonal contraceptives and their side effects.

Hormonal Contraception

The Pill	**Side effects include:**
Progestin-only Pill	
Injections (Depo-Provera)	**Menstrual difficulties,**
Norplant	**heart disease, blood clots,**
The Patch	**stroke, cancers, bone**
Vaginal Ring	**density loss, depression**
Emergency Contraception	

The side effects of hormonal contraceptives range from menstrual difficulties to heart disease, blood clots, stroke, cancers, bone density loss and depression. See pages 223–227 of the Reference Guide for more detailed information about how to determine the return of fertility after discontinuing them.

Some terminology is important with regard to the definition of pregnancy. Scientists and physicians agree that the biological components of a human person are in place at the moment of conception. While many individuals and organizations agree that human life begins at conception, several found a way decades ago to "morally justify" the use of hormonal contraceptives or various reproductive technologies such as in vitro fertilization. Thus, the medical definition of pregnancy was changed in the 1970s; instead of pregnancy beginning at the moment of conception, it was redefined as beginning once a new life has **implanted** in the uterus (the beginning of the embryonic stage of development)[2]. With this arbitrary definition of pregnancy encompassing only the time between implantation and the birth of a child, many individuals and organizations now justify various immoral behaviors up to the point of implantation. Regrettably there are several organizations in

---

[1] Larimore W, Stanford J,. Postfertilization Effects of Oral Contraceptives and Their Relationship to Informed Consent. *Arch Fam Med* 2000;9:126–133.

[2] Ibid.

the United States today that call themselves "pro-life," but avoid discussing contraceptives and procedures like in vitro fertilization simply by accepting this revised definition of pregnancy. CCL remains firm in its commitment to maintain the correct definitions of terms related to the beginning of life and to teach the truth about the human person.

There are some physicians in the United States who do not prescribe contraceptives for family planning purposes or offer assistance in procuring sterilizations or abortions. These physicians acknowledge that their patients who practice NFP are much healthier and have fewer reproductive system dysfunctions than their former patients who were contracepting and/or engaging in other harmful behaviors. The medical community clearly understands that there are serious medical side effects from the specific use of the injectable or non-injectable hormones. While some claim that the good outweighs the bad, too many health-care professionals continue to prescribe and/or assist with contraception and abortion with little concern for the consequences.

Pre-marital and extramarital sexual activities are partially responsible for the high percentage of sexually transmitted diseases in the United States. Many women are harming or destroying their reproductive systems under the guise of sexual freedom without really understanding the impact of their behavior, or gaining any knowledge of their fertility. Such knowledge is empowering. Women who can read their bodily signs of fertility and infertility can determine the fertile and infertile times of their cycle with high effectiveness.

Preventing Conception/Barriers

Withdrawal occurs when a man removes his penis from a woman's vagina prior to ejaculation. This action intentionally frustrates the completion of the marital act and thus frustrates openness to life. (It is also ineffective as a contraceptive method because it is likely some sperm will leak into the vagina prior to ejaculation.)

Barriers and other contraceptive devices also use direct physical action to prevent the natural completion of the marital act, and violate the self-giving and life-giving aspects of love. These include **condoms**, **diaphragms**, **spermicides**, and **vaginal sponges**. Aesthetically, these devices require a couple to act as if they are gearing up for war rather than preparing for what should be a complete self-donation through marital intercourse. All of these produce multiple side effects, from allergies to bladder infections to toxic shock syndrome (from sponges). Additionally, they are not as effective as NFP as a means of postponing a pregnancy.

The IUD

The **intrauterine devices (IUDs)** of today come in two basic categories — plain and hormone-embedded (laced with a hormone). The plain IUD is a device inserted in the uterus that does nothing to stop ovulation yet prevents the implantation of a newly conceived life.

It is strictly an abortifacient. Hormone-embedded IUDs are designed to emit progestin, which can sometimes inhibit ovulation; but if that fails, this IUD still acts as an abortifacient and terminates a new baby's life.

These devices can also cause ectopic pregnancies, increased menstrual bleeding and perforation of the uterus, and they are a leading cause of infertility due to infections in the uterus and the Fallopian tubes.

Sterilization

Other "permanent" procedures, such as **tubal ligations or occlusions** and **vasectomies**, treat the body as an object by removing or disabling a healthy, major functioning part of the body. If the reproductive system is healthy, it should never be altered through surgery, drugs or other devices because an attack on the body is an attack on the entire human person. Additionally, the side effects are numerous. In some cases after a vasectomy, a benign (non-cancerous) but painful and sensitive lump known as a granuloma may develop. This is a result of leakage of sperm from the cut end of the vas deferens. Some men report decreased sexual desire, and a small number of men experience long-term testicular pain. A side effect with regard to women is that many regret having tubal ligations because they feel like they have "lost their womanhood — their ability to conceive children." In fact, many women experience post-traumatic stress after a tubal ligation that is similar to the feelings of women who have had abortions. Some have even stated that they are grieving over "the babies that might have been."

Notes

Benefits of Breastfeeding and Its Effect on Fertility

Lesson 7

Since its inception, CCL has promoted breastfeeding because it is the ideal means of feeding a baby and because it affects a woman's return of fertility after childbirth. As a matter of fact, under certain conditions breastfeeding can extend the infertility of a **postpartum** (after childbirth) woman for several months. Many national and international organizations are encouraging women to breastfeed their babies because breastfeeding has so many advantages for the baby, the mother, the family, and society. In this lesson you will learn commonly-accepted terminology with regard to breastfeeding, many of the benefits of breastfeeding, and how breastfeeding can influence the return of your fertility. A separate supplemental class for postpartum women provides an in-depth understanding of how to interpret the signs of fertility no matter when they appear after the birth of a child, and no matter how you choose to feed your baby.

First, it is important to understand that there are different types of baby feeding, and each one will impact the health of both the infant and the mother in some way. Babies can be fed in one of four ways: formula feeding, mixed breastfeeding, exclusive breastfeeding, and continued breastfeeding. Each of these will be defined and discussed briefly.

Types of Baby Feeding

With **formula feeding**, baby receives only formula and no breast milk. The formula can range from cow's milk to specialty formulas. The method of feeding the baby is with a bottle.

Mixed breastfeeding is a combination of formula feeding and breastfeeding. **High mixed breastfeeding** means that 80% of the feeding comes from the breast. **Medium mixed breastfeeding** means that 20–79% of the feeding is from the breast, and **low mixed breastfeeding** occurs when less than 20% of the feeding comes from the breast.

Exclusive breastfeeding is defined by the World Health Organization (WHO) and the American Academy of Pediatrics (AAP) as the standard of care for babies during their first six months of life. It is characterized by breastfeeding whenever the baby indicates a desire (day and night), with each feeding fully emptying the breast of milk. Initially, a minimum of 8–12 feedings per day are required to establish the breastfeeding, with baby kept in close proximity to the mother.

Beyond six months, a baby needs additional nutrition over and above breast milk. Breastfeeding beyond six months is called **continued breastfeeding**, whereby the mother introduces other foods and liquids after nursing in order to complement the breast milk.

Nothing can duplicate or replicate mother's milk. Even evidence from re-formulated artificial milk products reveals that despite the best efforts of formula manufacturers to improve upon their artificial formulas, these substitutes remain significantly different and inferior to breast milk.[1] Human milk not only is a complete food, but it also acts as a medicine due to its immunological properties. For this reason, most authorities state that exclusive breastfeeding can completely satisfy a baby in every way for the first six months of life. The AAP and the WHO go even further and recommend continued breastfeeding as a standard of care for all babies at least up to 12 months and 24 months, respectively, from birth.[2]

---

[1] Uauy and Periano, Breast is best: human milk is the optimal food for brain development, *American Journal of Clinical Nutrition,* Vol 70 (4), 1999, 433.

[2] Lauwers, J. and Swisher, A., *Counseling the Nursing Mother, A Lactation Consultants Guide,* 2005, 167. *Pediatrics,* Vol. 115, No. 2 February 2005, 496–506. World Health Organization, *Infant and young child nutrition: Global strategy on infant and young child feeding,* Fifty-fifth World Health Assembly, 16 April 2002.

Benefits of Breastfeeding

1. Health benefits for baby and mother

Breastfed infants have better overall health records with fewer incidences and less severity of the following: acute infectious diseases such as ear, respiratory, urinary tract, and bowel infections; pneumonia; meningitis; and hospitalizations. Breastfeeding has been shown to lower rates of diabetes, some cancers, asthma, and Sudden Infant Death Syndrome (SIDS).

Breastfeeding enhances the development of a healthy oral structure because it improves shaping the hard palate which facilitates proper alignment of an infant's teeth. Infants subsequently have fewer problems which could result in future dental alignments with braces at later stages in life.

Breastfeeding mothers experience less postpartum bleeding and more rapid shrinking of their uterus after the baby's birth. Uterine contractions aided by breastfeeding are very productive in shrinking the uterus to its pre-pregnancy size.[3]

Exclusive breastfeeding in turn produces higher levels of **prolactin** (called "the mothering hormone") which helps to postpone the mother's return of fertility. This can enhance a mother's overall health by delaying ovulations and subsequent menstruations for a significant period of time while breastfeeding (see "Relative Return of Fertility" graph on page 150). It also can naturally space children, and allows mothers to rebuild energy and strength between pregnancies. In addition, it can reduce a woman's risk of anemia and breast,[4] ovarian and endometrial cancers.[5] In fact, her risk of breast cancer is reduced nearly 25% if she continues breastfeeding for 24 months or longer.[6]

2. Immunological benefits

Breast milk is not simply an inert, uniform nutrition source for a baby. Rather it is a living substance,[7] meaning that it changes in composition, pH, volume and immunological

---

[3] U.S. Department of Health & Human Services, Office on Women's Health, *HHS Blueprint for Action on Breastfeeding,* 2000, 11.

[4] Stuart-Macadam, P. and Dettwyler, K., *Breastfeeding, Biocultural Perspectives,* 1995, 9–11.

[5] Ibid, 11.

[6] Ibid, 12.

[7] Lawrence, Ruth and Lawrence, Robert, *Breastfeeding: A Guide for Medical Professionals,* 2005, 99.

factors on an on-going basis. Thus, breast milk helps infants develop their immune systems.

Breast milk is *species specific*. It is also *mother and baby specific*. Human milk is different from all other mammalian milk, and each mother's milk is different from another mother's milk. When babies are born **pre-term** (before full gestational age), mother's milk is biologically and immunologically appropriate for most of these early breastfeeding situations. In fact, milk from a mother nursing a pre-term baby is considerably different than milk from a mother nursing a full-term baby. It is specific to the pre-term baby's needs in order to provide the baby with the best chance for survival.

3. Psychological benefits

There is a basic need for babies to be close to their mothers. The child sees the mother as a protector, someone to return to when hurt or in need. This in turn reduces the baby's stress. His early dependence and trust that his needs will be met ultimately leads to independence, because the child knows that he can always return to mother for help and protection. Furthermore, breastfeeding enables the baby to experience the maternal heartbeat, a familiar intrauterine sound, while he satisfies his hunger. Breastfed infants are more advanced developmentally, more outgoing and assertive, and socialize better.

Breastfeeding eases mother-baby bonding and increases mother's attention to baby. This is explained by the release of prolactin and **oxytocin** while breastfeeding. (Oxytocin has been called "the hormone of love.[8]")The higher levels of prolactin and oxytocin also help decrease anxiety and are physiologically soothing to the lactating mother.

Although birthing a baby introduces multiple stressors (sore breasts, pain and discomfort, etc.), breastfeeding is protective against these stressors by inducing calm and confidence, lessening maternal reactivity to stressors and increasing nurturing behaviors.

---

[8] Stuart-Macadam, P. and Dettwyler, K., *Breastfeeding, Biocultural Perspectives,* 1995, p 8.

A mother's psychological outlook is also enhanced while exclusively breastfeeding.[9] In a study of 181 women, the breastfeeding mothers had a reduced incidence of perceived stress, anxiety, anger, and negative mood compared to the formula feeding mothers.

4. Cognitive benefits

Why breastfed babies have a cognitive edge over their formula-fed counterparts is somewhat of a mystery.[10] It is surmised that it could be the contents of the breast milk that makes the difference over formula-fed babies. This leads to a more rapid development of visual function and motor skills in breastfed babies, in addition to better neurological development. Such development is shown to increase the longer a baby is breastfed.

5. Nutrition benefits

Breast milk is the #1 food for most babies. It cannot be duplicated or replicated due to its living properties and ever-changing composition. It is easy to digest, and its essential nutrients are also easier for a baby to absorb. For approximately the first six months of life, this single food source offers optimum digestion and absorption as well as the proper concentrations of nutrients. (One study showed that infants absorb 57–70% of iron from breast milk compared to 10% of iron in cow's milk formulas.[11]) Breastfed babies' growth differs from formula-fed babies. A WHO study of data from 1997 to 2003 revealed that growth charts were developed generally from formula-fed babies and were inappropriate for assessing growth patterns in breastfed babies and young children.[12]

---

[9] Kendall-Tackett, K. A new paradigm for depression in new mothers: the central core of inflammation and how breastfeeding and anti-inflammatory treatments protect maternal mental health, *International Breastfeeding Journal,* Vol 2 (6), 2007, p 22.

[10] Uauy and Periano, ibid.

[11] Stuart-Macadam, P. and Dettwyler, K., *Breastfeeding, Biocultural Perspectives,* 1995, p 21.

[12] Onis, M. et al, Comparison of the WHO Child Growth Standards and the CDC 2000 Growth Charts, *The Journal of Nutrition,* 144.

The food a mother eats affects the composition and flavor of her breast milk, and these substances are transmitted to the child. In effect, baby eats what mother eats, modified for

baby's immature system. Baby is also exposed to flavors both in utero from the amniotic fluid and from breast milk after birth. Amniotic fluid is considered the "flavor bridge" to breast milk, and breast milk is considered the flavor bridge to solid foods.[13]

6. Environmental benefits

The costs to the environment are considerable for manufacturing infant formulas compared to breastfeeding. Breastfeeding is *free for mother and father, free for society and free from making a negative environmental impact*. With breastfeeding there is no burden on the environment due to manufacturing, the use of electricity, plastic, paper, etc. There is no increased demand for oil for production, transportation or refrigeration.

Mother's breast milk is always available and at the perfect temperature for feeding baby. In addition, breastfeeding saves mother time since there is no need to purchase, store and prepare the formula before feeding baby. Breast milk is ready to use, and excess is not wasted.

7. Economic benefits

Economically, everyone can benefit from breastfeeding babies — from individual families, to employers who help pay for their health care, to governments. Formula costs each family an average of $900–$1,200[14] per year in the United States. Breastfed babies are healthier babies and their health care costs are lower than formula fed babies. A 2010 cost analysis study also concluded that if 90% of U.S. families would breastfeed exclusively for six months, the U.S. would save $13 billion per year in health care costs and would prevent 911 excess deaths.[15] While the Women,

---

[13] Mennella, J., Mothers milk: a medium for early flavor experiences, *Journal of Human Lactation,* (3) 1995, Vol. 11, 39–45.

[14] Lauwers, J. and Swisher, A., *Counseling the Nursing Mother, A Lactation Consultants Guide,* 2005, 177.

[15] Bartick & Reinhold, *Pediatrics,* April 5, 2010 (10.1542/peds. 2009–1616).

Infants and Children (WIC) program[16] distributes free infant formula to families in need, there is a growing population who do not qualify for WIC, and the cost of baby formula is a significant burden on their income.

8. Social benefits

Finally, the diverse and often overlapping benefits of breastfeeding can be summarized by the social benefits: breastfed babies have lower death rates, and there is a significant societal impact from the collective increased quality of life (considering all of the benefits).

Role of Fathers in Breastfeeding

A father plays an important role in breastfeeding. While he cannot breastfeed, his caring attitude can help him realize the importance of breastfeeding in the health and development of his child. Studies show that fathers are one of the most important factors in determining whether or not a mother breastfeeds. The father's help, support and encouragement are vital, especially if family, friends or health care providers are unsupportive. Fathers can assist with changing/dressing/bathing the baby, help with their other children or with household duties that need additional fatherly attention, while mother temporarily attends more to the baby's needs.

The love of a father and mother (husband and wife) is a giving love — for the good of the other person. This love leads to a husband's involvement with his wife's unique nurturing of their baby, as he defers more to her needs and the needs of the family.

---

[16] WIC is a USDA program which purchases and distributes free infant formula to families in need. It is the largest purchaser of infant formula in the United States. In 1997, $567 million of infant formula was distributed through WIC. Every 10% increase in breastfeeding rates among WIC recipients would save taxpayers $750,000 annually. (Weimer, J, The Economic Benefits of Breastfeeding: A Review and Analysis, *United States Dept. of Agriculture Food Assistance and Nutrition Research Report Number 13,* 1.)

Baby Feeding and Fertility

How does breastfeeding affect fertility? Frequent breastfeeding produces higher levels of prolactin which suppresses estrogen and thus prevents a woman from ovulating. This is helpful to a mother's health because it can provide a rest from ovulations and subsequent menstruations for a significant period of time while breastfeeding.

Formula feeding is linked to an early return of fertility. Generally, mothers who feed their babies formula will have their fertility return by 12 weeks postpartum. Mixed breastfeeding mothers have a varied return of their fertility, depending upon the level of breastfeeding. Low mixed breastfeeding women can usually expect an early return, and high mixed breastfeeding can typically expect a later return. Mothers who exclusively breastfeed their babies can usually expect an extended length of infertility. Some studies show that approximately 98% of mothers who exclusively breastfeed and have not had a bleeding episode are infertile for the first six months postpartum. In addition, continued breastfeeding may result in extended infertility beyond six months for some mothers who remain in amenorrhea.[17] The length of infertility is dependent upon many factors that are addressed in CCL's postpartum class, and *Transitions Student Guide*.

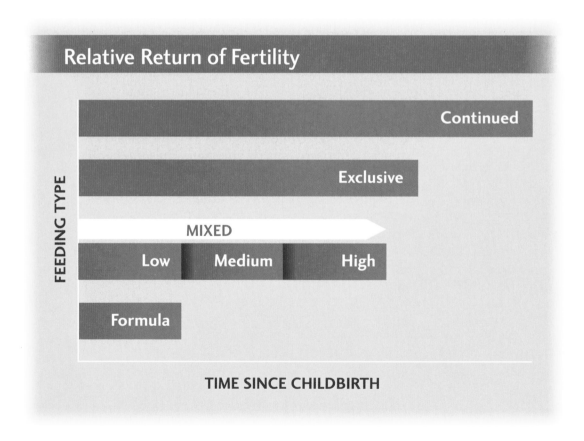

[17] Kennedy, K., Rivera, R. and McNeilly, A., Consensus statement on the use of breastfeeding as a family planning method, *Contraception*, Vol. 39 (5), May 1989, 477–496. From the Bellagio Consensus Conference on Lactational Infertility, Bellagio, Italy, August 1988.

Considerations

There are many factors that influence a couple's decision about how to feed their baby, and the decision to breastfeed a child is one of the prudential judgments of parents. The facts presented on the benefits of breastfeeding should help you discuss and prayerfully discern how this decision is best lived out in your own family. Based on the impact it made on their family life, many couples have shared with CCL their gratitude for being introduced to the idea of continued breastfeeding, a message they did not hear elsewhere. Regardless of the type of baby feeding a mother chooses, CCL offers assistance in identifying the return of fertility after childbirth.

There are several resources you can use to learn more about baby feeding and its impact on the return of your fertility, including CCL's *Transitions Student Guide*, and *The Art of Breastfeeding* by Linda Kracht and Jackie Hilgert.

It will be helpful for you to take CCL's supplemental postpartum class on the return of fertility after childbirth either prior to, or shortly after, the birth of your child. For more information, you can contact a Teaching Couple. As a member of CCL, you will find the *Family Foundations* magazine to be a regular useful resource for issues relating to your fertility and breastfeeding. The CCL website, *www.ccli.org*, is another source of information.

Notes

8 NFP During Premenopause

Lesson 8

For many women in their forties and fifties, the word "premenopause" evokes a cluster of negative experiences — hot flashes, irregular cycles, loss of bone density, headaches, mental confusion, low libido, and so on. While this transition from the fertile years to menopause can be difficult, women who are in tune with their fertility signs via NFP have a better understanding of what is happening to their fertility. They can still observe, record and interpret their overall fertility signs with confidence, and will be better able to understand their changing signs of fertility in the years preceding menopause, commonly referred to as premenopause.

Premenopause is the natural life progression, typically throughout a woman's forties, that occurs as her fertile years gradually come to a close. It can begin as early as age 35, although the average age is 45 years. For 95% of women, the last two to eight years of this transition is called **perimenopause**.[1] Premenopause begins with the onset of the decrease in fertility and ends one year after a woman's last menstrual period, at which time she enters **menopause**.[2] This stage of life is defined by the permanent cessation of menstruation and is officially reached after 12 months of no menstrual periods. The median age of

---

[1] Speroff, Lean, Glass, Robert H., Kase, Nathan G. *Clinical Gynecologic Endocrinology and Infertility,* 6th edition, Lippincott, Williams & Wilkins, Baltimore, MD 1999, 653.

[2] Ibid, 651. "Menopause is derived from the Greek words, *men* (month) and *pausis* (cessation)."

menopause usually occurs between ages 50 and 52. (The graph below illustrates these three changes from the fertile years to permanent infertility.)

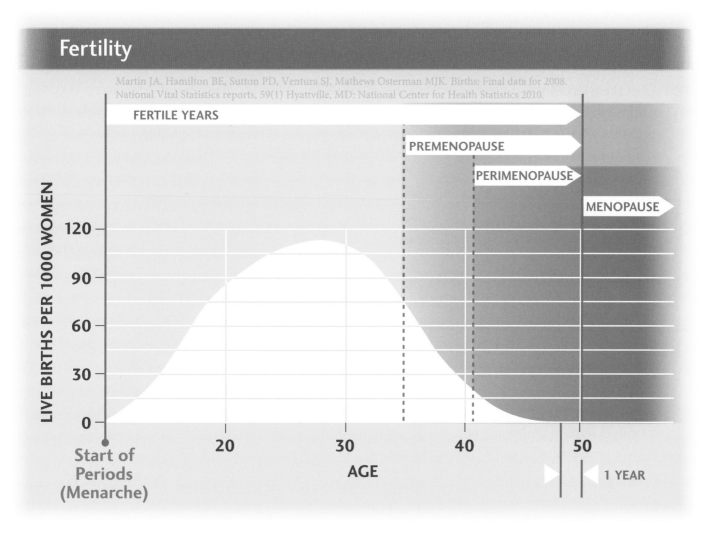

Hormonal Changes

The changes women experience during perimenopause are primarily caused by the reduced number of eggs available to ovulate, and the hormonal changes that are associated with this reduction in eggs. These hormonal fluctuations often result in ovulation being delayed, and women can have longer cycles than usual. However, with fewer follicles producing estrogen, the pituitary gland attempts to compensate for this — it produces higher levels of FSH (follicle stimulating hormone), which sometimes triggers a very short cycle.

The action of these hormones can lead to:

- Irregular cycles: longer or shorter
- Longer or shorter periods
- Heavier or lighter periods

A woman also experiences metabolic and emotional changes in response to these hormonal changes:

- "Hot flashes" or "night sweats" can be uncomfortable due to slight changes in the body's thermostat
- Mood swings can occur

All of these changes also affect a woman's measurable signs of fertility. For example, mucus quality and quantity may vary. It could be the same as during normal fertile years, or it may be absent, appear on and off in patches, occur during episodes of bleeding or spotting, or occur in unchanging patterns.

The temperature pattern will also change as the body produces less and less progesterone. Thermal shifts may get weaker, take longer to reach the HTL, or occur many days after Peak Day. A woman may experience shorter or longer luteal phases than normal.

Women who are proficient in checking the cervix may find this sign helpful during perimenopause. If both the mucus and temperature recordings seem confusing at times, a woman should consider checking and recording her cervix sign as well.

Some women pass through premenopause and encounter nothing more than irregular cycle lengths, but all women will experience a substantial reduction in fertility. No matter what changes occur, women who are familiar with reading the body language regarding their own fertility are less likely to become anxious during this time of transition. CCL offers a special supplemental class and Student Guide on premenopause, which provides the necessary details to help women pass from the reproductive stage of life through the premenopause transition and into menopause.

Benefits of NFP 9

Lesson 9

Since its founding in 1971, CCL has heard from thousands of couples whose lives have changed because they practiced Natural Family Planning, and this same experience is corroborated by other NFP organizations. This knowledge of fertility awareness has been used by many couples to make responsible decisions about family size. It has also been credited with improving the general health of women (especially their fertility), helping to identify potentially life-threatening diseases, and cultivating marital intimacy through better communication. Furthermore, many couples avow that NFP saved their marriage by restoring a mutual respect for each other as persons to be loved and gifts to be appreciated.

Natural Family Planning can lead couples to become *other*-centered rather than *self*-centered when making decisions about themselves and their relationship with each other. In the words of one couple, "NFP helped us realize that the body is holy and sacred, and if we are truly made in the image of God, then we should treat each other that way."

Many women have shared anecdotes explaining different ways in which their knowledge of fertility awareness has helped them. One woman was checking her cervix sign and noticed an abnormality. She went to her physician and told her that she had a growth on her cervix. The physician asked her how she knew that, and she said that she was using NFP and making the cervix observation. Surely enough, she was right! The medical problem was detected and resolved before it became life-threatening.

Several years ago, an NFP teacher was having multiple physical problems and temporary infertility because her thyroid was not functioning properly. She and her husband desired another child, and she was scheduled to undergo thyroid surgery. Then, CCL published Marilyn Shannon's book *Fertility, Cycles & Nutrition*. Following the author's advice, the teacher changed her diet, and within a few weeks, she achieved pregnancy. No surgery was necessary.

Another couple was sent to CCL by an infertility specialist because their difficulty conceiving was related to the timing of intercourse rather than infertility. They just needed to learn how to determine which days were most fertile. The wife was able to conceive during her second cycle of charting.

Perhaps the most significant benefit of NFP within marriage is that it enhances marital respect and communication. The decision to postpone or to try to achieve a pregnancy — bringing a new child into the world — profoundly touches the physical, psychological and spiritual levels of the marital relationship. The power of procreation is central to marriage and the act of marital relations. As you have seen throughout this course, a woman's body is designed to prepare for and protect a newly-conceived life after each ovulation during her fertile years. Making a prayerful decision in marriage to postpone bringing a child into the world requires not only ongoing spousal communication, but also discernment of God's will. This regular deep communication and prayer enables couples to address topics that can be sensitive or difficult. These could include subjects such as: changing jobs, buying a home, moving to another state, etc. Couples who use the information gained from NFP to virtuously make decisions concerning family size continue to tell us how that process has made them better spouses and parents, and has enabled them to communicate more intimately.

With NFP, knowing that you are fertile on a given day raises the act of marital relations to a spiritual level. What a powerful event when a husband and wife come together at a time when they both know that at that moment, they are beginning a process that may bring new life into the world!

Marriage is thus about love *and* life. These are the norms of marriage and not the exceptions. Loving one's spouse is not something that an individual does "every once in a while;" rather, it is something that should be "24/7." Openness to life is not something that is occasional either; it, too, is "24/7." How can a couple be open to life, but defer a pregnancy for a time? They do so by jointly deciding to abstain during the fertile days of a cycle. In this way, the integrity of their physical, psychological and spiritual personhood remains intact. They do not alter themselves in any way; rather, they refrain from the marital embrace for a time, and express their permanent love for each other in non-genital ways. By doing so, husbands and wives become virtuous role models for their children and for others. Their example demonstrates that true love involves sacrifice — giving for the good of another. If the greater good at a particular time is postponement of a new life, then the spouses refrain from the actions that would lead to conception and continue to show their love in other ways. Their marital love thus becomes not only a gift from spouse to spouse, but a gift to others as well, as children, family, and friends witness the beauty of marriage that is truly a union of wills, based on the knowledge of human dignity, and a self-gift that is both permanent and life-giving.

Notes

Benefits of CCL Membership

This completes the three classes on the Sympto-Thermal Method of Natural Family Planning (NFP), but we hope your relationship with the Couple to Couple League continues for many years.

Maintaining membership in CCL affords you several privileges based on your level of support:

- All levels of membership grant you assistance with personal charting and interpretation when needed, as long as you have taken a CCL course. After this class, feel free to contact your Teaching Couple if you have questions or need help in any way.

- Certain levels of membership provide additional CCL class-related benefits:

  - Discounted rates on a refresher course in the future if you feel that would be helpful;

  - If you are pregnant or will be pregnant in the next few months, the Postpartum Class is available for free your convenience to prepare you for the return of fertility after childbirth and to augment resources and support for a successful breastfeeding experience if you decide to nurse your baby;

  - As you transition into the years of reduced fertility, the Premenopause Class is available for free to help you prepare for this change from fertility to the infertility of menopause.

- Ongoing support through *Family Foundations* — CCL's award-winning bi-monthly magazine. This is a one-of-a-kind magazine strictly dedicated to couples and families who use NFP. In it, you will find many articles of interest, to include first-person stories from NFP couples, chart reviews and current scientific information on NFP-related news. Available in print and online editions.

Staying in touch with the Couple to Couple League is easy via website, social media or mail, electronic or postal.

Couple to Couple League • 4290 Delhi Avenue • Cincinnati, Ohio 45238-5829
1-800-745-8252 • 513-471-2000 (local) • 513-557-2449 (fax)
www.ccli.org • info@ccli.org

Find us on: Facebook • Twitter • Instagram

Share this Information with Others

The Couple to Couple League has been teaching The Art of Natural Family Planning® and promoting faith-filled marriages since 1971. During that time, tens of thousands of couples across the United States and around the world have benefited from this instruction. Volunteer couples have been the core of the Couple to Couple League since its inception. Additionally, new generations of Teaching Couples provide NFP instruction as the number of volunteers continues to grow with a greater need to provide classes in the United States and in other parts of the world.

The volunteer Teaching Couples and Promoters of NFP who make up the CCL team range in education from high school graduates to graduates in all the professions. They are generally family people with all of the time-consuming obligations of ordinary family life. Yet they have volunteered their time and effort to share their knowledge of NFP with others through the standardized teaching program of the League. If you are willing to help us in this ministry — to either teach or promote NFP — please contact a Teaching Couple or the CCL central office directly. The Couple to Couple League's professional training program is provided at no charge, and will adequately prepare you to teach the materials. It also provides you with a deeper insight about NFP and how its virtuous use can improve your marriage. If you cannot teach, there are many needs in the CCL promoter program...or perhaps you would like to pray for the League or help us help others by donating since CCL is a non-profit organization. There is a place for you in CCL. Take up the challenge!

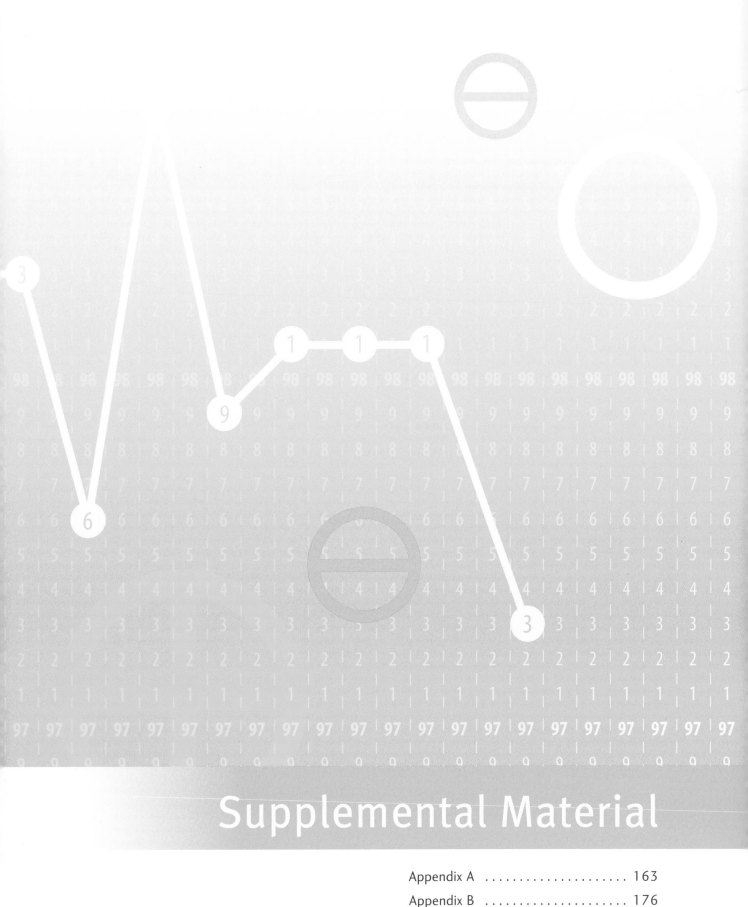

Supplemental Material

Appendix A

The Appendix contains selected practice exercises, practice charts and all of the homework exercises, along with the answers for each of the three basic classes. The selected practice exercises are for the Home Study students who will not be provided the necessary information to complete the exercise in the Student Guide. Other students will have most of the data for the practice exercises provided to them in the classes.

Class 1

Recording Mucus Sensations › Practice

Using the data provided below, record the descriptions of mucus sensations with "d," "m," "w" and/or "sl" in the Sensations row of the chart on page 22. (Remember that the descriptions may require more than one of the letters.) Answers to this exercise can be found in Appendix B on page 177.

Cycle Days	Description
5	felt dry
6	felt dry; toilet paper met with friction when wiping
7	vaginal area was dry throughout the day
8	felt rough and scratchy when wiping
9	felt moist during the day
10	same as previous day
11	felt wet during the day
12	felt wet during the day and slippery when wiping
13	felt really wet while up and about; very slippery when wiping
14	same as yesterday
15	felt sticky; slipperiness gone
16	felt sticky
17	rough feeling; produced friction when wiping
18	scratchy feeling when wiping
19–28	dry; no lubrication

Recording Mucus Characteristics › Practice

Using the data provided below, record the descriptions of mucus characteristics with "n," "t" and/or "s" in the Characteristics Row of the chart on page 25. Answers to this exercise can be found in Appendix B on page 177.

Cycle Days	Description
5	nothing on the toilet paper
6	nothing on the toilet paper
7	nothing on the toilet paper
8	sticky mucus
9	thick mucus
10	stretched a little, but broke easily
11	elastic, stringy
12	thin and stringy
13	mucus resembled raw egg-white
14	nothing on the toilet paper
15	thicker, less stretchy mucus; definitely different from Cycle Days 11–13
16	glob of mucus
17	nothing on toilet paper
18	sticky glob
19	thick mucus
20–22	nothing on toilet paper
23	sticky mucus
24	thick glob
25–28	nothing on toilet paper

Recording the Cervix Sign › Practice

Using the data provided below, record the cervix sign with "•" or "o," "h" or "so" in the Cervix Row of the chart on page 29. Answers to this exercise can be found in Appendix B on page 178.

Cycle Days	Description
5	closed and hard
6	closed and hard
7	closed and hard
8	cervix open a little and soft
9	a little open and soft
10	open, somewhat soft
11	same as yesterday
12	more open, soft
13	more open, soft
14	very soft, very open
15	not as soft, closing a little
16	closed, hard
17	closed, hard
18–28	closed, hard

Homework › Charts 1–4
(Complete between Class 1 and Class 2)

For Homework Charts 1–4, determine the start of Phase III using the Sympto-Thermal Rule. Be sure to follow the steps below. These charts are discussed as part of the Review in Class 2.

Steps for Applying the Sympto-Thermal Rule

1. Find Peak Day and number the three days of drying up after it from left to right.

2. Close to Peak Day, find three temperatures that are higher than the six preceding temperatures.

3. Number the pre-shift six from right to left.

4. Draw the Low Temperature Level (LTL) on the highest of the pre-shift six temperatures.

5. Draw the High Temperature Level (HTL) at 0.4° F above the LTL.

6. Find the third of three normal post-peak temperatures that are all above the LTL ("post-peak" means temperatures occurring after Peak Day). If this temperature is at or above the HTL, Phase III begins on the evening of that day.

7. If the third normal post-peak temperature does not teach the HTL, check the cervix sign (if recorded). If there are three days of a closed, hard cervix, then it is not necessary for the third normal post-peak temperature to reach the HTL. Phase III begins on the evening of that day.

8. If the requirements in steps #6 and #7 are not met, wait for an additional normal post-peak temperature above the LTL; Phase III begins that evening.

9. After you apply the ST Rule and determine the start of Phase III, draw a vertical phase division line through the temperature dot on the first day of Phase III.

Homework › Chart 1

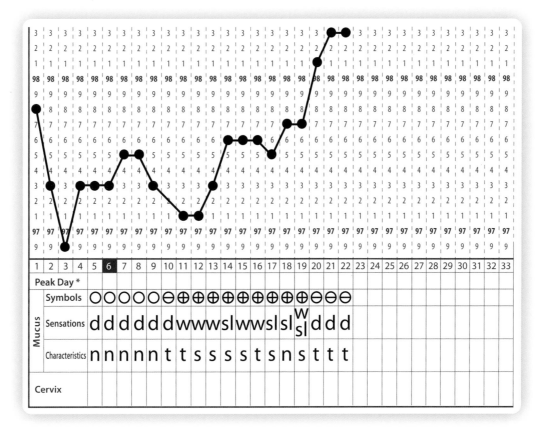

Homework › Chart 2

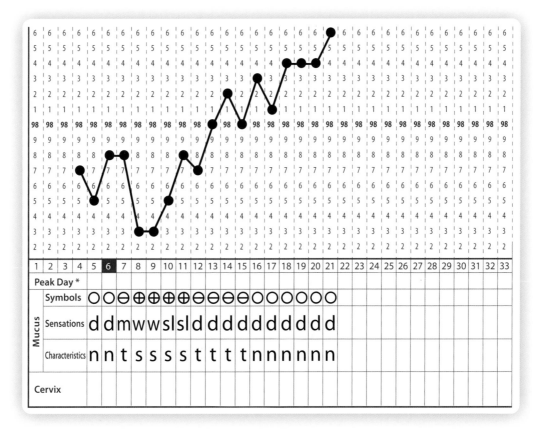

Homework › Chart 3

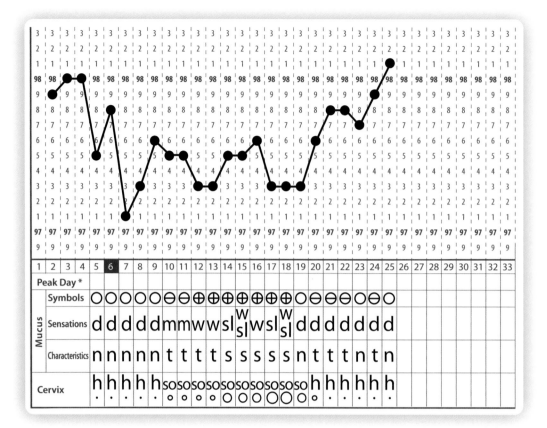

Homework › Chart 4

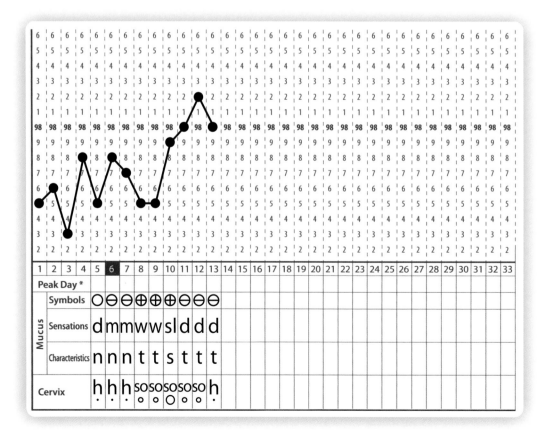

Class 2

Phase I Rules › Practice (page 88)

1. Using the cycle history provided on page 88, determine the end of Phase I with the Day 5/6 Rule and the Doering Rule. Circle those cycle days on the chart.

2. Record the data in the box below in the appropriate places on Chart No. 7.

Cycle Days	Menstruation	Coitus	Temperature	Mucus Sensations	Mucus Characteristics
1	X		97.5° F.		
2	X	✓	97.2 ° F.		
3	X	✓	97.3 ° F.		
4	/		97.3 ° F.	d	n
5	/	✓	97.4 ° F.	d	n
6			97.3 ° F.	d	sr
7		✓	97.4 ° F.	d	n
8			97.2 ° F.	d	t, sr

3. Enter the correct symbol for each day in the Symbols row on the chart.

4. Determine the last day of Phase I and the first day of Phase II; draw the phase division line between those two cycle days.

Class 3

Homework › Charts 5–7
(Complete between Class 2 and Class 3)

For Homework Charts 5–7, determine the following:

Phase I and Phase II

- Day 5/6 Rule

- Doering Rule

- Last Dry Day Rule

- Circle the appropriate day(s), if applicable

- Determine the end of Phase I and draw a line between Phase I and Phase II

Phase III

- Determine Phase III by applying the Sympto-Thermal Rule using the steps outlined on page 168 in Appendix A or page 48 of the Student Guide.

These charts will be discussed as part of the review in Class 3.

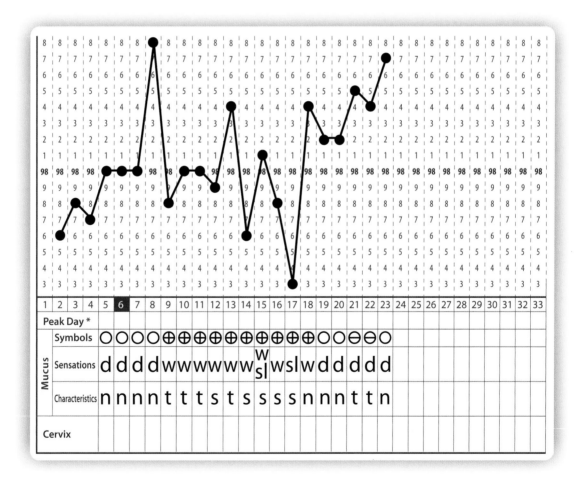

CYCLE HISTORY   Chart No. **2**

Previous cycle variation: Short ____26____ Long ____32____

Cycle variation based on ____12____ recorded cycles

Earliest "first day of temperature rise" ____18____

based on last ____1____ cycles (up to 12)

End of Phase I: Day 5/6 Rule 5   6   Doering Rule _____

Last Dry Day =

	1	2	3	4	5	6	7	8	9	10	11	12	13	14	15	16	17	18	19	20	21	22	23	24	25	26	27	28	29	30	31	32	33
Peak Day *																																	
Symbols	O	O	O	O	O	⊕	⊕	⊕	⊕	⊕	⊕	⊕	⊕	⊕	⊕	O	O	O	⊖	⊖	O												
Mucus Sensations	d	d	d	w	w	w	w	w	w	w sl	w	s	l	w	d	d	d	d	d														
Characteristics	n	n	n	n	t	t	t	s	t	s	s	s	s	n	n	n	t	t	n														
Cervix																																	

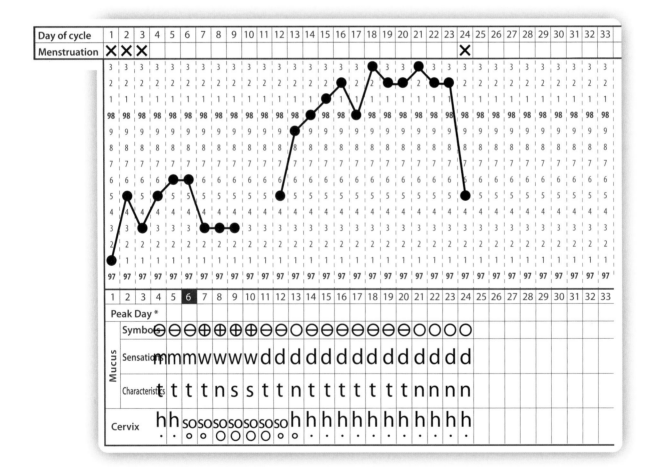

CYCLE HISTORY   Chart No. **4**

Previous cycle variation: Short __24__ Long __26__

Cycle variation based on __3__ recorded cycles

Earliest "first day of temperature rise" __14__

based on last __3__ cycles (up to 12)

End of Phase I: Day 5/6 Rule 5 6   Doering Rule _____

Last Dry Day =

Day of cycle	1	2	3	4	5	6	7	8	9	10	11	12	13	14	15	16	17	18	19	20	21	22	23	24	25	26	27	28	29	30	31	32	33
Menstruation	X	X	X																					X									

	1	2	3	4	5	6	7	8	9	10	11	12	13	14	15	16	17	18	19	20	21	22	23	24	25	26	27	28	29	30	31	32	33
Peak Day *																																	
Mucus — Symbol	⊖	⊖	⊖	⊕	⊕	⊕	⊖	⊖	○	⊖	⊖	⊖	⊖	⊖	⊖	⊖	○	○	○	○													
Mucus — Sensation	m	m	m	w	w	w	d	d	d	d	d	d	d	d	d	d	d	d	d	d													
Mucus — Characteristics	t	t	t	t	n	s	s	t	t	t	n	t	t	t	t	t	t	n	n	n													
Cervix	h	h	so	so	so	so	so	so	so	so	h	h	h	h	h	h	h	h	h	h													
Cervix	·	·	o	o	O	O	O	O	O	o	o	·	·	·	·	·	·	·	·	·													

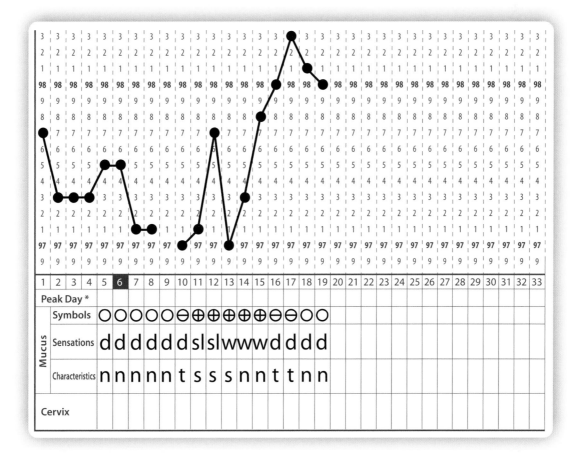

CYCLE HISTORY — Chart No. 10

Previous cycle variation: Short __27__ Long __29__

Cycle variation based on __9__ recorded cycles

Earliest "first day of temperature rise" __14__

based on last __9__ cycles (up to 12)

End of Phase I: Day 5/6 Rule 5 6   Doering Rule _____

Last Dry Day =

Appendix B: Answers to Practice Exercises and Practice Charts

Class 1

Recording Mucus Sensations › Practice (page 22)
(See data on page 165 in Appendix A)

	1	2	3	4	5	6	7	8	9	10	11	12	13	14	15	16	17	18	19	20	21	22	23	24	25	26	27	28	29	30
Peak Day *																														
Symbols																														
Mucus — Sensations	d	d	d	d	m	m	w	w sl	w sl	w sl	m	m	d	d	d	d	d	d	d	d	d	d	d	d	d	d				
Characteristics																														

Recording Mucus Characteristics › Practice (page 25)
(See data on page 166 in Appendix A)

	1	2	3	4	5	6	7	8	9	10	11	12	13	14	15	16	17	18	19	20	21	22	23	24	25	26	27	28	29	30
Peak Day *																														
Symbols																														
Mucus — Sensations	d	d	d	d	m	m	w	w sl	w sl	w sl	m	m	d	d	d	d	d	d	d	d	d	d	d	d	d	d				
Characteristics	n	n	n	t	t	t	s	s	s	n	t	t	n	t	t	n	n	n	t	t	n	n	n	n						

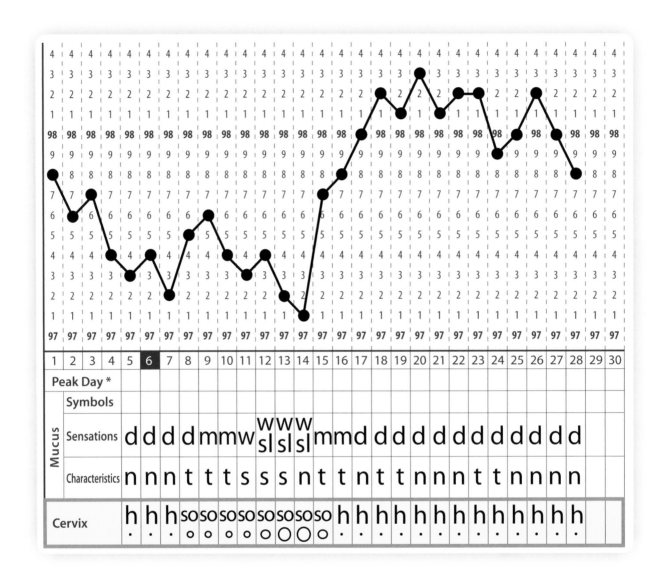

Recording Mucus Symbols › Practice (page 35)

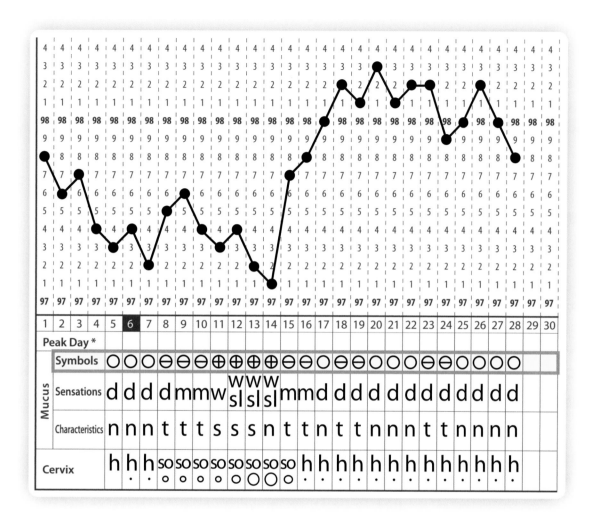

Identifying Peak Day › Practice (page 39)

1 of 3 Peak Day	—	Cycle Day 15
2 of 3 Peak Day	—	Cycle Day 18
3 of 3 Peak Day	—	Cycle Day 19

Interpreting the Temperature Sign › Practice (page 44)

Three Thermal Shift Temperatures	—	Cycle Days 16–18
Pre-shift six	—	Cycle Days 10–15
LTL	—	97.9° F.
HTL	—	98.3° F.

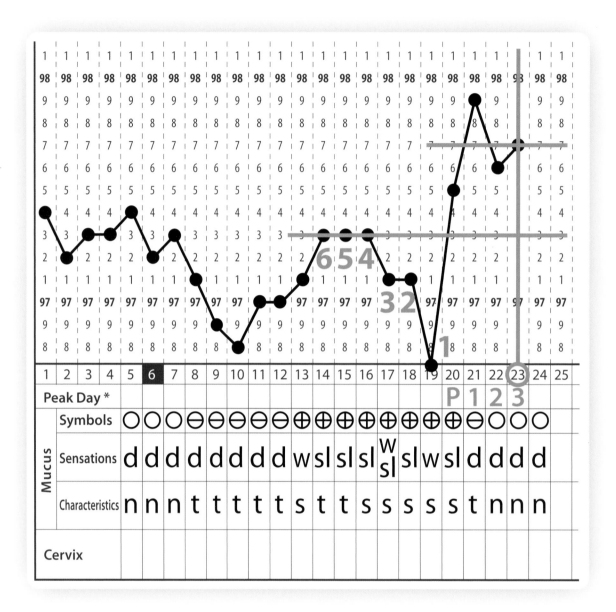

The third day of drying up past the Peak Day is Cycle Day 23, and the three normal post-peak temperatures above the LTL are Cycle Days 21, 22, and 23. The third of these temperatures (Cycle Day 23) is at (or above) the HTL. Thus, Phase III begins on the evening of Cycle Day 23.

Note: Even though the temperatures on Cycle Days 14, 15, 16 are higher than the previous six temperatures, it is clear that they are not associated with the Peak Day.

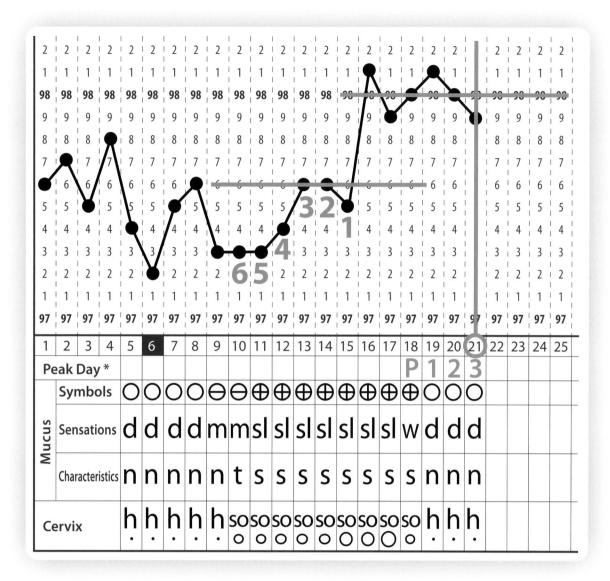

The third day of drying up past the Peak Day is Cycle Day 21, and the three normal post-peak temperatures above the LTL are Cycles Days 19, 20, and 21. The third of these temperatures (Cycle Day 21) is below the HTL, but the cervix is closed and hard for three days (Cycle Days, 19, 20 and 21). Thus, Phase III begins on the evening of Cycle Day 21.

Note: Sometimes temperatures rise before Peak Day. Use only post-peak temperatures to apply the ST Rule.

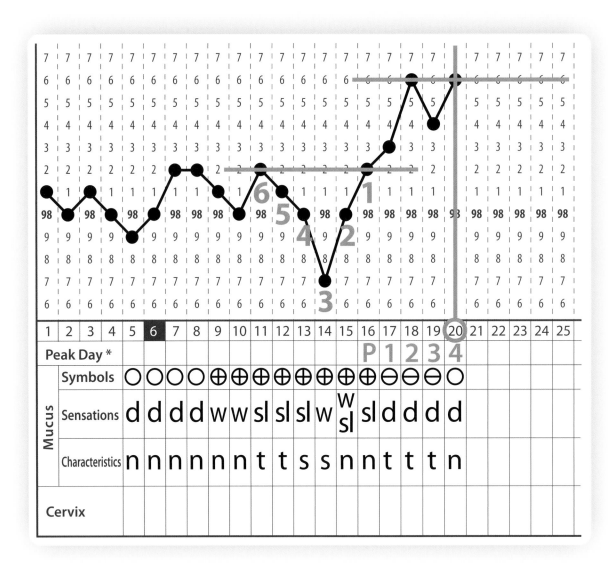

The third day of drying up past the Peak Day is Cycle Day 19, and the three normal post-peak temperatures above the LTL are Cycle Days 17, 18, and 19. The third of these temperatures (Cycle Day 19) is below the HTL, and there is no cervix data. Thus, Phase III begins after waiting an additional post-peak day for another temperature above the LTL on the evening of Cycle Day 20.

Note: The third temperature does not reach the HTL and no cervix sign is recorded, so it is necessary to wait a fourth day. While in this example the fourth post-peak temperature reaches the HTL, it does not have to, as long as it is above the LTL.

Class 2

Identifying Peak Day › Practice (page 70)

Peak Day	—	Cycle Day 15

Review › Practice Chart (page 72)

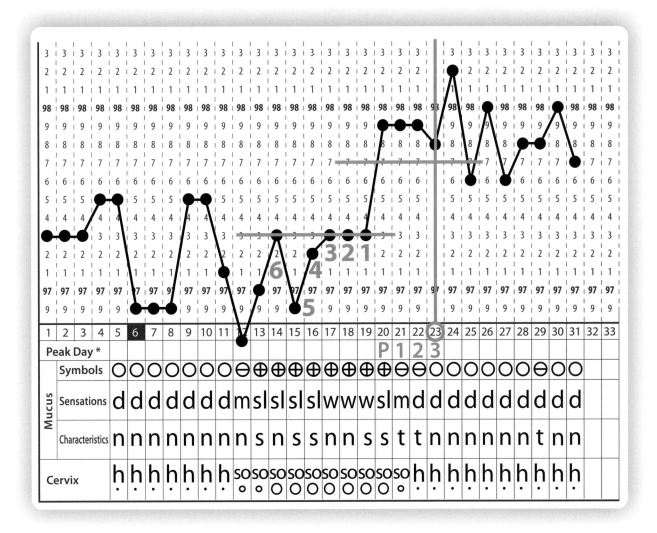

The third day of drying up past the Peak Day is Cycle Day 23, and the three normal post-peak temperatures above the LTL are Cycle Days 21, 22, and 23. The third of these temperatures (Cycle Day 23) is (at or) above the HTL. Thus, Phase III begins on the evening of Cycle Day 23.

Homework › Chart 1

(See instructions and chart on pages 168–169 of Appendix A)

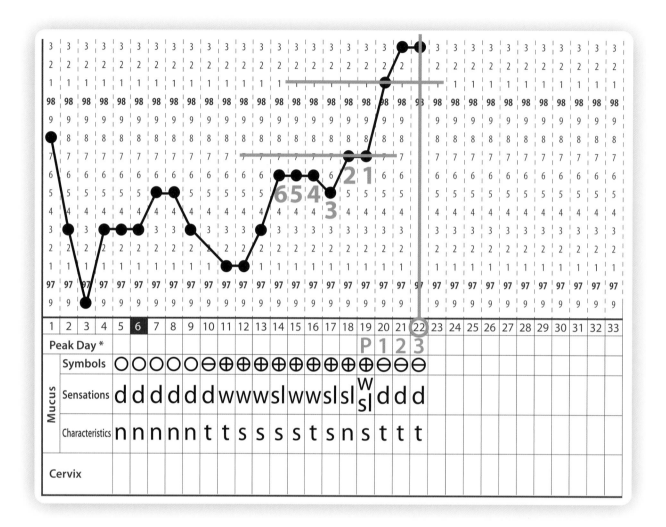

There are two ways to interpret this chart, based on how the thermal shift is interpreted. The first way is to consider that the thermal shift is found closest to Peak Day, which would be Cycle Days 20, 21, and 22. That makes the pre-shift six temperatures Cycle Days 14–19. The third day of drying up past the Peak Day is Cycle Day 22, and the three normal post-peak temperatures above the LTL are Cycle Days 20, 21, and 22. The third of these temperatures (Cycle Day 22) is (at or) above the HTL. Thus, Phase III begins on the evening of Cycle Day 22.

The second way to interpret this chart is to consider the thermal shift to be on Cycle Days 18, 19, and 20. That makes the pre-shift six temperatures Cycle Days 12–17, and the LTL and HTL to be 97.6° F and 98.0° F respectively. The rest of the interpretation is the same, and this yields the evening of Cycle Day 22 as the beginning of Phase III as well.

Homework › Chart 2

(See instructions and chart on pages 168–169 of Appendix A)

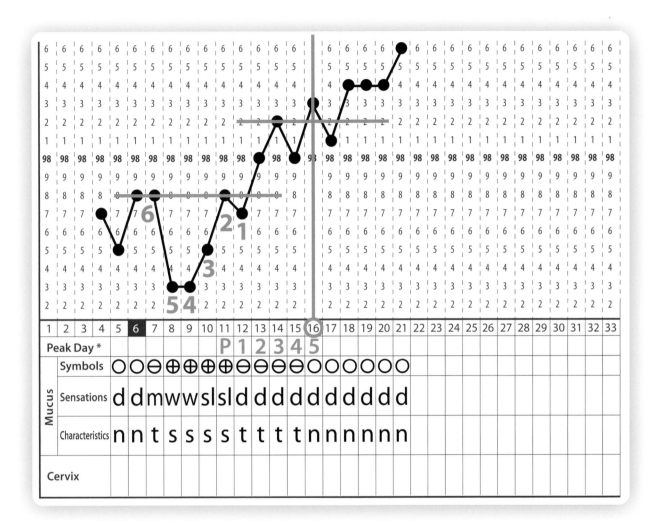

	1	2	3	4	5	6	7	8	9	10	11	12	13	14	15	16	17	18	19	20	21	22	23	24	25	26	27	28	29	30	31	32	33
Peak Day *						P	1	2	3	4	5																						
Symbols	O	O	⊖	⊕	⊕	⊕	⊕	⊖	⊖	⊖	⊖	⊖	O	O	O	O	O	O															
Sensations	d	d	m	w	w	s	l	s	l	d	d	d	d	d	d	d	d	d															
Characteristics	n	n	t	s	s	s	s	t	t	t	t	n	n	n	n	n	n	n															
Cervix																																	

The third day of drying up past the Peak Day is Cycle Day 14, and the three normal post-peak temperatures above the LTL are Cycle Days 13, 14, and 15. The third of these temperatures (Cycle Day 15) is below the HTL, and there is no cervix data. Thus, Phase III begins after waiting an additional post-peak day for another temperature above the LTL on the evening of Cycle Day 16.

Homework › Chart 3

(See instructions and chart on pages 168 and 170 of Appendix A)

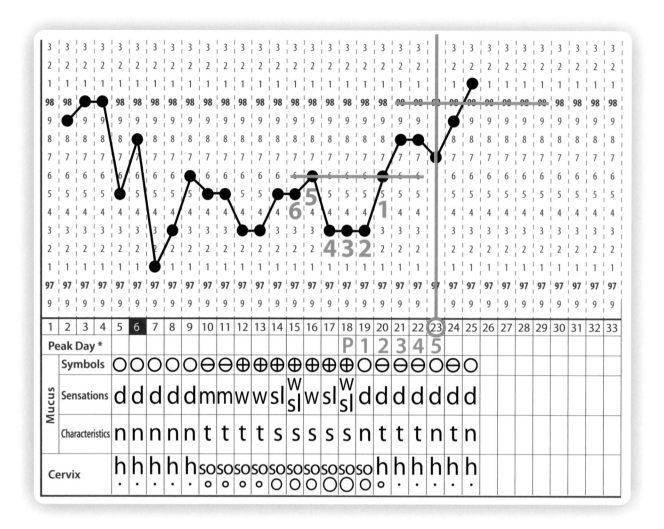

The third day of drying up past the Peak Day is Cycle Day 21, and the three normal post-peak temperatures above the LTL are Cycle Days 21, 22, and 23. The third of these temperatures (Cycle Day 23) is below the HTL but the cervix is closed and hard for three days (Cycle Days 21, 22, and 23). Thus, Phase III begins on the evening of Cycle Day 23.

Homework › Chart 4

(See instructions and chart on pages 168 and 170 of Appendix A)

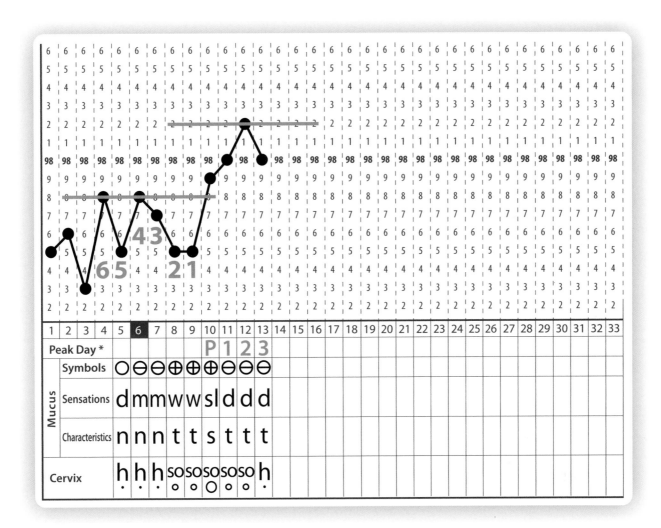

The third day of drying up past the Peak Day is Cycle Day 13, and the three normal post-peak temperatures above the LTL are Cycle Days 11, 12, and 13. The third of these temperatures (Cycle Day 13) is not at or above the HTL, nor has the cervix been closed and hard for three days. Thus, the start of Phase III cannot be determined until we observe and record the signs for at least one more day.

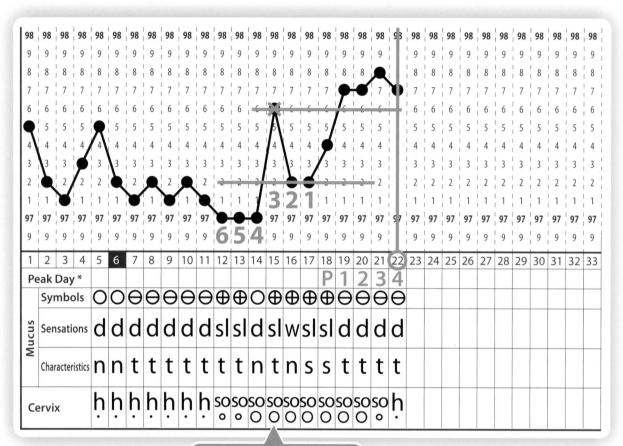

Temp 2 hours late

Because there was one abnormal temperature in the pre-shift six (Cycle Day 15), Phase III begins after waiting for four post-peak temperatures above the LTL. Thus, Phase III begins on the evening of Cycle Day 22.

Applying the ST Rule: Abnormal/Missed Temperatures › Practice Chart 2 of 2 (pages 75–76)

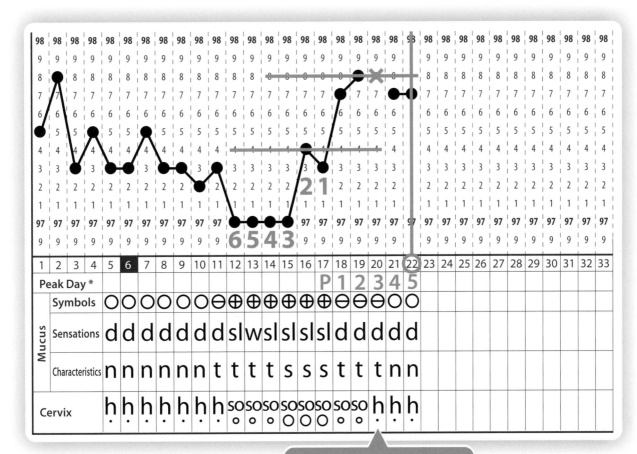

Forgot Temperature

Because there was a missed temperature within the thermal shift, the pre-shift six cannot be established until there are three elevated normal temperatures (Cycle Days 18, 19 and 21). Because the third temperature (Cycle Day 21) is not at or above the HTL and the cervix is only closed and hard for two days, Phase III cannot begin until after waiting an additional post-peak day for another temperature (Cycle Day 22) above the LTL. Thus, Phase III begins on the evening of Cycle Day 22. Note that the fourth temperature (Cycle Day 22) need not be at or above the HTL.

Day 5/6 Rule › Practice (page 80–81)

Cycle History	Shortest Cycle	Infertile Days
12	26 days	Cycle Days 1–6
12	24 days	Cycle Days 1–5
10	28 days	Cycle Days 1–5

Doering Rule › Practice (page 82)

Earliest first day of temperature rise	Infertile Days
14 days	Cycle Days 1–7
18 days	Cycle Days 1–11
12 days	Cycle Days 1–5

Last Dry Day Rule › Practice (page 83–84)

1 of 3

Cycle Day 7	Mucus Symbol = ◯
Cycle Day 8	Mucus Symbol = ⊖

- Last Dry Day is Cycle Day 7
- Phase division line is drawn between Cycle Days 7 and 8

2 of 3

Cycle Day 11	Mucus Symbol = ⊕

- Last Dry Day is Cycle Day 10
- Phase division line is drawn between Cycle Days 10 and 11

3 of 3

Cycle Day 10	Mucus Symbol = ⊖

- Last Dry Day is Cycle Day 9
- Phase division line is drawn between Cycle Days 9 and 10

Days of Infertility in Phase I › Practice (page 84)

False
True
True
True

Setting Up a New Chart › Practice (page 86–87)

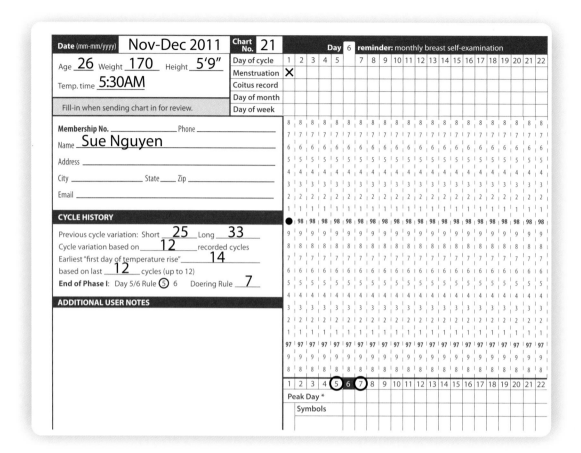

1. **Cycle Length:** Since menstruation began on Cycle Day 26, the length of the previous cycle is 25 days.

2. **Data Transferred:**
   - Date: Nov–Dec 2011
   - Age, weight, height remain same
   - Chart No. = 21
   - Data for Cycle Day 1: "X" for menstruation — Temperature = 98.0° F

3. **Cycle History**
   - Previous cycle variation: Since Cycle No. 20 was 25 days long, the previous cycle variation for short or long cycles becomes 25 (new short cycle) and 33, respectively.
   - Earliest "first day of temperature rise" is Cycle Day 14 which is now a day earlier than it was before.
   - End of Phase I:
     - Day 5/6 Rule = Cycle Day 5 because now the woman does not have cycles 26 days or longer in her last 12 cycles
     - Doering Rule = Cycle Day 7

4. **Circle Cycle Days 5 & 7** at the bottom of the chart.

Phase I Rules › Practice (page 88)

Chart No.	7				Day	6																							
Day of cycle	1	2	3	4	5		7	8	9	10	11	12	13	14	15	16	17	18	19	20	21	22	23	24	25	26	27	28	29 30 31 32 33
Menstruation	✕	✕	✕	╱	╱																								
Coitus record		✓	✓		✓		✓																						
Day of month																													
Day of week																													

CYCLE HISTORY

Previous cycle variation: Short __26__ Long __30__

Cycle variation based on __6__ recorded cycles

Earliest "first day of temperature rise" __16__

based on last __6__ cycles (up to 12)

End of Phase I: Day 5/6 Rule ⑤ 6   Doering Rule __9__

Peak Day *

Mucus Symbol	◉	◯	?	◯	⊖				
Mucus Sensation	d	d	d	d	d				
Mucus Characteristic	n	n	sr	n	t sr				

Cervix

End of Phase I:

- Day 5/6 Rule = Cycle Day 5 because the woman has only 6 recorded cycles

- Doering Rule = Cycle Day 9

- Circle Cycle Days 5 and 9 on the chart.

- End of Phase I is Cycle Day 7

Since the couple had relations on Cycle Day 5, seminal residue (sr) was recorded on Cycle Day 6 and the absence or presence of mucus could not be confirmed. The couple had relations on Cycle Day 7 and recorded "sr" for Cycle Day 8. However, the woman also detected some tacky mucus. The presence of mucus (⊖ symbol) is the positive indication of the start of Phase II.

Note: The phase division line is drawn after Cycle Day 7.

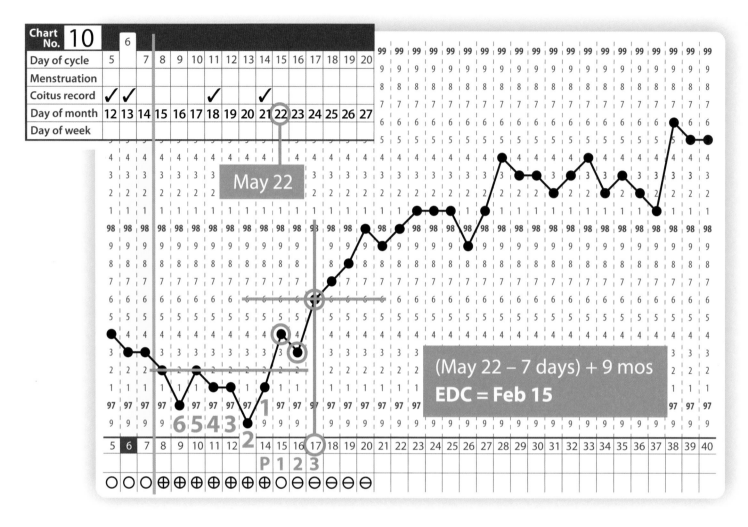

End of Phase I: Cycle Day 7.

The third day of drying up past the Peak Day is Cycle Day 17, and the three normal post-peak temperatures above the LTL are Cycle Days 15, 16, and 17. The third of these temperatures (Cycle Day 17) is at (or above) the HTL. Thus, Phase III begins on the evening of Cycle Day 17.

The Estimated Date of Childbirth (EDC) using the Prem Rule is the first day of the temperature rise (Cycle Day 15, May 22) minus seven days, plus 9 months. Thus, the EDC is February 15.

Note: Generally, a luteal phase of at least 21 days is an indication of pregnancy.

Class 3

Review › Practice Chart (page 117)

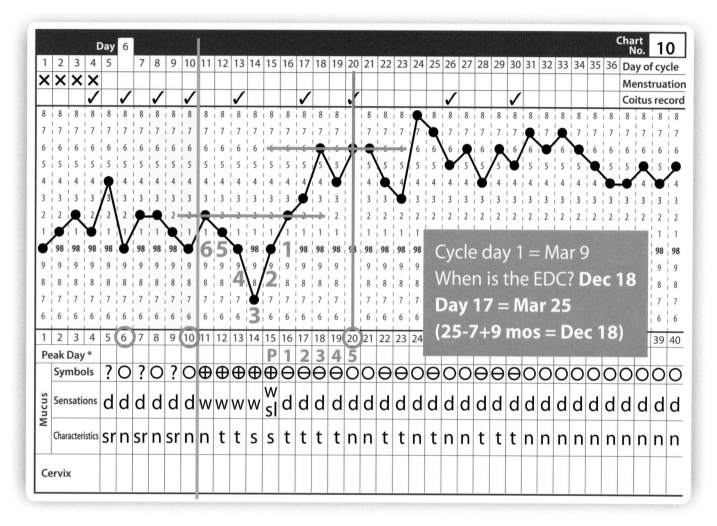

Chart No. 10

Cycle day 1 = Mar 9
When is the EDC? **Dec 18**
Day 17 = Mar 25
(25-7+9 mos = Dec 18)

Phase I and Phase II:

- Day 5/6 Rule = Cycle Day 6
  Note: There is seminal residue "sr" on Cycle Days 5, 7 and 9 which could mask the presence of mucus. Thus, these are not known infertile days. So the mucus symbols are not shown.

- Doering Rule = Cycle Day 10

- Last Dry Day = Cycle Day 10

- End of Phase I = Cycle Day 10
  (Even though the couple had marital relations on Cycle Day 10, the wet "w" sensation on Cycle Day 11 indicates fertility and the start of Phase II.)

Phase III:

The third day of drying up past the Peak Day is Cycle Day 18, and the three normal post-peak temperatures above the LTL are Cycle Days 17, 18, and 19. The third of these temperatures (Cycle Day 19) is not at or above the HTL and there is no cervix data. Thus, Phase III begins after waiting an additional post-peak day for another temperature above the LTL on the evening of Cycle Day 20.

Estimated Date of Childbirth = December 18.

– Calculation: First day of thermal shift = March 25

March 25 – 7 days = March 18

March 18 + 9 months = December 18

The luteal phase for a typical cycle is between 10 and 14 days. Since the luteal phase is well beyond that number, it could be assumed that this woman is pregnant.

Homework › Chart 5

(See instructions and chart on pages 172–173 of Appendix A)

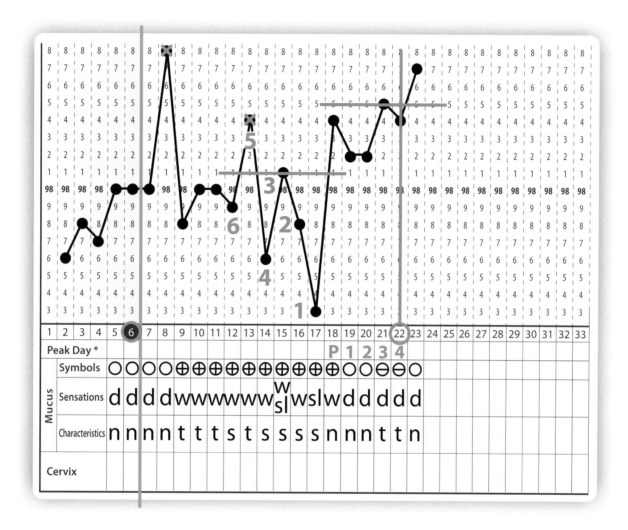

Phase I and Phase II:

- Day 5/6 Rule = Cycle Day 6
  Note: Although this is only her second cycle using the Sympto-Thermal Method, she knows that in the last 12 cycles, her shortest cycle length was 26 days. Thus, she can use Cycle Day 6.

- Doering Rule = N/A (< 6 cycles of experience)

- Last Dry Day Rule = N/A (< 6 cycles of experience)

- End of Phase I = Cycle Day 6

Phase III:

Because there was one abnormal temperature in the pre-shift six (Cycle Day 13), Phase III begins after waiting for four post-peak temperatures above the LTL, on the evening of Cycle Day 22.

Phase I and Phase II:

- Day 5/6 Rule = Cycle Day 5
  Note: Since mucus was observed on Cycle Day 4, this indicates that Phase I has ended and Phase II has started.

- Doering Rule = N/A (< 6 cycles of experience)

- Last Dry Day Rule = N/A (< 6 cycles of experience)

- End of Phase I = Cycle Day 3

Phase III:

Because there were two missed temperatures (Cycle Days 10 and 11), Phase III begins after waiting for four post-peak temperatures above the LTL on the evening of Cycle Day 16.

Note: Remember that when using the ST Rule, the pre-shift six are the temperatures taken on the six days immediately preceding the three thermal shift temperatures. If there are up to two abnormal or missed temperatures during this time, the LTL is derived from the remaining normal temperatures.

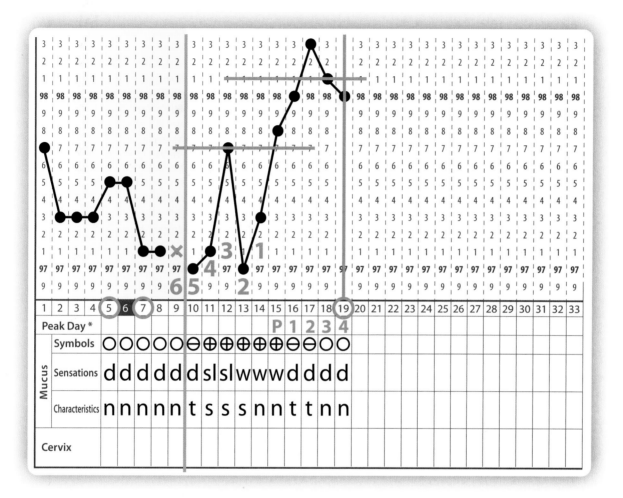

Phase I and Phase II:

- Day 5/6 Rule = Cycle Day 5

  Note: Since 12 cycle lengths have not been observed, the Day 5/6 Rule is still limited to Cycle Day 5.

- Doering Rule = Cycle Day 7

- Last Dry Day Rule = Cycle Day 9

- End of Phase I = Cycle Day 9

Phase III:

Because there was one missing temperature in the pre-shift six (Cycle Day 9), Phase III begins after waiting for four post-peak temperatures above the LTL on the evening of Cycle Day 19.

Calendar Rhythm › Practice Chart (page 121)

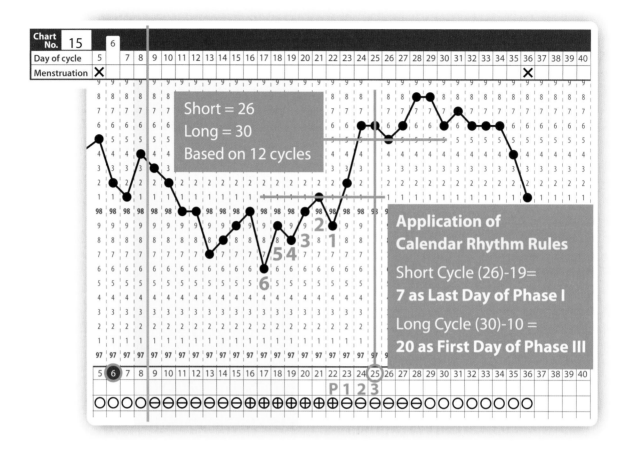

Phase I and Phase II:

Sympto-Thermal Method

- Day 5/6 Rule = Cycle Day 6
- Doering Rule = N/A (Not enough information)
- Last Dry Day Rule = Cycle Day 8
- End of Phase I = Cycle Day 8

Phase III:

Sympto-Thermal Method

- Start of Phase III = Evening of Cycle Day 25

This cycle is a 35-day cycle, which is five days longer than her previous longest cycle. Note the ⊕ symbols on Cycle Days 20–22, yet Calendar Rhythm yields Cycle Day 20 as the start of Phase III. When the current cycle is significantly longer or shorter than the previous cycles, the Calendar Rhythm method does not give an accurate determination of fertile and infertile days.

CCL Mucus-Only Rule › Practice Chart (page 123)

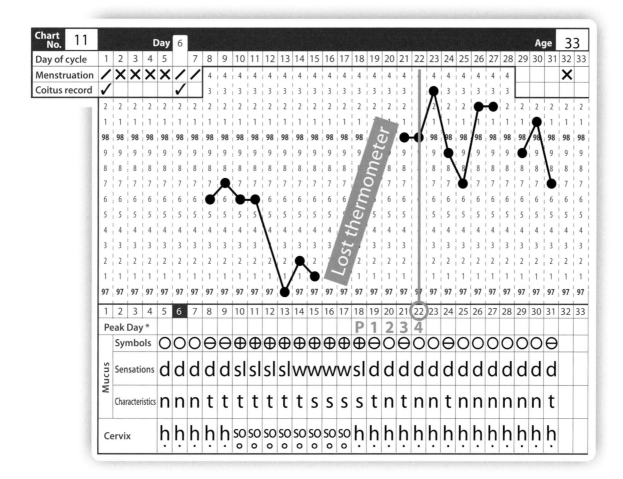

Phase III:

> Using the CCL Mucus-Only Rule, Phase III begins on the evening of the fourth day of drying-up past the Peak Day, which is Cycle Day 22.

Note: More than two temperatures are missing during the pre-shift six and likely some temperatures are missing in the thermal shift. Therefore, the ST Rule cannot be applied.

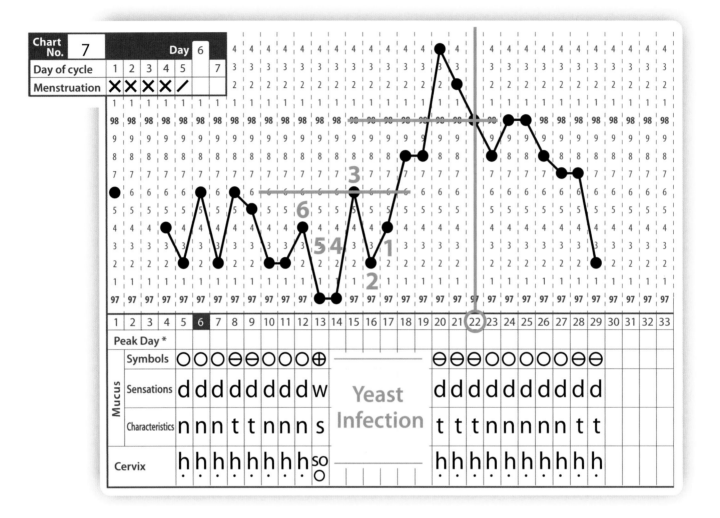

Phase III:

Since the mucus sign could not be used, the CCL Temperature-Only Rule is applied. The fourth day of normal temperatures above the LTL is Cycle Day 21, and the last three consecutive temperatures at or above the HTL are Cycle Days 20, 21 and 22. Thus, Phase III begins on the evening of Cycle Day 22.

Breakthrough Bleeding › Practice Chart (page 132)

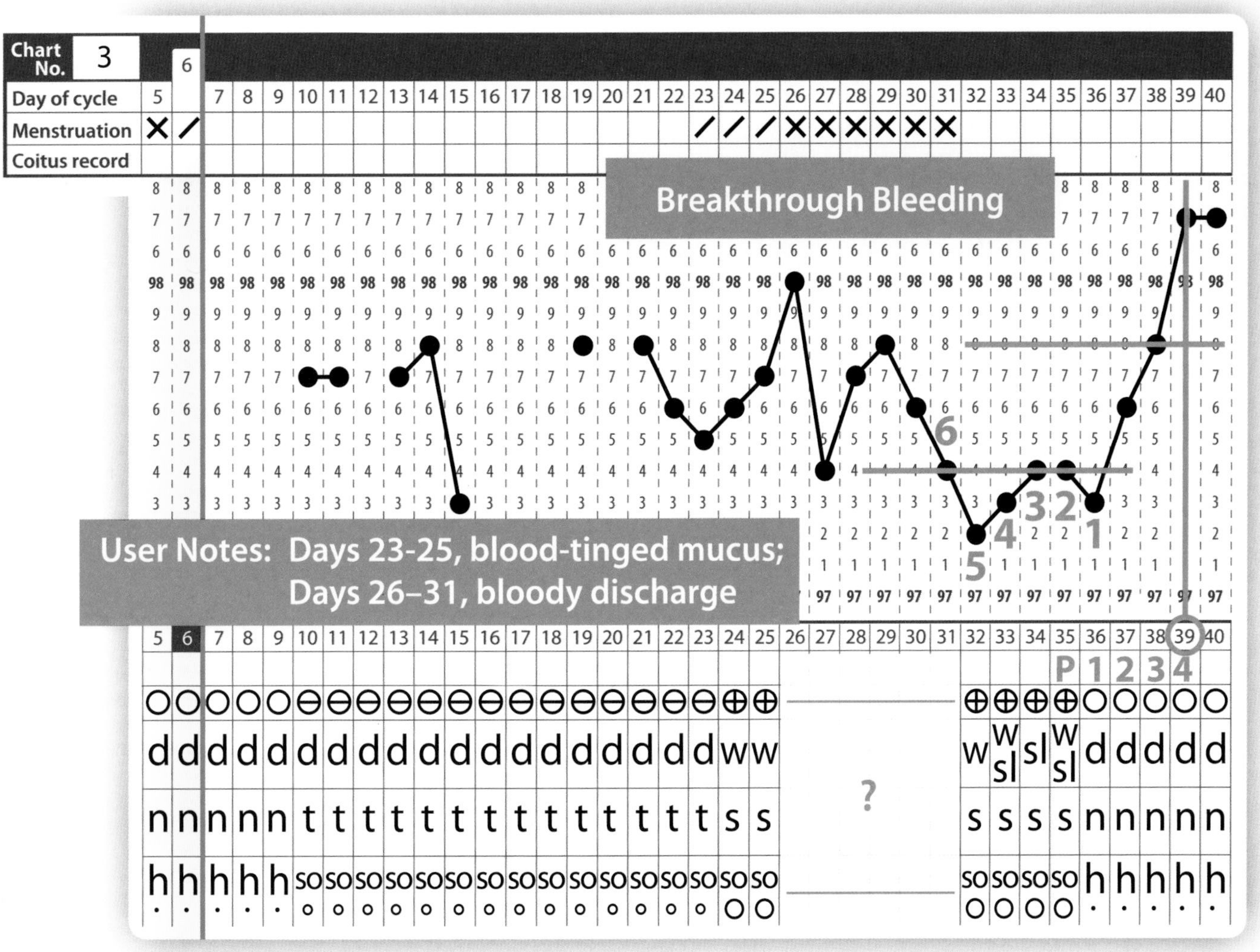

Chart No. 3

Day of cycle	5	6	7	8	9	10	11	12	13	14	15	16	17	18	19	20	21	22	23	24	25	26	27	28	29	30	31	32	33	34	35	36	37	38	39	40
Menstruation	✗	╱																	╱	╱	╱	✗	✗	✗	✗	✗	✗									
Coitus record																																				

Breakthrough Bleeding

User Notes: Days 23–25, blood-tinged mucus; Days 26–31, bloody discharge

Phase III:

The third day of drying up past the Peak Day is Cycle Day 38 and the three normal post-peak temperatures above the LTL are Cycle Days 37, 38, and 39. The third of these temperatures is (at or) above the HTL. Thus, Phase III begins on the evening of Cycle Day 39.

Stress › Chart (page 133)

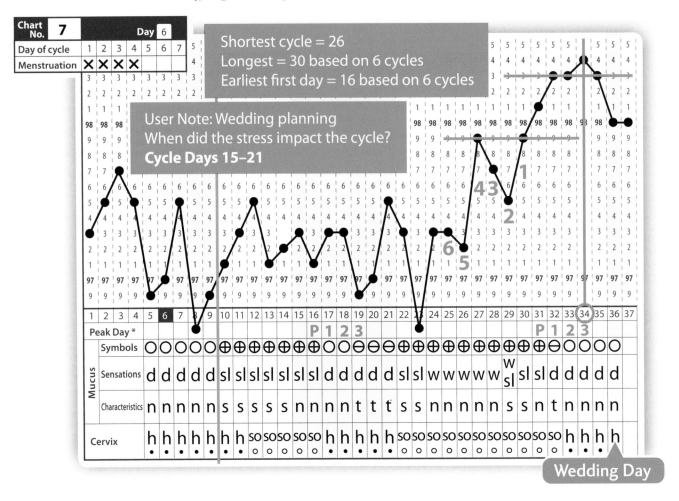

Chart No. 7 — Day 6

Day of cycle	1	2	3	4	5	6	7
Menstruation	✕	✕	✕	✕			

Shortest cycle = 26
Longest = 30 based on 6 cycles
Earliest first day = 16 based on 6 cycles

User Note: Wedding planning
When did the stress impact the cycle?
Cycle Days 15–21

Wedding Day

- End of Phase I = Cycle Day 9

Phase III:

This chart shows two patches of mucus. The first mucus patch occurs on Cycle Days 10–16 followed by two dry, nothing days. At first glance it may seem that Peak Day may have occurred on Cycle Day 16. However, there is no thermal shift to confirm an ovulation. Another mucus patch begins on Cycle Day 19 and it progresses from less-fertile mucus on Cycle Days 19–21, becomes more-fertile on Cycle Days 22–31, and ends in Peak Day (Cycle Day 31), accompanied by a thermal shift.

The third day of drying up past the Peak Day is Cycle Day 34, and the three normal post-peak temperatures above the LTL are Cycle Days 32, 33, and 34. The third temperature past the Peak Day is (at or) above the HTL. Thus, Phase III begins on the evening of Cycle Day 34.

Note: In cycles that are long, due to stress or other reasons such as PCOS, etc., mucus may come and go in mucus patches. This is a sign that ovarian activity starts and then stops. In this chart it is probably due to the stress of wedding planning.

Illness › Practice Chart (page 134)

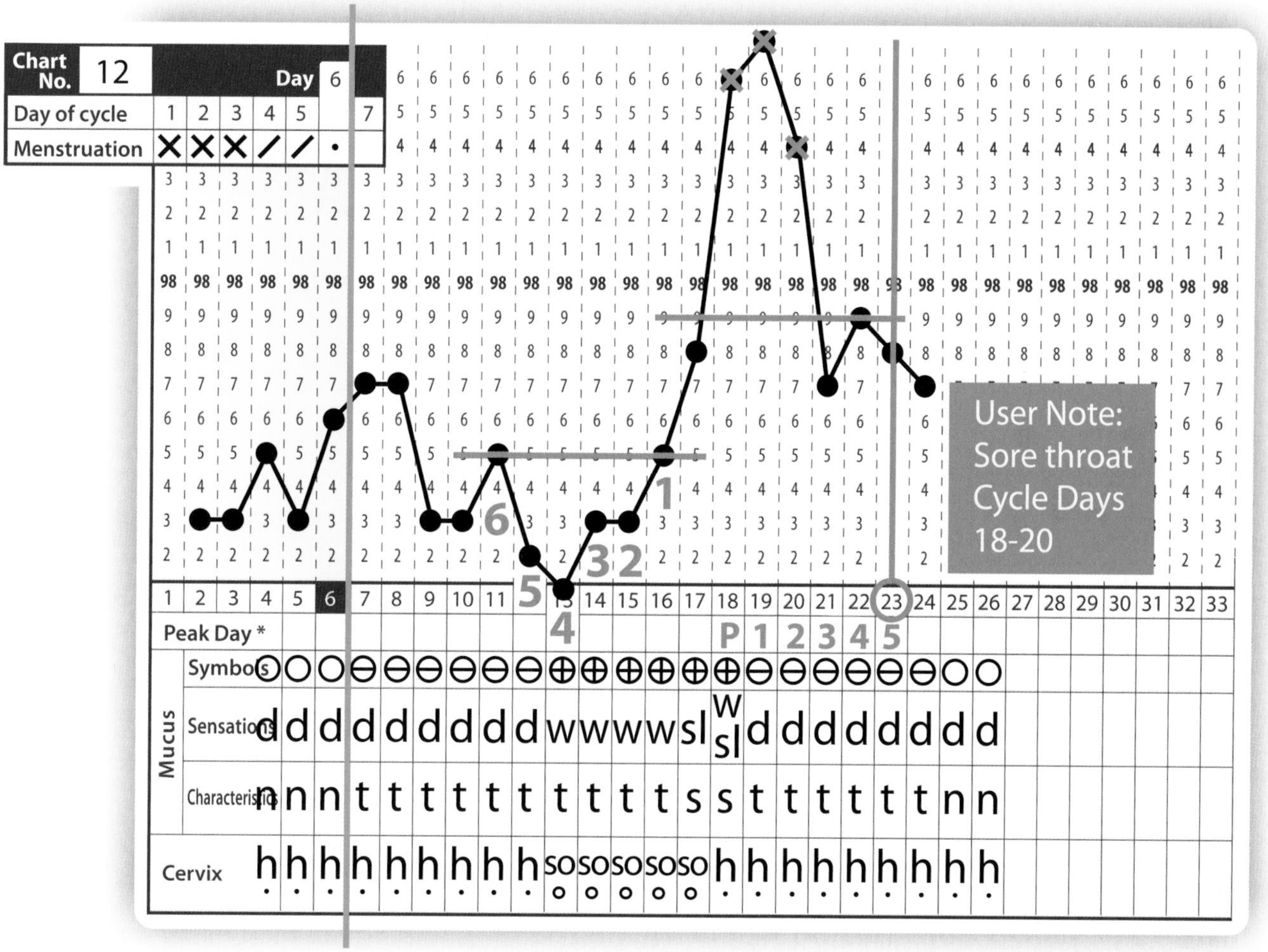

Chart No. 12 — Day of cycle / Menstruation chart with temperature graph.

User Note: Sore throat Cycle Days 18-20

Phase III:

There are abnormal temperatures on Cycle Days 18, 19, and 20. The three normal temperatures of the temperature rise thus are Cycle Days 17, 21, and 22. The third day of drying up past the Peak Day is Cycle Day 21, and the three normal post-peak temperatures above the LTL are Cycle Days 21, 22, and 23. The third of these temperatures is below the HTL, but the cervix is closed and hard for three days. Thus, Phase III begins on the evening of Cycle Day 23.

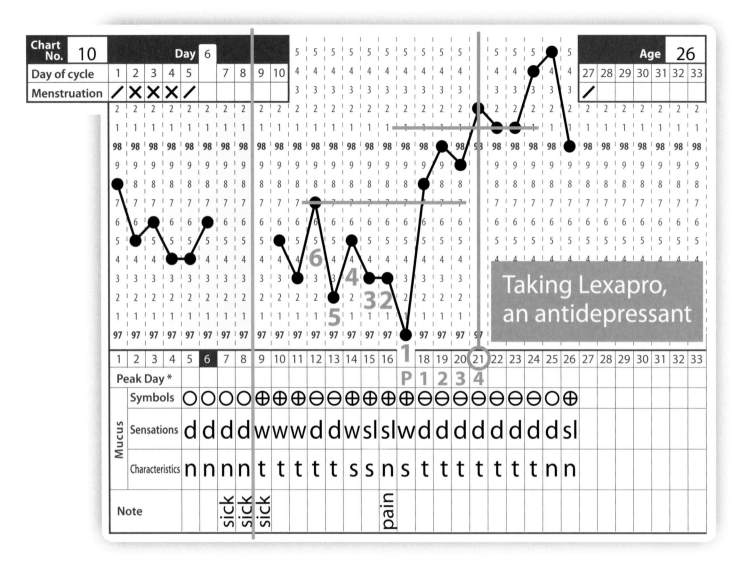

- End of Phase I = Cycle Day 8

Phase III:

The third day of drying up past the Peak Day is Cycle Day 20, and the three normal post-peak temperatures above the LTL are Cycle Days 18, 19, and 20. The third of these temperatures is below the HTL, and there is no cervix data. Thus, Phase III begins after waiting an additional post-peak day for another temperature above the LTL on the evening of Cycle Day 21.

Reference R

Biological Clock

When trying to achieve a pregnancy, it is important to acknowledge the well-known fact that women have a "biological clock" or biological rhythms. Although age is a factor in the time it takes a woman to conceive, an increasing number of couples today are unnecessarily alarmed because of a misunderstanding about how long it naturally takes for conception to occur.

The graph on the next page illustrates the possibility of conception in various age groups for couples using "focused fertility awareness." It shows that "although fecundity [fertility] seemed to decrease with age, the cumulative pregnancy rates were not statistically different."[1] After 12 cycles, all women reached an estimated plateau of a 90–98% pregnancy rate, including the women who were older than 35.

Thus…age per se was not associated with any statistically significant reduction in CPC (cumulative probabilities of conception)."[2] The significance of this information is that while a small minority of couples will have their fertility start to decrease as they leave their twenties, the vast majority of couples are still quite fertile well into their mid- to late-thirties.

---

[1] Gnoth et al., "Time to Pregnancy: results of the German prospective study and impact on the management of fertility," *Human Reproduction*, 18(9), 2003, 1959–66.

[2] Ibid.

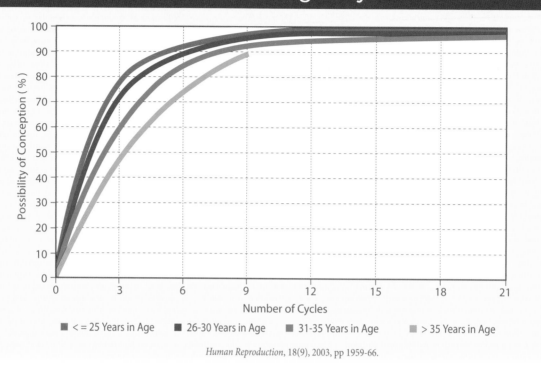

Human Reproduction, 18(9), 2003, pp 1959-66.

Breakthrough Bleeding

Class 3 briefly mentioned "breakthrough bleeding," and that occasionally during the times of puberty, postpartum, premenopause, or infrequently during the most fertile years, bleeding may occur which begins like menstruation but really is not. This breakthrough bleeding can be a potentially fertile time because it could occur just before ovulation, or it might not be fertile at all.

Breakthrough bleeding can happen when the endometrium builds up so much that the top layer cannot be sustained just by estrogen, so it breaks down. The result may be only spotting, or it may be like a normal menstrual flow. A mucus discharge could occur at the same time.

How can you distinguish breakthrough bleeding from a true menstruation? Breakthrough bleeding is a bloody discharge not preceded by a sustained thermal shift, whereas, menstruation is a bloody discharge that follows ovulation and is confirmed by a preceding, sustained thermal shift. (A sustained thermal shift would be at least three temperatures above the LTL close to Peak Day.)

In the postpartum transition a bleed may begin without any previous signs of fertility.

Thus, women may not have charted their fertility signs and will not know if it is a breakthrough bleed or a menstruation. If this occurs, consider the bleed to be a breakthrough bleed for interpretation purposes.

(See the breakthrough bleeding explanation and chart in the Student Guide — Class 3, Lesson 4, *Applying NFP in Special Situations*, page 131, and in Appendix B, page 203.)

If you experience a bleeding episode that is not preceded by a thermal shift (breakthrough bleeding), you should consider it a potentially fertile time, even if mucus sensations and/or characteristics do not appear to be present. Record the bleeding on the Menstruation row of your chart and continue charting your fertility signs on the same chart. The bleeding may or may not be accompanied by mucus. In either case, if you observe a thermal shift shortly after the bleeding subsides, mark the last day of bleeding or the last day of more-fertile mucus, whichever comes later, as your Peak Day. Couples seeking to avoid or postpone a pregnancy should abstain during these days of bleeding and any mucus until a thermal shift occurs, confirming the start of Phase III infertility. Then, apply the Sympto-Thermal Rule to determine the start of Phase III. When your true menstruation returns after a sustained thermal shift, then you can start a new chart.

Breakthrough bleeding is uncommon, but it does happen. Women who frequently experience breakthrough bleeding and are not postpartum or in premenopause may find it helpful to examine their overall health with regard to nutrition, exercise and stress level. It may be necessary to consult with a nutritionist and/or physician. In addition, women who have a long, continuous bleeding episode should also consult with a physician.

Calendar Rhythm

As explained in Class 3, Calendar Rhythm was based on the discovery that ovulation occurs about two weeks before the next menstruation. It was first presented as a systematic method of family planning by Dr. Jan N. J. Smulders in 1930. While the Calendar Rhythm method is morally acceptable, it is not as effective as modern methods of NFP because it relies solely on past cycle history and not on a woman's current signs of fertility.

Calendar Rhythm used the following rules to determine the end of Phase I and the beginning of Phase III:

1. The last cycle day of pre-ovulation infertility (Phase I) is the shortest previous cycle minus 19, and

2. The first cycle day of post-ovulation infertility (Phase III) is the longest previous cycle minus 10.

Cervix Exam

As you learned in Class 1, although optional, the cervix can be a very helpful sign of fertility. As a woman starts to become fertile, the cervix begins to soften, open a bit, and may become more difficult to reach because it will rise up in the vagina. It may feel like your lower lip. Once ovulation occurs and fertility disappears, the cervix will harden, close up, and lower in the vagina, and it may feel like the tip of your nose.

The cervix is sometimes compared to the narrow end of a pear with the stem removed. (The illustration shows what the cervix looks like when viewed from below.)

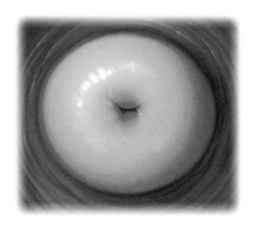

The easiest way to observe changes in the cervix is to perform a personal examination. It is important for women to find the technique that works best for them, but most women tend to use one of the following three techniques.

1. Sit on an open toilet. Insert the index finger into the vaginal canal and gently touch the cervix. If reaching it is difficult, try pressing down on the abdomen with the other hand.

2. Stand with one foot on the toilet seat cover, insert the index finger into the vagina to touch the cervix, and press down on the abdomen, if necessary.

3. Squat down, and insert the index finger into the vagina, etc.

Note: If a woman pushes down on her abdomen to help locate the cervix, then for consistency, she should use this same technique each time she checks her cervix.

When inserting the index finger, know that the only structure in the vagina will be the cervix. If needed, a woman can move the finger around a bit at the back end of the vagina, and she should be able to discern the cervix. The easiest time for beginners to learn this observation is during Phase III. This will be the baseline infertile position of the cervix; it will be the most closed and hard during this time, and is easier to reach.

CCL History

In *Humanae Vitae*, Pope Paul VI wrote about the need for married couples to become apostles to other married couples: "…it is married couples themselves who become apostles and guides to other married couples. This is assuredly, among so many forms of apostolate, one of those which seem most opportune today."[3]

John and Sheila Kippley felt strongly called to address this prophetic statement from Pope Paul VI by providing the practical help of Natural Family Planning. They created an apostolate based on a "couple to couple" approach — married couples volunteering to teach NFP to other married and engaged couples. Thus, the Couple to Couple League (CCL) was founded in 1971.

CCL taught a method of NFP that the Kippleys had developed in consultation with Dr. Konald A. Prem, professor and chairman of the Department of Obstetrics and Gynecology at the University of Minnesota School of Medicine. The method used temperature, mucus observations and cervical observations to form a comprehensive system that cross-checked all the proven indicators of pre- and post-ovulation infertility.

In the very first course, CCL's "triple strand" approach was put into place:

1. Sympto-Thermal Method (STM) of NFP based on cross-checking signs of fertility

2. Promotion of breastfeeding through "ecological" breastfeeding and the return of fertility after childbirth

3. Traditional Catholic Church teaching on marriage and sexuality to include John Kippley's Covenant Theology

Since its founding over 40 years ago, the League has grown into an extensive network of volunteers located throughout the United States and in various countries throughout the world. In that time, some of the specifics have changed. For example, the method has been streamlined, simplified and adapted using current best medical evidence. The term "ecological" is no longer used when referring to breastfeeding, and the Catholic Church's teaching on marriage and sexuality is presented based on Pope John Paul II's Theology of the Body. But CCL's basic "triple strand" approach — method, breastfeeding and morality — is still in place today.

Literally thousands of couples have found that practicing NFP can have an incredibly positive effect on their marriages…for some it has been a life-changing experience. That is why many of these couples have chosen to volunteer their time to share this wonderful teaching and experience with others. If you are interested in volunteering for CCL, visit our website at **www.ccli.org** and click on "Teach/Promote."

---

[3] *Humanae Vitae*, 26

CycleProGo®

CCL's mobile app charting, known as CycleProGo®, tracks and electronically charts the mucus, temperature and cervix signs of fertility. Note that the purpose of CycleProGo® is to help couples identify the fertile time to assist in achieving pregnancy. CycleProGo® automatically keeps an electronic history of cycle lengths and assists in applying CCL's rules to identify the fertile time of a woman's cycle.

CycleProGo® is easy to use for couples who know how to observe and assess a woman's signs of fertility. CycleProGo® can be accessed via a mobile app or a web browser. For more information, visit ***www.ccli.org***

Day 5/6 Rule

See Reference Guide, *Rules Summary*, pages 245–246, and Student Guide, Class 2, Lesson 4, *The Transition from Phase I to Phase II*, page 77.

Daylight Savings Time (DST)

If a woman is in Phase I or Phase III when the time changes to or from Daylight Savings Time (DST), she should have no problem adjusting to the time change with regard to interpreting her signs of fertility. But what if she is in Phase II? Will the change to or from DST affect her charting?

The short answer is that while the temperature may be affected, it is unlikely to be of significant impact. For most women, taking a temperature up to ½ hour before or after the normal waking time will not adversely affect their charting. In his book *Natural Conception Regulation (Natuerliche Empfaengnisregelung)*[4], Dr. Josef Roetzer states that variations up to 1½ hours between measuring times are of no consequence, so it is unlikely that the time change of one hour will have a dramatic effect. However, if couples have reason to suspect their temperature readings are off, it is easy to just add an extra day to the ST Rule for Phase III.

Doering Rule

See Reference Guide, *Rules Summary*, pages 245–246, and Student Guide, Class 2, Lesson 4, *The Transition from Phase I to Phase II*, page 77.

Effectiveness

As outlined in Class 2, effectiveness of contraception and effectiveness of NFP — both method and user effectiveness — are percentages derived from studies that have determined an **unintended pregnancy rate**. However, there are some basic limitations and underlying factors that affect studies of family planning methods. These include the quality of the study's design, execution and analysis, couples consistently and correctly using a particular method, the actual frequency of marital relations, the underlying fertility of couples, and even the country or culture where the study was conducted. For example, sometimes method effectiveness is interpreted to mean that all women participating in the study

---

[4] Joseph Roetzer, M.D., *Natural Conception Regulation* (*Natuerliche Empfaengnisregelung*) (Freiburg: Herder, 2006), 18. Note that Dr. Roetzer also adds that "Large variations after 7:30 a.m. must be noted on your chart."

could have gotten pregnant; however, there are always some couples who will not become pregnant no matter what method they use or do not use simply because of the infertility rate of the population. Also, if there is only one birth per 100 couples using a particular method for one year, it does not necessarily follow that the method used was the only reason the other 99 couples did not conceive. Consider another example: a study based on rural women in Uganda may show markedly different results than one based on farm families in California or families from New York City. The overall point is that effectiveness rates are not perfect and have certain biases that are extremely difficult to factor out.

While NFP (fertility awareness) is as effective as contraception, like contraception it is not 100% effective. There are only three 100% effective means of preventing a pregnancy:

- Total abstinence from sexual intercourse

- Complete removal of the male testicles (which is not a vasectomy)

- Complete removal of the female ovaries (which is not a tubal ligation or occlusion)

Just as every method of contraception has some rate of unintended pregnancy associated with it, so also does NFP. The following charts are examples of unintended pregnancies.

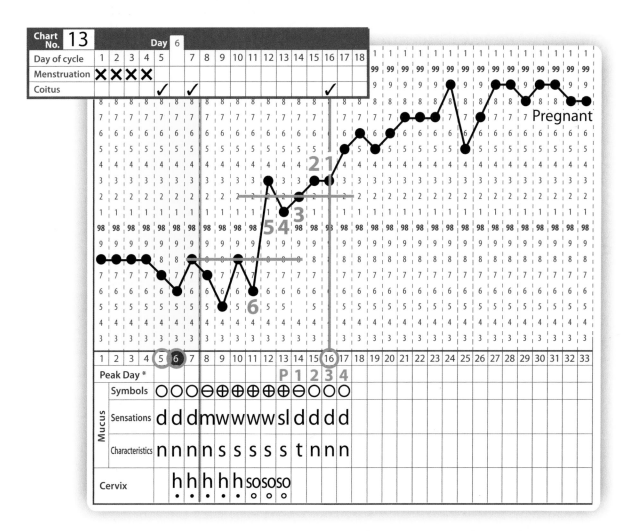

This pregnancy most likely occurred as a result of coitus on a dry day, Cycle Day 7. The mucus and cervix signs did not warn this couple in sufficient time that fertility had begun. In the future this couple could use the Day 5/6 Rule or the Doering Rule, which are more conservative. This is a method-related unintended pregnancy.

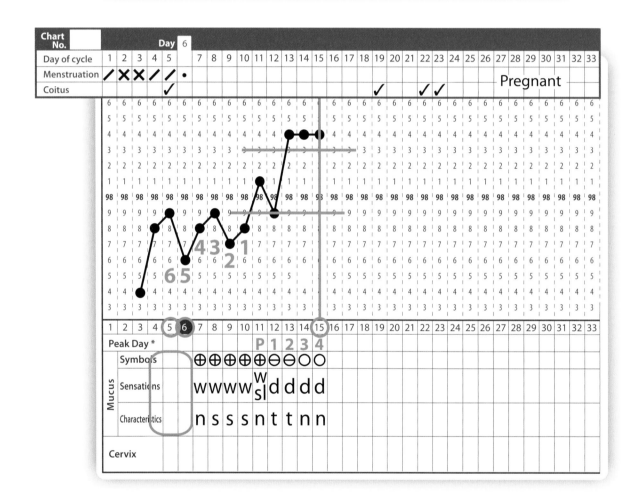

The Day 5/6 Rule yields Cycle Day 5 according to previous cycle history. Despite decreased menstrual flow, the mucus observations for Cycle Days 4–6 were not made. An essential part of Phase I infertility, including the Day 5/6 Rule, is ensuring there are no signs of mucus throughout the day. This is a user-related unintended pregnancy.

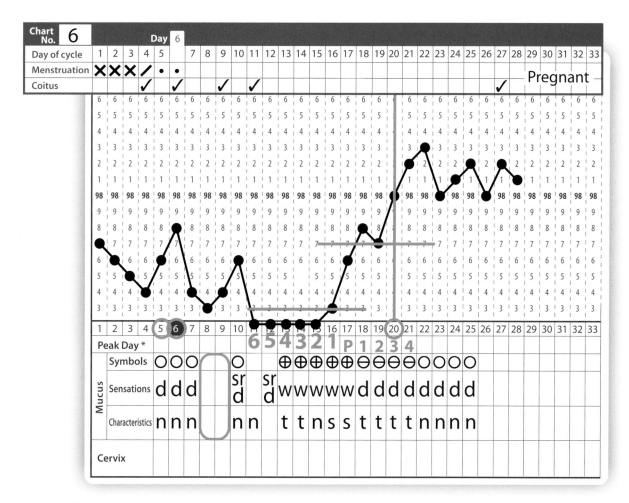

This couple used the Doering Rule to determine the end of Phase I with only one cycle of temperature history. They did not have sufficient experience to use the Doering Rule (six cycles required) and should have ended Phase I on Cycle Day 6. There were also no mucus observations on Cycle Days 4, 8 and 9, incomplete mucus observations on Cycle Days 11 and 12, and they had marital relations on Cycle Days 9 and 11. This is a user-related unintended pregnancy.

Even though unintended pregnancies do happen, NFP is still up to 99% effective if the rules are followed. The data that follows provides more detailed information on the 2007 German study, since the majority of CCL's method is based on this source of data.

2007 German Study. The Sympto-Thermal Method (STM) study conducted by Dr. Petra Frank-Herrmann et al. included 900 women contributing 17,638 cycles. The study showed a 99.6% method effectiveness rate, and a 98.2% user effectiveness rate.

The STM rules used in this study varied slightly from CCL's method. For the last day of Phase I, Cycle Day 5 was used for the first 12 cycles of experience, and a modified Doering Rule subtracting eight from the earliest day of temperature rise was used after 12 cycles. Both rules assumed the absence of mucus; i.e., when cervical mucus was observed, Phase II began. For the first day of Phase III, the later of three days of drying up after Peak Day and three temperatures above the LTL with the last temperature 0.2° C (~ 0.4° F) or higher was used.

Other large clinical trials support the effectiveness of the STM. For example, a large study conducted in nine European countries evaluated the effectiveness of four methods of NFP in 900 women with over 9,000 cycles. Of this group, 620 women used the STM for more than 7,000 cycles and had just 15 unintended pregnancies. There were no method-related pregnancies in the STM group, and user effectiveness was found to be 97.6%.[5] The group led by Dr. Frank-Herrmann also reported on a study conducted in 1997 involving more than 750 women contributing over 14,000 cycles. Method effectiveness in this study was 99.4% and user effectiveness was 97.8%.[6]

Effectiveness of CCL Rules. While the 2007 German study influences CCL's method the most, there are other studies supporting various portions of CCL's method with differing effectiveness rates. The table highlights each of CCL's rules and summarizes the effectiveness and supporting study.

---

[5] The European Natural Family Planning study groups, "Prospective European multi-center study of natural family planning (1989–1992): interim results," *Advances in Contraception* (1993); 9:269–283.

[6] Frank-Hermann, et. al., "Natural family planning with and without barrier method use in the fertile phase: efficacy in relation to sexual behavior: a German prospective long term study," *Advances in Contraception* (1997); 13:179–189.

Day 5/6 Rule

Effectiveness: 99.6 % method | 98.2 % user

Summary:

The effectiveness of Cycle Days 1–5 is based on the Frank-Herrmann study. The Frank-Herrmann study did not include women with cycles less than 22 days; therefore, efficacy of the Day 5/6 Rule for these women is unknown.

The method effectiveness of Cycle Day 6 (99.8%) is based on Dr. Josef Roetzer. Roetzer did not report user effectiveness of this rule.

Studies:

"The effectiveness of a fertility awareness based method to avoid pregnancy in relation to a couple's sexual behavior during the fertile time: a prospective longitudinal study," Frank-Herrmann et al, *Human Reproduction*, 2007;22(5):1310–1319.

"A Prospective Sympto-Thermal Trial in Austria, Germany and Swtzerland," Roetzer, Presentation III International Congress IFFLP/FIDAF, Hong Kong, Nov 20–30, 1983.

Doering Rule

Effectiveness: % method — not reported | 96.9 % user

Summary:

The Frank-Herrmann study and Roetzer required 12 cycles of experience and subtracted 8 days from the earliest first day of temperature rise. CCL's rule follows Doering's original study by requiring only 6 cycles of experience and subtracting 7 from the earliest first day of temperature rise. While CCL's Doering Rule is slightly less than 97% effective, it should be noted that Doering's study was based solely on temperature — women did not check for mucus. By checking for mucus, CCL's Doering Rule is more conservative than the approach used in the Doering study, and thus is as effective and may be more effective than 96.9%.

Studies:

"About the Dependability of the Temperature Method to Avoid Conception," Doering, Translated from the original article in *Deutsche medizinische Wochenschrift* (9 Jun 1967); 92: 1055–1061.

Last Dry Day Rule

Effectiveness: unknown method and user effectiveness

Summary:

CCL's Last Dry Day Rule is based primarily on mucus-only methods, such as the Billings Ovulation Method (BOM). There are differences, however, between how Billings and CCL teach the mucus sign. With regard to experience, BOM requires fewer cycles of experience to begin using their mucus rule, whereas CCL requires 6 cycles of experience. These differences affect the ability to correlate the studies' effectiveness with CCL's Last Dry Day Rule.

There have been many studies on the effectiveness of the BOM to include the studies shown above with reported effectiveness rates between 97.1% and 99.5%. Independent studies throughout the years, however, have reported effectiveness rates much lower. Because of the variability in reported effectiveness, combined with differences in teaching methods, until CCL can conduct its own effectiveness research we consider the effectiveness of the Last Dry Day Rule to be unknown.

Having said this, there is still great physiological evidence to warrant using this rule, and using it with confidence. The Wilcox study (see Class 3 page 95) estimated that the probability of conception on the sixth day preceding ovulation was zero. Thus, women with a normal mucus patch of 6 days or more through Peak Day have a very high probability of preventing conception.

Studies:

"Evaluation of the Effectiveness of a Natural Fertility Regulation Program in China," Qian et al, Paper presented at a Congress organized by the Center for Study and Research in the Natural Regulation of Fertility, Universita Cattolica del Sacro Cuore, Rome, Italy, 8 Sep 2000.

"Timing of sexual intercourse in relation to ovulation," Wilcox et al, *The New England Journal of Medicine* (7 Dec 1995); 333, 23:1517–1521.

Sympto-Thermal Rule

Effectiveness: 99.6 % method | 98.2 % user

Summary:

The effectiveness of the Sympto-Thermal Rule is well documented. It is based on both the Frank-Herrmann study and over 40 years of experience in Dr. Josef Roetzer's clinical practice. The effectiveness rates above were published in the Frank-Herrmann study, and Roetzer did not observe any method-related Phase III pregnancies with over 300,000 cycles.

Studies:

"The effectiveness of a fertility awareness based method to avoid pregnancy in relation to a couple's sexual behavior during the fertile time: a prospective longitudinal study," Frank-Herrmann et al, *Human Reproduction,* 2007;22(5):1310–1319.

Natural Conception Regulation, Roetzer, Freiburg: Herder, 2006.

Post-Hormonal Rule (non-injectable)

Effectiveness: 98.4 % method | 98.4 % user

Summary:
CCL's Post-Hormonal Rule is supported by Gnoth's longitudinal cohort study, where he compared a group of women immediately discontinuing oral contraceptives with a control group of women who had never taken oral contraceptives. Women in both groups were learning NFP for the first time. Although not the primary purpose of the study, it reported a 98.4% method and user effectiveness rate for the group of women discontinuing oral contraceptives.

Studies:
"Cycle characteristics after discontinuation of oral contraceptives," Gnoth et al, *Gynecological Endocrinology* 2002; 16:307–317.

Temperature-Only Rule

Effectiveness: 100 % method | 99.2 % user

Summary:
A very effective rule based upon Doering's original work. Phase III method effectiveness was 100% (no method failures) and Phase III user effectiveness was 99.2%.

Studies:
"About the Dependability of the Temperature Method to Avoid Conception," Doering, Translated from the original article in *Deutsche medizinische Wochenschrift* 92: 1055–1061, 9 Jun 1967.

Mucus-Only Rule

Effectiveness: 98.8 % method | 98.0 % user

Summary:
Although there are differences between CCL's instruction on mucus and that of the mucus-only methods, the CCL Mucus-Only Rule's use of "Peak + 4" is generally accepted as the beginning of Phase III by Creighton and other top mucus-only methods. Further, CCL teaches that this rule should only be used when temperatures are unavailable or unreliable. The League's primary focus for Phase III is a sympto-thermal approach and normally is based on the Sympto-Thermal Rule. Couples who desire to practice NFP based solely on mucus should learn from a mucus-only method.

Studies:
"Use Effectiveness of the Creighton Model Ovulation Method of Natural Family Planning," Fehring et al, Marquette Unversity, *College of Nursing Faculty Research and Publications*, 1994.

"Evaluation of the Effectiveness of a Natural Fertility Regulation Program in China," Qian et al, Paper presented at a Congress organized by the Center for Study and Research in the National Regulation of Fertility, Universita Cattolica del Sacro Cuore, Rome, Italy, 8 Sep 2000.

Post-Injectable Patch Rule (more-fertile mucus or bleeding)

Effectiveness: Unknown % method | Unknown % user

Summary:	Studies:
This rule was developed by CCL in consult with physicians on the CCL Board of Directors and Advisory Council to assist women who have discontinued injectable hormonal contraceptives (i.e. Depo-Provera). We know of no studies that have looked specifically at rules associated with discontinuing injectable hormones, thus the effectiveness of this rule is unknown until CCL can conduct its own effectiveness research.	N/A

Post-Injectable Patch Rule (less-fertile mucus)

Effectiveness: Unknown % method | Unknown % user

Summary:	Studies:
As with the Post-Injectable Patch Rule for more-fertile mucus or bleeding, this rule was developed by CCL to assist women who have discontinued injectables. Again, effectiveness is unknown.	N/A

Hormonal Contraceptives

Hormonal contraceptives are the most common form of contraceptives in women under 30 in our society, even though they have a great deal of health risks associated with them (stroke, heart attack, etc.). There are two primary categories of hormonal contraceptives: non-injectables and injectables.

Non-Injectables. For most women discontinuing non-injectable hormones, their signs of fertility and natural cycles return quickly— typically within a month or two, but in some cases longer. The following describes the most common forms of non-injectable hormones and when couples should begin charting their signs of fertility after discontinuation.

Pills. Primarily of two types: **combination** (combined estrogen and synthetic progestin) and **progestin-only** (mini-pill). For combination pills, begin charting after discontinuing the pills and when withdrawal bleeding begins. (*Withdrawal bleeding is bleeding from the vagina that occurs at the end of the pill regimen when withdrawing the hormones. It is NOT menstruation.*) For progestin-only mini-pills, begin charting immediately after the last pill is taken.

Vaginal rings. Thin, usually transparent, flexible polymer rings that contain both estrogens and progestins which are inserted into the vagina (NuvaRing is one example). Begin charting after the ring is removed and when withdrawal bleeding begins.

Topical patches. Commonly referred to as "The Patch," these are square adhesive patches worn on the body and embedded with both estrogen and progestin. Begin charting after the patch is removed and when withdrawal bleeding begins.

There are two forms of non-injectable hormones that require a physician for placement and removal — IUDs and implants.

Hormone-embedded intrauterine devices (IUDs). IUDs are plastic devices shaped like a "T" that contain only progestin. The most common types include Progestasert and Mirena. Begin charting immediately after the IUD is removed.

Implants. Implants are thin flexible plastic rods containing progestin that are surgically placed under the skin of the upper arm, such as Jadelle and Implanon. Begin charting immediately after the implant is removed.

Couples should abstain from relations during Phases I and II for the first cycle after discontinuation of non-injectable forms of hormonal contraceptives. To determine the end of Phase I, couples may use the Day 5/6 Rule (limited to Cycle Day 5) in cycles two through six, and from cycle seven onward, they may use any Phase I rule (Day 5/6 Rule, Doering Rule or Last Dry Day Rule).

The **Post-Hormonal Rule** (non-injectable) for determining the beginning of Phase III (see page 60) requires identification of Peak Day; therefore, it is important for women to make mucus observations and record them daily so that Peak Day can be determined. If a woman checks for mucus and consistently does not see or feel any, then she and her husband can use the Temperature-Only Rule to identify the beginning of Phase III (just as any couple would who does not observe mucus).

Injectables. An injectable hormone is a liquid contraceptive hormone that is injected into a woman's body with a needle (a shot). There are generally two types of injectable hormonal contraceptives — those that require monthly shots (Lunelle) and those that require a shot every three months (Depo-Provera). These hormones disrupt a woman's natural fertility signs for quite some time after discontinuation. Therefore, the post-hormonal rules for injectables are different because they deal with patches of mucus and bleeding during the transition to normal menstrual cycles. The timing of the returning fertility varies a great deal, especially when discontinuing Depo-Provera (i.e., from three months up to as long as 18 months after the last shot). Therefore, these rules are conservative. Even though the rules for discontinuing injectables are presented here, we recommend couples do not apply these rules without first consulting with a CCL Teacher or taking a CCL class.

For monthly shots, like Lunelle, couples should begin charting (mucus sensations and characteristics and the temperature) one month after the last shot was administered, and for longer term shots like Depo-Provera, couples should begin charting three months after the last shot was administered. In both cases, this is when the next shot would otherwise be "due." Couples should then abstain for the next four weeks while observing and charting mucus and temperature signs.

After discontinuing injectable hormones, patches of mucus will likely be experienced on and off for several months. For this reason, a patch rule for mucus can be used. Although a woman's temperature should be taken and recorded during this time, couples will be relying mainly on the mucus sign and applying these patch rules to determine the transition from Phase I infertility to Phase II fertility and back to Phase I infertility again. Thus, the mucus sign is the best way to determine the fertile and infertile phases, whereas, the temperature sign is necessary to determine the start of Phase III when cycles return. Note that it could take many months — six months or even longer — for cycles to return to normal.

During this transition back to cycles, if a woman does not observe any mucus, the couple is considered in Phase I. *They should use Phase I guidelines — evenings only and not on consecutive days — for marital relations.* In the presence of mucus patches, there are two Patch Rules: one for less-fertile mucus and one for more-fertile mucus or bleeding.

Post-Injectable Patch Rule (less-fertile mucus)

To apply the Post-Injectable Patch Rule during patches of *less-fertile* mucus (i.e., when *more-fertile* mucus or bleeding is NOT part of the patch), couples should abstain on any days of mucus. Mark the last day of less-fertile mucus with a Δ (delta) and count four days after. On the evening of the fourth day of no mucus after Δ, Phase I resumes. (Note: Δ is a symbol that means change)

Post-Injectable Patch Rule (more-fertile mucus or bleeding)

To apply the Post-Injectable Patch Rule during patches of *more-fertile mucus or bleeding/ spotting* followed by a change to *less-fertile* mucus, couples should still abstain on those days. However, *less-fertile* mucus days can be used as part of the "dry-up" count. Mark the last day of the more-fertile mucus or bleeding/spotting with a Δ and apply the same Δ + 4 rule if there is no thermal shift.

Phase I infertility begins when the woman returns to days with no mucus, but no earlier than Δ + 4. That means that *at a minimum* there must be no mucus on Δ + 4. (In other words, if on Δ + 4, less-fertile mucus is still present, continue the count. If on Δ + 5 no mucus is present, Phase I infertility starts on the evening of that day.)

Note that use of the term Δ is somewhat different than what you learned in the main CCL course for normal cycles. In normal cycles, Peak Day in conjunction with a thermal shift determines the beginning of the post-ovulatory infertile phase, or Phase III. With the Post-Injectable Patch Rules, we are still determining an infertile phase by using Δ. But now Δ does not refer to ovulation; rather, it is used to determine the return to *Phase I* infertility instead of the *beginning of Phase III* infertility. The following diagram should help you understand how Δ is used to determine whether or not a woman is in Phase I or Phase II.

Date	Apr-May 2005																						
Day of cycle	1	2	3	4	5	6	7	8	9	10	11	12	13	14	15	16	17	18	19	20	21	22	23
Menstruation			/	•																			
Phase of cycle	1	1	2	2	2	2	2	1	2	2	2	2	2	1	2	2	2	2	2	2	2	2	1

In and out of Phase I and Phase II

	1	2	3	4	5	6	7	8	9	10	11	12	13	14	15	16	17	18	19	20	21	22	23
		Δ	1	2	3	4		Δ	1	2	3	4			Δ	1	2	3	4	5			
	O	O	O	O	⊖	⊖	O	⊖	O	⊖	⊖	O	O	O	O	⊕	⊕	⊕	⊖	⊖	⊖	⊖	O
	d	d	d	d	d	d	d	d	d	d	d	d	d	d	w	w	w	d	d	d	d	d	
	n	n	n	t	t	n	t	n	t	t	n	n	n	n	s	t	t	t	t	t	t	n	

Note that on Cycle Day 4, Δ is marked at the beginning of a dry-up count because it was the last day of spotting, which is considered *more-fertile*. Applying the Post-Injectable Patch Rule (more-fertile mucus or bleeding), Phase I returns on the evening of Cycle Day 8. With this rule, days of less-fertile mucus can be used as part of the drying up count. However, the count must continue until a cycle day occurs where there are no mucus sensations or characteristics present at all.

Another Δ occurs on Cycle Day 10 because it is the last day of another mucus patch. In this case of a *less-fertile* mucus patch, when applying the Post-Injectable Patch Rule (less-fertile mucus), Phase I returns on the evening of Cycle Day 14.

Mucus is observed on Cycle Day 15 so Phase II begins again. This more-fertile mucus patch continues until a Δ occurs on Cycle Day 17. Using the Post-Injectable Patch Rule (more-fertile mucus), Phase I returns again on the evening of Cycle Day 22.

At some point a thermal shift should occur in conjunction with Peak Day indicating the beginning of the return to normal fertility. Once that happens, the following rules apply.

- From the first true menstruation onward, couples can use the Last Dry Day Rule for the end of Phase I, because by the time a woman discontinues injectable hormones and her cycles return, she will typically have months of experience observing her mucus sign.

- For Cycles 2–6, couples may use the Day 5/6 Rule (limited to Cycle Day 5) or the Last Dry Day Rule.

- After six cycles of experience, couples may add the Doering Rule. (This will allow for a sufficient history of thermal shifts to use the Doering Rule.)

- To determine the beginning of Phase III, apply the standard Sympto-Thermal Rule. It is not necessary to apply the same Post-Hormonal Rule that is used for non-injectables.

Last Dry Day Rule

See Reference Guide, *Rules Summary*, pages 245–246, and Student Guide, Class 2, Lesson 4, *The Transition from Phase I to Phase II*, page 82.

Medications and NFP

In general, most pharmacists understand how hormones work in the body, but they usually are not familiar with how mucus and temperature are used in conjunction with determining fertility or infertility. Nevertheless, the pharmacist remains an accessible source of information on medications. Some questions follow that you might ask your pharmacist to help you determine a particular medication's possible effect on fertility.

Does the medication cause a dry mouth?

Is the medication safe for use during pregnancy and/or breastfeeding?

Are any of the following listed as adverse effects of the medication?

- Amenorrhea (lack of menstrual periods)

- Dysmenorrhea (painful periods)

- Menstrual disturbances

- Oligomenorrhea (infrequent or light periods)

- Menorrhagia (abnormally heavy or prolonged periods)

Does this medication cause any of the following?

- Impotence

- Erectile dysfunction

- Gynecomastia (breast enlargement in men)

- Decreased libido

Does this medication affect the thyroid? If so, what is the effect?

How long will it take for the body to eliminate the medication?

Does this medication produce galactorrhea (presence of breast milk in non-nursing women)?

If the pharmacist is not able to provide the information you request, there are also resources on the internet. One online resource that contains drug information is **www.rxlist.com**. Many of the national pharmacy chains have online access to fact sheets and comparisons, and often provide up-to-date information on drugs, their uses and effects. One good reference for the effect of medications on pregnancy or nursing is the book *Medications & Mother's Milk* by Thomas W. Hale, Ph.D.

Look for adverse effects on *reproductive or urogenital* systems. Information about the effects on the menstrual cycle will sometimes mention amenorrhea, oligomenorrhea or menstrual disturbances as possible side effects. If searching for product information sheets on the internet, search for the brand name drug site and then look for its complete prescribing information.

While it is impossible to provide data on all medications that could possibly affect a woman's fertility signs, information on some common medications is captured within the tables that begin on page 230.

Although drug manufacturers do not focus specifically on a medication's potential effect on a woman's signs of fertility, we have made every effort to document possible side effects through the assistance of a licensed pharmacist who is also a CCL NFP Teacher. Nevertheless, you may or may not actually encounter any of these side effects.

Some of the side effects listed are *probable* and are inferred based on their documented effects on other body systems. (For example, if a medication produces a dry mouth, cervical mucus may also be affected.) It is also important to note on your chart when medications begin, end or change. This will help you to evaluate whether or not a particular medication might be affecting your fertility signs. When searching for the possible effects on fertility, be aware that depending on the drug, short-term treatments may not adversely affect fertility; reactions may occur only with chronic use. In other cases, after the body adjusts to the medication, fertility signs may be helpful despite being altered. It may even mean recalibrating your understanding of fertility signs and using close observation to determine changes. But in most cases, if careful mucus, temperature and cervix observations are made, couples can still successfully practice NFP.

The tables that follow primarily show how a woman's signs of fertility could *potentially* be affected. Some medications that affect men — to include the potential effect on male fertility — have been mentioned as well.

The following terms are used in the table:

Amenorrhea: lack of periods

Dysmenorrhea: painful periods

Galactorrhea: presence of breast milk in non-nursing women

Gynecomastia: breast enlargement in men

Menorrhagia: abnormally heavy or prolonged menstrual period

Menometrorrhagia: irregular or excessive bleeding

Metrorrhagia: vaginal bleeding not associated with a menstrual period

Oligomenorrhea: infrequent or light menstrual periods

Oligospermia: < 20 million sperm/ml ejaculate

Vulvovaginitis, Vaginitis: irritation & inflammation of the vulvo-vaginal area

Common generic names are lower case followed by (Brand name) in parentheses and in **bold type**.

Drug Classification	Generic/(Brand) Drugs	Effects
Acne Relief		
Retinoid (Vitamin A derivative)	isotretinoin (**Claravis, Amnesteem**)	Potentially dry cervical mucus, birth defects, abnormal menses
Antibiotics	doxycycline, ampicillin, tetracycline, minocycline (**Solodyn, Dynacin**)	No documented effect on fertility signs
Anti-Anxiety		
Benzodiazepines	diazepam (**Valium**) lorazepam (**Ativan**) clonazepam (**Klonopin**)	No documented effect
	alprazolam (**Xanax**)	Menstrual disorder (10%) Sexual dysfunction (7%)
Non-Benzodiazepines	buspirone (**Buspar**)	No documented effect
Antibiotics		
Major Antibiotic Classes	tetracycline, cephalosporins, penicillins, macrolides, quinolones, sulfonamides, antibacterials	No documented effect on fertility, but may disrupt vaginal flora and cause a vaginal infection
Anticonvulsant		
	topiramate (**Topamax**)	<3% occurrence: dysmenorrhea amenorrhea, menorrhagia, breast pain
	gabapentin (**Neurontin**) carbamazepine (**Carbatrol, Tegretol**)	Potentially dry mucus
	valproate (**Depakote**)	Avoid in pregnancy; affects neural tube development, 1–5% occurrence: dysmenorrhea, amenorrhea
	lamotrigine (**Lamictal**)	Potentially dry cervical mucus (2–7%), dysmenorrhea, vaginitis, amenorrhea
Antidepressants		
Selective Serotonin Reuptake Inhibitors (SSRI)	sertraline (**Zoloft**) fluoxetine (**Prozac**) paroxetine (**Paxil**) escitalopram (**Lexapro**) citalopram (**Celexa**)	1–7% occurrence: Prohibit/delay ovulation, amenorrhea, bleeding without ovulation, dysmenorrhea, breast pain, breast enlargement, may cause PMS symptoms, may dry or decrease flow of cervical mucus *Effects on Male*: Decreased libido (2–6%), ejaculatory disorders (3–13%), anorgasmia (2%), impotence (3%)

Drug Classification	Generic/(Brand) Drugs	Effects
Antidepressant (*continued*)		
Selective Serotonin Norepinephrine Reuptake Inhibitors (SSNRI)	venlafaxine (**Effexor**) atomoxetine (**Strattera**)	1–7% occurrence: Prohibit/delay ovulation, amenorrhea, bleeding without ovulation, dysmenorrhea, breast pain, breast enlargement, may cause PMS symptoms, may dry or decrease flow of cervical mucus *Effects on Male*: Decreased libido (2–6%), ejaculatory dysfunction (5%), impotence (3%)
Tricyclic Antidepressants (TCA)	amitriptyline, imipramine, nortriptyline	1–7% occurrence: Prohibit/delay ovulation, amenorrhea, bleeding without ovulation, dysmenorrhea, breast pain, breast enlargement, may cause PMS symptoms, may dry or decrease flow of cervical mucus *Effects on Male*: 1–10%: sexual dysfunction, impotence, decreased orgasm
	Doxepin (**Sinequan**)	Effects on female as above in (TCA) *Effects on Male*: Gynecomastia, libido changes (+/−)
Tricyclic Antidepressant (TCA)	clomipramine	Galactorrhea (50%) *Effects on Male*: Change in libido (+/−) (21%), ejaculatory failure (42%), impotence (20%)
Other	trazadone (**Desyrel**)	1–7% occurrence: Prohibit/delay ovulation, amenorrhea, bleeding without ovulation, dysmenorrhea, breast pain, breast enlargement, may cause PMS symptoms, potentially dry/decrease flow of mucus
Anti-Diarrhea Agents/ Antispasmodic Agents		
	loperamide (**Imodium AD**), diphenoxylate/atropine (**Lomotil**), dicyclomine (**Bentyl**)	Potentially dry/decrease mucus signs

Drug Classification	Generic/(Brand) Drugs	Effects
Anti-Estrogen Agents		
Treatment of Endometriosis	leuprolide (**Lupron, Depot**) gonadotropin releasing hormone (GnRH or LH-R), danocrine (**Danazol**)	Flushing (6%), vaginal dryness, irritation (4%), sweating (3%), lowering of estrogen; create a false state of menopause with no fertile signs detectible
Antifungal Agents		
	Ketoconazole (**Nizoral Shampoo, Neutrogena T_Gel**)	Potentially cause gynecomastia, impotence and oligospermia
Antihistamines		
Standard Antihistamines	diphenhydramine (**Benadryl**), chlorpheniramine (**Chlor-Trimeton**), promethazine (**Phenergan**), hydroxazine (**Atarax**), fexofenadine (**Allegra**), clemastine (**Tavist**)	Potentially dry/decrease mucus signs
Antiserotonin Antihistamines	cyproheptadine (**Periactin**)	Potentially dry cervical mucus, potentially causes amenorrhea or cycle disruption due to possible prolactin production
Anti-Inflammatory Agents		
Non-Steroidal (NSAIDS)	Ibuprofen (**Motrin IB, Advil, Pamprin IB, Nuprin**), naproxen (**Naprosyn, Aleve, Anaprox**), Indomethacin (**Indocin**), diclofenac (**Voltaren**), ketoprofen (**Orudis**), Etodolac (**Lodine**), Piroxicam (**Feldene**)	Potentially affects menstrual bleeding patterns due to effect on platelets
Non-Steroidal (NSAIDS) COX-2 Inhibitor	Celecoxib (**Celebrex**)	0.1–1.9% occurrence: breast pain, dysmenorrhea, vaginitis *Effects on Male:* prostatic disorders
Corticosteroids	prednisone, methylprednisolone, betamethasone, dexamethasone, triamcinolone, plus many variations	Dry mucus and false temperature rise; consider all symptoms disturbed until 4 days after discontinuing oral treatment
Anti-Nausea /Anti-Vertigo		
	Promethazine (**Phenergan**), Prochlorperazine (**Compazine**), Meclizine (**Antivert, Bonine**), Diphenhydramine (**Benadryl**), Scopolamine-Transdermal (**Transderm-Scop**)	Potentially dry cervical mucus

Drug Classification	Generic/(Brand) Drugs	Effects
Antipsychotics		
Typical Antipsychotics	haloperidol, thiothixene, chlorpromazine fluphenazine, perphenazine	Galactorrhea (50%)
D_2-$5HT_{2A}$ Antagonist	paliperidone (**Invega**), olanzapine (**Zyprexa**)	Potentially dry cervical mucus, delay/suppress ovulation (<0.1%), gynecomastia (1%)
	risperidone (**Risperidal**)	Galactorrhea (50%), dry vagina (1%)
Partial Dopamine Agonist Antipsychotics	aripiprazole (**Abilify**)	May dry cervical mucus, Rare occurrence: amenorrhea, menstrual irregularities, menorrhagia
5HT Agonist-Dopamine Antagonist Antipsychotics	ziprasidone (**Geodon**)	May dry cervical mucus, thyroid effect (rare), galactorrhea (rare)
$5HT_2$, $5HT_3$ Antagonist-Histamine Antagonist Antipsychotics	mirtazipine (**Remeron**)	May dry cervical mucus, decreased thyroid function (rare), <1% occurrence: amenorrhea, dysmenorrhea
Serotonin, Dopamine Histamine Antagonists Antipsychotics	quetiapine (**Seroquel**)	Potentially dry cervical mucus, galactorrhea (small possibility)
Basic Antipsychotic	lithium	Adversely affects thyroid, associated with birth defects
Anti-Viral Agents		
	acyclovir (**Zovirax**)	No documented effect on fertility
	valacyclovir (**Valtrex**), famciclovir (**Famvir**)	Dysmenorrhea: ≤ 1% in basic acute genital herpes treatment, 4–8% in chronic genital herpes suppression treatment
	amantadine (**Symmetrel**)	Potentially dry cervical mucus
Blood Pressure Regulation		
Beta Blockers	propranolol, bisoprolol	No documented effect on fertility signs
	atenolol	Potentially increase prolactin levels, potentially delay ovulation or cause amenorrhea
ACE Inhibitors	lisinopril, benazepril	Potentially dry mucus, Avoid in pregnancy, Impotence (1%)
Angiotensin Receptor Blockers (ARB)	valsartan (**Diovan**), losartan (**Cozaar**)	Potentially dry mucus, Avoid in pregnancy, Impotence (1%)

Drug Classification	Generic/(Brand) Drugs	Effects
Blood Pressure (*continued*)		
Renin Inhibitors (RI)	aliskiren (**Tecturna**, **Rasilez**)	Potentially dry mucus, avoid in pregnancy
Calcium Channel Blockers	amlodipine (**Norvasc**)	No documented effect on fertility
	verapamil	Potentially increase prolactin and delay ovulation, amenorrhea
Cancer Agents (Oral)		
	tamoxifen (**Nolvadex**), exemestane (**Aromasin**), anastrozole (**Arimidex**)	Frequent symptoms: hot flashes/flushes, altered menses, amenorrhea, oligomenorrhea, breast pain, altered mucus sign
Cholesterol Lowering Agents		
	gemfibrozil (**Lopid**), fenofibrate (**Tricor**), "Statins": atoravastin (**Lipitor**), pravastatin (**Pravachol**), rosuvastatin (**Crestor**)	No documented effect on fertility
Diuretics		
	bumetanide (**Bumex**), furosemide (**Lasix**), hydrochlorothiazide (**HCTZ**)	Potentially dry mucus
	spironolactone (**Aldactone**), spironolactone/HCTZ (**Dyazide**)	Spironolactone interferes with progesterone production, increasing estrogen levels, potential to cause amenorrhea *Effect on Males*: Gynecomastia, inability to achieve/maintain erection
Expectorants		
	guaifenesin (**Robitussin**, **Mucinex**, **Humabid**)	Thins mucus, may help facilitate sperm migration
Gastrointestinal Agents		
H$_2$ Antagonists	cimetidine (**Tagamet**), famotidine (**Pepcid**)	Galactorrhea & delayed ovulation due to possible prolactin production, gynecomastia
	ranitidine (**Zantac**)	No documented effects on fertility
Proton Pump Inhibitors	omeprazole (**Prilosec**), lansoprazole (**Prevacid**), esomeprazole (**Nexium**), pantoprazole (**Protonix**), rapeprazole (**Aciphex**)	No effect on fertility signs *Effect on Males*: impotence (<1%)

Drug Classification	Generic/(Brand) Drugs	Effects
Gastrointestinal Agents *(continued)*		
Upper GI Stimulants	metoclopramide (**Reglan**)	Potential galactorrhea 50% due to prolactin, amenorrhea due to prolactin, gynecomastia, impotence
Insomnia Agents		
Benzodiazepines	temazepam (**Restoril**)	
Non-benzodiazepines	zolpidem (**Ambien**), zalepion (**Sonata**), eszopiclone (**Lunesta**)	Potentially dry cervical mucus, dysmenorrhea (3%), amenorrhea, breast pain < 0.1%
Migraine Agents		
	almotriptan (**Axert**), sumatriptan (**Imitrex**), rizatriptan (**Amerge**), eletriptan (**Relpax**), zolmatriptan (**Zomig**)	Potentially dry cervical mucus
Ovulation Stimulants (Oral)		
	clomiphene (**Clomid, Serophene**)	Anti-estrogen effect, potentially dry mucus, hot flushes
Pain Control Agents		
	tramadol, hydrocodone, oxycodone, codeine, fentanyl patch, morphine	Potentially dry mucus
Progesterone		
	progesterone (**Prometrium**)	Breast pain, artificially elevated temperature pattern, drying of mucus, may also affect cervix sign
Low Thyroid Treatment		
	Levothyroxine, L-thyroxine (**Synthroid, Levoxyl, Levothroid**) Thyroid USP (**Armour**)	Improve fertility symptoms in cases of low thyroid function
Wakefulness Agents		
	modafinil (**Provigil**) dextroamphetaimne, methyphenidatemixed amphetamine salts (**Adderall**)	No documented effect on fertility signs

Method Effectiveness

See Reference Guide, *Effectiveness*, pages 213–222, and Student Guide, Class 2, Lesson 5, *Effectiveness of NFP*, page 90.

Miscarriage

Experiencing a miscarriage can be very difficult for a family. A miscarriage occurs when a developing young baby dies in utero (in the uterus). Some physicians estimate that approximately 10% to 20% of all clinically recognized pregnancies end in miscarriage.[7]

Before resuming marital relations after a miscarriage, you should consult with your physician. Usually women are instructed to abstain from sexual intercourse and using tampons until their normal menses returns. This usually occurs four to six weeks after the completion of the miscarriage. To know that fertility is returning a woman should observe and chart her fertility signs by taking her basal body temperature each day and by making mucus observations, both sensations and characteristics. In some cases, the temperature will remain high for some time during and immediately following a miscarriage (as it was during the pregnancy), but it should then drop down to the usual pre-ovulation levels. You normally should wait two or three cycles before attempting pregnancy again, but consult with your physician. If you have two or more consecutive miscarriages, seek competent medical expertise in the evaluation of your hormones, physiology and anatomy. You may need progesterone support to help maintain subsequent pregnancies.[8]

Mucus

Mucus Sensations

A description of mucus would be incomplete without emphasizing the importance of sensation in the overall context of the presence or absence of mucus for the day's observations. In this section we are showing actual photos of mucus; however, the **sensations** that mucus produces are **equally** important, especially if a woman doesn't actually see any mucus characteristics. Therefore, don't forget to become aware of sensations at the vaginal opening throughout the day while going about your daily activities and also when wiping at your bathroom visits.

---

[7] American College of Obstetricians and Gynecologists, *Causes of Recurrent Pregnancy Loss*, 2001.
[8] *http://www.naprotechnology.com/progesterone.htm*

The main sensations of mucus are listed here as reminders that these occur along with the visual aspects of mucus characteristics shown in the photos that follow.

DRY — A sensation or feeling of dryness while going about daily activities; may produce a rough feeling or friction when wiping.

MOIST—a feeling of moistness, dampness, or stickiness while going about daily activities. Women who feel sticky notice that the labia stick together. A LESS-FERTILE sensation.

WET — A sensation of wetness at the vaginal opening or at the vulva while going about daily activities. A MORE-FERTILE sensation. When close to and/or on Peak Day, it is often a watery, runny sensation, signaling that ovulation is imminent.

SLIPPERY — A sensation of slipperiness when wiping; the toilet paper glides or slides across the vaginal opening. A MORE-FERTILE sensation. When close to and/or on Peak Day, the slippery sensation becomes intense signaling that ovulation is imminent.

Mucus Characteristics

There are many different characteristics of mucus; only a few are represented here during one cycle from one woman.

NOTHING — No mucus is observed.

TACKY — Mucus is sticky, thick, pasty, creamy, clumpy, and/or breaks when stretched repeatedly.

STRETCHY — Mucus is elastic, thin, stringy, similar to raw egg-white, and/or stretches repeatedly when pulled apart.

No mucus

NO MUCUS [1] — After wiping, nothing is seen on the paper.

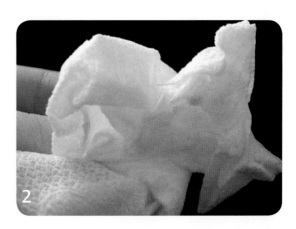

[2] — Note that crumpled toilet paper inhibits seeing mucus; fold toilet paper before wiping. Also **mucus sits on the toilet paper; urine soaks in the paper.**

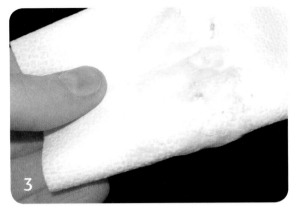

Less-fertile mucus

LESS-FERTILE [3] — This mucus is tinged with pink, appearing right at the end of the menses on Cycle Day 6. When lifted off the toilet paper, it did not hold a stretch, but fell back to the paper. This type of mucus is tacky.

LESS-FERTILE [4] — This mucus has very little stretch.

LESS-FERTILE [5] — Note the thicker consistency and opaque color.

LESS-FERTILE [6] — Note that this mucus is still thick and opaque (compare to more-fertile mucus pictures 10 and 11), and it is losing its stretch after being pulled apart. This picture was taken just as the mucus was breaking away from the woman's thumb. Tacky mucus may stretch some but tends to break apart, and it does not have the same elastic qualities as more-fertile mucus.

LESS-FERTILE [7] — Note that this opaque mucus has increased in thickness.

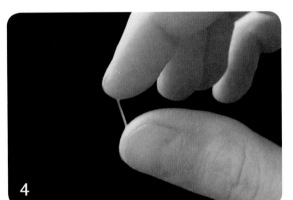

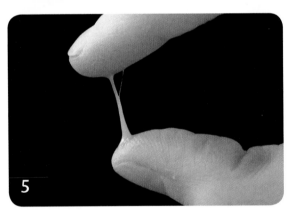

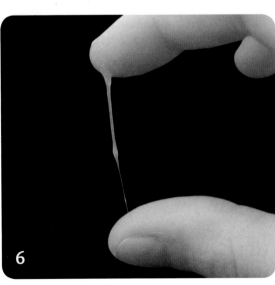

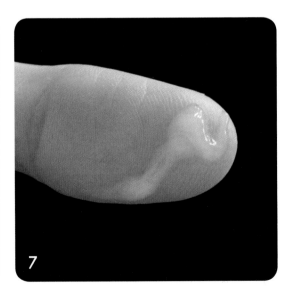

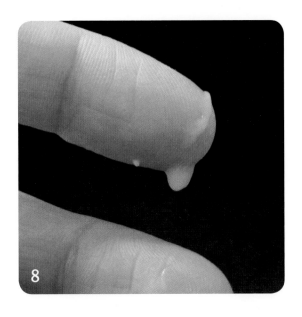

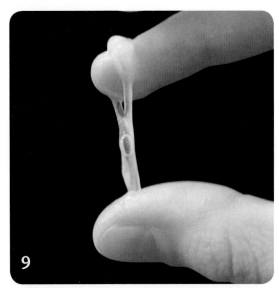

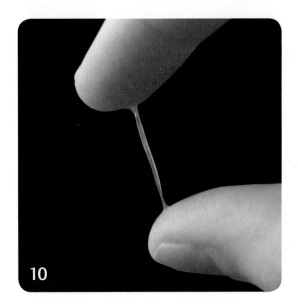

LESS-FERTILE [8] — This mucus is tacky and sticky.

More-fertile mucus

MORE-FERTILE [9] — Clear mucus, like raw egg-white.

MORE-FERTILE [10] — Clear, stretchy mucus. Note that the mucus thins as it becomes more-fertile. Mucus like this is elastic and can be stretched repeatedly without breaking.

MORE-FERTILE [11] — Stretchy mucus with clear areas.

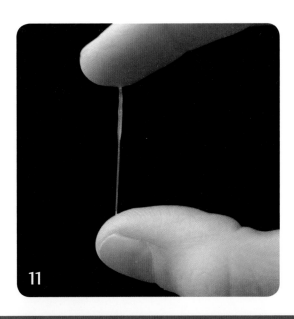

Less-fertile mucus (after Peak Day)

LESS-FERTILE [12] — This picture was taken soon after Peak Day and coincided with the temperature shift. This particular mucus has some stretch, but has a thick consistency and opaque color. It also does not stretch repeatedly and is losing elasticity. Like picture 6, this one was taken just as the mucus was breaking apart.

LESS-FERTILE [13] — Another example of less-fertile mucus after Peak Day.

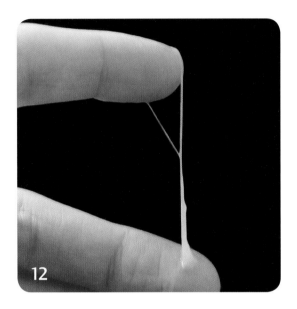 

Scant mucus

Scanty or poor quality mucus was briefly addressed in Class 3. Scant mucus is characterized by the lack of definition in both quantity and quality. However, young, healthy women should normally have a good mucus sign. In many cases, scant mucus can be improved with dietary changes and/or supplements; refer to *Fertility, Cycles & Nutrition* by Marilyn Shannon for nutritional suggestions.

NFP-Supportive Physicians

There are some physicians who do not prescribe or recommend contraception, sterilization or abortion. Some will also not refer to another physician for these services. Instead, these NFP-supportive physicians use treatments that address a woman's underlying condition rather than trying to mask or further complicate them by prescribing hormones as a method of family planning. Such physicians are hard to find.

If you are interested in finding an NFP-supportive physician in your area, visit One More Soul's website at **www.omsoul.com**. One More Soul maintains a database of NFP-supportive physicians, which they term *NFP-Only*, and is one of the best single sources for this information.

In addition to the above, there are many physicians who are supportive of NFP, but who also prescribe hormones as a method of family planning. Sometimes, such physicians can read an NFP chart and provide sound counsel to women. If you cannot find an NFP-Only physician in your area, seek one who fits this description. There are many instances in which these physicians eventually discontinued prescribing or recommending contraception, sterilization or abortion after seeing many patients who understand their fertility signs and apply NFP. Prayer and subtle encouragement are common actions that can lead to conversion.

If you would like your physician or a physician in your area to learn more about NFP, suggest they take a CCL NFP course.

Patch Rule, Mucus (for Post-Injectables)

See Reference Guide, *Hormonal Contraceptives*, pages 223–227, and *Rules Summary*, pages 245–246.

Phase I Guidelines and Rules

See Reference Guide, *Rules Summary*, pages 245–246, and Student Guide, Class 2, Lesson 4, *The Transition from Phase I to Phase II*, page 77.

Postpartum, Fertility Return

As you learned in Class 3, the return of fertility after giving birth varies greatly depending on how you decide to feed your baby (i.e. formula feeding, mixed breastfeeding, exclusive breastfeeding, continued breastfeeding). While CCL promotes exclusive and continued breastfeeding, a separate supplemental class is available to provide you a deeper understanding of the return of fertility after childbirth no matter how you choose to feed your baby. Visit *www.ccli.org* to register for a Postpartum Class and/or order a *Transitions Student Guide.*

Pregnancy, Practical helps for Achieving

The following practical suggestions to help in achieving a pregnancy are based on CCL's 40+ years of experience in the NFP field and are meant to supplement the information provided in the Student Guide, Class 2, Lesson 6, *Using NFP to Achieve a Pregnancy*, page 94. *These suggestions should not be construed as medical advice. Consult with your physician about any self-help measure you would like to try to help achieve pregnancy.*

Good Health Considerations

1. **Well-balanced meals.** Well-balanced meals can go a long way in maintaining a healthy reproductive system. As much as possible, minimize eating foods with additives. Iodine from iodized salt or other reliable sources, such as kelp tablets, is helpful. Iodine is essential for proper functioning of the thyroid gland, and thyroid function affects fertility.

2. **Weight.** Ten or 15 pounds of excess weight usually does not impair fertility, but too much body fat can upset the balance of estrogen and progesterone in some women.

3. **Exercise.** Exercise can be a part of living a healthy lifestyle. However, over-exercising can negatively affect a woman's fertility. A woman needs a certain percentage of body fat to maintain normal fertility. Excessive exercise can cause infertile cycles even in the presence of continued menstruations, or it can cause **runner's amenorrhea** — the absence of both ovulation and menstrual periods.

4. **Smoking.** Women who smoke are estimated to have only 72% of the fertility of non-smokers and are 3½ times more likely to take an entire year to conceive.

5. *Fertility, Cycles & Nutrition* by Marilyn Shannon. This is an excellent book for relating nutrition to fertility and infertility. It has chapters on cycle irregularities and female infertility, pregnancy-related problems, repeated miscarriages and birth defects, and male infertility. It also has suggestions for proper diets and balanced multi-vitamin/mineral supplements, as well as several references for other resources.

Tips for Husbands

1. **Balanced diet and multivitamin/mineral supplements.** *Fertility, Cycles & Nutrition* points out how **Vitamin C, zinc, B vitamins** and other nutrients can help with proper male fertility. Note that it may take three to six months of better nutrition before male fertility improves.

2. **Clothing.** Some men find it helpful to wear boxer shorts instead of jockey shorts. The testicles are external reproductive organs. Jockey style underwear forces the testicles closer to the body, making them subject to higher temperatures; whereas, boxer shorts can help maintain a slightly cooler temperature which is conducive to better male fertility. A very hot working environment can also damage male fertility.

3. **Smoking and alcohol.** For men, nicotine may impair sexual function, and alcohol in great excess can cause infertility which may be irreversible.

4. **Hot tubs.** Frequent hot tub use has been shown to lower sperm count.

General Tips

1. **Timing.** As mentioned in Class 2, the days of highest probability to achieve a pregnancy are Peak Day and the two days preceding Peak Day. Although Peak Day is determined in hindsight, consider marital relations on days when the mucus produces very slippery sensations, very wet (runny, watery) feelings, and/or has very stretchy characteristics. The temperature sign can also be used to help with timing. The first day of temperature rise is closely associated with ovulation, and on days of more-fertile mucus, the temperature sometimes "dips" right before ovulation. Fertility monitors can also help pinpoint the day of ovulation.

2. **Maximize sperm count.** Abstaining for a few days before Phase II could increase the probability of achieving a pregnancy.

Premenopause, Fertility Awareness

Premenopause is the natural life progression that occurs as a woman's fertile years come to a close. A reduction in the number of eggs available to ovulate and the hormonal changes associated with this reduction can cause cycle irregularities, changes in menstrual bleeding, and changes to the signs of fertility. CCL offers a separate supplemental class to help you practice NFP as you transition through premenopause. Visit *www.ccli.org* to register for a Premenopause Class and/or order a *Transitions Student Guide*.

Questions to Ask Your Pharmacist

See Reference Guide, *Medications and NFP*, page 241.

Reproductive Technologies

Class 2 provided hints to help couples achieve a pregnancy. There are acceptable technologies that can assist couples without violating the dignity of the spouses or the baby.

Unfortunately, there are also many technologies today that do not respect the dignity of the human person. How does a couple know what is acceptable and what is not? As a general rule of thumb, any procedure that *assists a couple in achieving the full procreative potential of marital relations* is **acceptable**. Any procedure that *adds an additional "participant" into the act of conception*, or which *substitutes a laboratory procedure for the marital embrace*, is **not acceptable**.[9]

It is morally acceptable to apply the knowledge gained through NFP (fertility awareness), fertility monitors and basic medical evaluations to time sexual relations during the days of highest fertility (nearest ovulation). Post-coital tests that examine the interaction between sperm and mucus at the cervix after marital relations, uterine and tubal assessments conducted with ultrasound or x-ray technologies, or injections that stimulate a woman's ovaries are all considered moral. There are helpful surgical procedures and medical approaches like NaproTECHNOLOGY that do not interfere or replace marital relations that are acceptable as well, and have success rates equal to or greater than immoral technologies like in vitro fertilization. A semen analysis can be accomplished if the sperm is collected by obtaining a seminal fluid sample from a non-lubricated, "perforated" condom used during normal marital relations. A small hole should be made at the tip of the sheath so that a substantial amount of the ejaculate is allowed to be projected into the wife during marital relations.

Drugs that help men engage in marital relations are also acceptable if they do not go against the nature or the dignity of the husband. So there are many acceptable options to help couples who struggle with infertility.

Some of the methods that are considered immoral and violate the dignity of the spouses or the baby include masturbation, artificial insemination and surrogate motherhood in which a woman's uterus is used in order to reproduce a baby for someone else.

Other technologies like in vitro fertilization and zygote-intra-fallopian transfer (ZIFT) are also immoral. Conception occurs outside the wife's body and several fertilized embryos (human persons) are selected for implantation into the woman's uterus, but the other ones are destroyed.

To learn more about the morality of various reproductive technologies, visit the website of the U.S. Conference of Catholic Bishops (USCCB): ***www.usccb.org.*** CCL also carries an easy-to-read booklet titled *The Human Body…a sign of dignity and a gift* by Rev. Richard M. Hogan, which provides a framework for evaluating why certain behaviors violate dignity and others are genuine gifts of love.

---

[9] USCCB Fact Sheet, "Reproductive Technology (Evaluation & Treatment of Infertility Guidelines for Catholic Couples)," *http://www.usccb.org/prolife/issues/nfp/treatment.htm*

Rules Summary

Following is a summary of the rules taught throughout the course. For details on each of the rules, see the applicable lesson.

Phase I Rules & Guidelines

Phase I Guidelines

• Once menstruation decreases, marital relations occur only in the evenings during Phase I.

• Once menstruation lessens, abstain on any day that follows marital relations in Phase I unless you are experienced and can positively detect the absence of mucus.

Day 5/6 Rule

Assume infertility on Cycle Days 1–5.

For women with cycles 26 days or longer in the last 12 cycles, assume infertility on Cycle Days 1–6.

Conditions for use

This rule assumes the absence of mucus.

Doering Rule

Subtract seven from the earliest first day of temperature rise in the last 12 cycles. Mark that cycle day as the last day that you can assume Phase I infertility.

Conditions for use

This rule assumes the absence of mucus.

This rule requires six cycles of temperature history.

Last Dry Day Rule

The end of Phase I is the last day without mucus sensations or characteristics.

Conditions for use

This rule requires six cycles of experience.

Women should have at least six days of mucus from its onset through Peak Day.

Phase III Rules

Sympto-Thermal (ST) Rule

Phase III begins on the evening of:

1. The third day of drying-up after Peak Day, combined with

2. Three normal post-peak temperatures above the LTL, and

3. The third temperature at or above the HTL or the cervix closed and hard for three days.

If the above conditions are not met, then Phase III begins after waiting an additional post-peak day for another temperature above the LTL

Mucus-Only Rule

Phase III begins on the evening of the fourth day of drying up or thickening of the mucus after Peak Day.

Temperature-Only Rule

Phase III begins on the evening of the fourth day of normal temperatures above the LTL. The last three temperatures must be on consecutive days, and at or above the HTL.

Post-Hormonal Rules

Post-Hormonal Rule (for non-injectables)

For the first cycle after stopping the hormones, Phase III begins on the evening of:

1. The fourth day of drying-up after Peak Day, combined with

2. Four normal post-peak temperatures above the LTL

Post-Injectable Patch Rule (less-fertile mucus)

Phase I returns on the evening of the fourth consecutive day of no mucus after a less-fertile mucus patch.

Post-Injectable Patch Rule (more-fertile mucus or bleeding)

Phase I returns on the evening of the fourth day of drying-up after Peak Day, where Peak Day is the last day of more-fertile mucus or bleeding. The drying-up days can be less-fertile mucus; however, there cannot be any mucus on the fourth day.

Shift work

When should a woman's temperature be taken if she works evenings or night shifts? A general rule is: *Take the temperature when awakening from the longest best rest.*

Will working different shifts affect a temperature pattern? There is no universally valid answer to this question — it may, but it may not. Whether a temperature pattern is affected may depend on how often a woman changes from one sleeping time to another (e.g., CCL has seen charts from a substitute nurse who changed shifts almost every day and took her temperature whenever she awoke from her best sleep time each day. Her temperature pattern was still easy to interpret). If you suspect your temperature pattern may be affected by your schedule, try to be *even more consistent and precise with your mucus observations.*

To determine if your sleep schedule is having an effect on your temperature pattern, pay particular attention to what happens to the pattern when your schedule changes during *Phase III.* Remember, any difference you see during Phase III is not caused by a change in hormones.

Experimenting with the best time for taking the temperature may help as well. For one or two cycles, take your temperature at two or three different times each day and record each reading in a different color. Suggested times to try are when you wake up from the best sleep of the day; before you go to bed; at some other fixed time when you are not too active and have not just finished eating or drinking. At the end of the complete cycle, compare the different patterns with your mucus and/or cervix patterns to see which one gives you the most accurate picture.

Software, Charting

See Reference Guide, CycleProGo™, page 212.

Sympto-Thermal Rule

See Reference Guide, *Rules Summary*, page 245–246, and Student Guide, Class 1, Lesson 5, *Interpreting the Signs of Fertility*, page 46.

Time Zones

Traveling across time zones during Phase I or Phase III will usually not affect your chart interpretation because temperatures during those phases are normally not needed. However, if you are in Phase II during these times, it could possibly affect your temperature pattern and the ability to interpret the beginning of Phase III.

As with shift work, this is a time to *be as precise as possible with mucus observations.*

You should take your temperature whenever you awake from restful sleep, and keep that time as your "normal" temperature-taking time for the remainder of the trip if possible. The main point is to take your "resting" temperature, before getting up for the day, similar to the advice for those working different shifts.

Indicate the change in time zone(s) in the User Notes section of your chart for those days and see whether those temperatures are in conformity with the level of the temperatures prior to the trip. Again, emphasis can always be placed on the mucus sign, and/or if in doubt, add an extra day to the ST Rule for determining the beginning of Phase III, or use the Mucus-Only Rule.

Unintended Pregnancy Rate

See Reference Guide, *Effectiveness*, p. 227–236.

User Effectiveness

See Reference Guide, *Effectiveness*, pages 213–222, and Student Guide, Class 2, Lesson 5, *Effectiveness of NFP*, page 90.

Vaginal Discharges

There are other types of vaginal discharges besides cervical mucus. For example, **arousal fluid** can be detected when a woman is sexually stimulated. It is similar to cervical mucus because it can produce a slippery sensation and/or it can appear stretchy. However, when rolled between the fingers it appears to be absorbed into the skin, or when placed in water it dissipates (See Reference Guide, Mucus, *Water Test*, page 240). It does not remain long unless stimulation is continuous.

Seminal residue may appear after marital relations, but usually disappears within hours or the next day. It can also look similar to stretchy mucus and/or produce a slippery sensation, but like arousal fluid, when rolled between the fingers, it too will dissipate and appear to be absorbed. Nevertheless, it can cause confusion with observing mucus. Seminal residue should be recorded on the chart as "sr."

Candida (yeast) is an organism that is normally present in the vagina. However, changes in the vaginal environment due to improper nutrition, frequent antibiotic use, douching, poorly-controlled diabetes, or the general lowering of a woman's immune system can cause the Candida to proliferate. The resulting discharge will be thick and white, like cottage cheese, and it may produce itching at the vulva and/or redness in the vaginal area. Over-the-counter treatments are available in stores and/or through a physician.

Other vaginal discharges may be the result of infections and/or sexually transmitted diseases and should be treated by a physician. If you experience any of the following symptoms, you should contact your doctor.

- Itching, burning sensation, profuse discharge that is sometimes foul-smelling or containing pus
- Warts, ulcerations, reddish patches, or sores in the vaginal area
- Grayish-green and pasty discharge
- Inflamed genital areas
- Painful intercourse and/or painful urination
- Frequent wet sensation without any slippery feeling even during what should be Phase I infertility and/or Phase III infertility.[10]

Other considerations. Most women can learn to interpret their mucus signs without difficulty. Nevertheless, some women experience continuous discharges that are not due to an infection or related to fertility. Usually a woman should still seek the advice of a physician; however, changes in clothing and/or personal hygiene may help in some cases.

If a continuous, unexplained discharge is causing difficulty in interpreting mucus, some women have found that wearing cotton instead of synthetic underwear, and/or loose-fitting instead of tight-fitting clothing, can help. Women often use a sanitary pad when they have an annoying discharge; however, this can sometimes lead to more discharges. Sanitary pads close off the entrance to the vagina, which can block in heat and create an environment conducive to bacterial growth. Women should consider limiting the use of pads or panty liners to days when truly necessary if they are having trouble interpreting their mucus signs. Some perfumed products, such as soaps, lotions, sprays, disinfectants, and fabric softeners can possibly irritate the vaginal opening and/or potentially cause an abnormal discharge. Women who experience an abnormal discharge may find it helpful

---

[10] Hilgers, Tom, M.D. *Medical and Surgical Practice of NaProTECHNOLOGY*, 300

to use products free of added fragrances and perfumes. Lastly, incorrect wiping after a bowel movement can potentially cause an abnormal discharge. Women can prevent intestinal bacteria from entering the vagina by wiping from front to back, not back to front. Wiping after urination should also be done from front to back.

Water Test

Sometimes other fluids not related to fertility, like seminal residue or arousal fluid, may appear similar to cervical mucus. If you are concerned as to whether or not you are observing true cervical mucus, there is a test that may help. With some of the suspected mucus on your finger, run water over your finger and deposit the sample into a clear glass of water. Note what happens. *True cervical mucus retains its structure in water,* so if the sample forms into strands or webs, then it can be presumed to be real mucus. Other vaginal discharges and seminal residue will usually dissipate and cloud the water. *If the sample dissolves, it is not cervical mucus.*

Glossary C

Abnormal temperature: A basal body temperature among the pre-shift six, or within the thermal shift, that is clearly out of the range of the surrounding temperatures.

Abortion: The deliberate termination of a newly conceived life. Not to be confused with *spontaneous abortion* (miscarriage).

Abortifacient: A drug or device used to cause an abortion.

Abstinence: The practice of refraining from indulging an appetite or desire, e.g., marital relations.

Amenorrhea: Lack of menstrual periods.

Anovulatory cycle: A cycle without ovulation.

Basal body temperature: The temperature of the human body at rest or upon awakening, unaffected by food, drink or activity.

Blastocyst: The beginning stage of new life immediately after conception, when the cells begin to divide and grow.

Breakthrough bleeding: A bleeding episode that is not part of menstruation. It can appear as spotting or days of bleeding in the middle of a cycle, and it can also occur as a regular period following an *anovulatory* cycle. Breakthrough bleeding can mask the presence of mucus, and it can be a potentially fertile time.

Breastfeeding, continued: Nursing beyond six months when the introduction of other foods and liquids are added to complement the breast milk.

Breastfeeding, exclusive: The standard of care for babies during their first six months of life, characterized by nursing whenever the baby indicates a desire (day or night), with each feeding fully emptying the breast of milk.

Breastfeeding, mixed: *High mixed:* 80% of the feeding comes from the breast; *medium mixed:* 20–79% of the feeding comes from the breast; *low mixed:* less than 20% of the feeding comes from the breast.

Calendar Rhythm: The 1930s forerunner of modern NFP based on an assumption that ovulation occurred around Cycle Day 14. It took into account a woman's past cycle history, but did not take into account any activity occurring during the current cycle.

Cervical mucus: A natural fluid of the body that is necessary for the proper functioning of a woman's reproductive system and is an aid to fertility.

Cervical os: The opening of the cervix.

Cervix: The lower, narrow part of the uterus that

extends slightly into the vagina; the opening to the uterus.

Clitoris: A part of the female genitalia consisting of a small elongated highly sensitive erectile organ at the front of the vulva.

Coitus: A Latin term for *sexual intercourse*.

Conception: The union of one male sperm and one female ovum; the beginning of a new human life. Also called *fertilization*.

Condom: A sheath made of thin rubber or latex, to cover the penis as a contraceptive during sexual intercourse.

Contraception: The use of mechanical, chemical or medical procedures to prevent *conception* resulting from sexual intercourse. Not to be confused with *responsible parenthood*.

Corpus luteum: A yellow, progesterone-secreting structure that forms from an ovarian follicle after the release of a mature egg. If the egg is not fertilized, the corpus luteum secretes progesterone for approximately 14 days after ovulation.

Day 5/6 Rule: A rule to determine the infertile time at the beginning of a woman's menstrual cycle. In the absence of mucus infertility is assumed on Cycle Days 1–5. For women, with cycles 26 days of longer in the last 12 cycles, infertility is assumed on Cycle Days 1–6.

Diaphragm: A contraceptive device consisting of a flexible disk that covers the cervix.

Doering Rule: A formula to determine the infertile time at the beginning of a cycle based on the earliest day of temperature rise in previous cycles. In the absence of mucus, the last day of Phase I infertility is seven days before the earliest first day of temperature rise.

Ejaculation: The spasmodic expulsion of semen from the penis.

Embryo: The stage of human life from implantation through the eighth week of development.

Encyclical: A letter address by the Pope to all the bishops of the Church to explain the Church's teaching on an important matter.

Endometrium: The inner lining of the uterus.

Epididymis: The comma-shaped male sexual organ attached to the top and to the back of the testicles that assists in the storage and maturation of the sperm.

Estrogen: A fertility hormone that causes the cervix to undergo physical changes and to secrete mucus, and which causes the development of the endometrium.

Estimated Date of Childbirth: See Naegele Rule and Prem Rule.

Fallopian tubes: The pair of tubes that transport female eggs from either ovary to the uterus.

Fertile time: The time of a woman's menstrual cycle leading up to and including the time of ovulation, characterized, in part, by the presence of mucus. Sexual intercourse during this time (Phase II) could result in conception.

Fertility: The quality or condition of being able to produce offspring.

Fertility awareness: Use of physical signs and symptoms that change with hormonal fluctuations throughout a woman's menstrual cycle to predict a woman's fertility.

Fertility monitor: A device that measures hormone levels, such as estrogen or luteinizing hormone (LH), to detect the fertile time of a woman's cycle.

Fertilization: The union of one male sperm and one female ovum; the beginning of a new human life. Also called *conception*.

Fetus: The stage of life development beginning at eight weeks after implantation and continuing until birth.

Five characteristics of divine and marital love: A (1) *freely-chosen*, (2) *permanent*, (3) *self-gift* that is (4) *based on knowledge* and (5) *open to life*.

Follicle: One of thousands of small ovarian sacs containing an immature ovum; each cycle, one follicle fully matures and is released at ovulation. Upon release of its egg, the follicle becomes a structure called the *corpus luteum*.

Follicle Stimulating Hormone (FSH): A fertility hormone secreted by the pituitary gland to stimulate the maturation of ovarian follicles.

Formula feeding: A baby is fed with a bottle and receives only formula (no breast milk).

High Temperature Level (HTL): The temperature level that is 0.4° degrees Fahrenheit (0.2° degrees Celsius) above the Low Temperature Level (LTL). Used when establishing the beginning of Phase III with the Sympto-Thermal Rule.

Hormonal contraception: Any drug, device, or implant that utilizes synthetic hormones to alter fertility in an effort to disrupt the natural process of conception.

Hormone: A chemical substance produced by a gland or organ of the body and carried by circulation to other areas where it produces an effect.

Human Chorionic Gonadotropin (hCG) hormone: A hormone produced by the placenta that maintains the corpus luteum and stimulates it to continue producing progesterone for the first 10–12 weeks of pregnancy.

Humanae Vitae (*On Human Life*): Pope Paul VI's 1968 encyclical letter explaining the duty of the transmission of life for married couples.

Implantation: The process of an embryo attaching to the lining of the uterus.

Infertile time: The time of a woman's menstrual cycle both before the ovulation process begins as well as after ovulation, characterized, in part, by the absence of mucus. Sexual intercourse during these times (Phases I and III) does not result in conception.

Infertility: The quality or condition of being unable to produce offspring.

Injectable hormonal contraceptives: A liquid artificial hormone that is injected into a woman's body with a needle (a shot). Examples include Depo-Provera and Lunelle.

Intrauterine device (IUD): A metal or plastic loop, ring, or spiral inserted into the uterus to prevent conception; acts as an abortifacient by preventing the implantation of a newly conceived life.

In vitro fertilization: A specialized technique by which an ovum is fertilized by sperm outside the body, with the resulting embryo later implanted in the uterus.

Labia: The inner and outer lips of the vulva; the outermost parts of the female genital sex organs.

Last Dry Day Rule: A formula to determine the infertile time at the beginning of a cycle based on the appearance of mucus. The end of Phase I is the last day without mucus sensations or characteristics.

Less-fertile mucus: Less-fertile mucus is usually present both before and after a woman experiences more-fertile mucus leading up to ovulation. Sensations are often described as moist, damp or sticky, and characteristics are often described as tacky, sticky, opaque, or thicker than the more-fertile mucus.

Libido: Feelings of sexual desire.

Low Temperature Level (LTL): The highest of the normal pre-shift six temperatures. The LTL is the level from which the High Temperature Level (HTL) is determined.

Luteal phase: A stage of the menstrual cycle, lasting about two weeks, measured by counting the days from the first day of temperature rise to the last day of the cycle.

Luteinizing hormone (LH): A fertility hormone produced by the pituitary gland that helps to stimulate ovulation in females.

Menarche: The first menstrual period; the establishment of menstration.

Menopause: The period marked by the natural and permanent cessation of menstruation; officially reached after 12 months of no menstrual periods.

Menstruation: The periodic discharge of blood and tissue from the uterus in non-pregnant women from menarche to menopause (following a sustained thermal shift).

Method effectiveness: The effectiveness of a method intended to deploy/postpone pregnancy assuming *perfect use*; when calculating, it includes only those unintended pregnancies that resulted from correct and consistent use of the method.

Missed temperature: A basal body temperature that is not recorded on a woman's menstrual cycle chart on a given day.

More-fertile mucus: Mucus that is present during the most-fertile time prior to ovulation (Phase II) in a woman's menstrual cycle. It is identified by sensations of wetness and/or slipperiness, and/or characteristics that are stretchy, stringy or resembling raw egg-white.

Mucus characteristics: The qualities of mucus that a woman *sees* and/or *touches* when making observations.

Mucus-Only Methods: Methods of natural family planning based on reading and interpreting the cervical mucus of a woman's menstrual cycle. Mucus-only methods provide the underpinning for CCL's Mucus-Only Rule for those situations in which a couple may not have a reliable temperature sign in a particular cycle.

Mucus-Only Rule: The CCL formula to determine the infertile time of a woman's menstrual cycle following ovulation using just the mucus data. Phase III begins on the evening of the fourth day of drying up or thickening of the cervical mucus after Peak Day.

Mucus sensations: The qualities of mucus that a woman *feels* and *senses* throughout the day and when wiping at bathroom visits.

Mucus symbols: The graphic symbol used to describe the day's most-fertile mucus observation: $\bigcirc$ = no mucus, $\ominus$ = less-fertile, $\oplus$ = more-fertile.

Naegele Rule: A rule traditionally used by the medical community to calculate the Estimated Date of Childbirth (EDC); calculated by adding seven days to the first day of the last menstrual period, and then adding nine months.

Natural Family Planning (NFP): A means of reading a woman's signs of fertility and infertility; also known as *fertility awareness.*

Non-Injectable hormonal contraceptives: All forms of birth control that introduce artificial hormones into a woman's body in ways other than injection (e.g., pills, patches, ring, etc.).

Normal temperatures: Basal body temperatures that were taken properly at the usual time — uninfluenced by factors such as alcohol, illness, medications, travel, or some other condition.

Ovary: The female reproductive organ containing the ova, or eggs.

Ovulation: The process of an ovarian follicle releasing its ovum, thus making a woman fertile and able to become pregnant.

Ovum: The female reproductive cell, or egg; plural: ova.

Oxytocin: A hormone released from the pituitary gland that stimulates the contraction of the smooth muscle of the uterus during labor and facilitates release of milk during nursing; called the "hormone of love."

Patch Rule, Mucus, Post-Injectables: A formula to determine the change in fertility status during the times of transition to fertile cycles following the discontinuation of injectable hormonal contraceptives. *With less-fertile patches,* Phase I infertility begins on the evening of the fourth consecutive day of no mucus after a less-fertile mucus patch. *With more-fertile patches,* Phase I returns on the evening of the fourth day of drying up after Peak Day, where Peak Day is the last day of more-fertile mucus or bleeding. The drying-up days can be less-fertile mucus; however, there cannot be any mucus on the fourth day.

Peak Day: The last day of the more-fertile mucus before the drying-up process begins. Peak Day can only be identified in retrospect.

Penis: The male external sexual organ.

Perimenopause: The last two to eight years of the premenopause transition, ending one year after a woman's last menstrual period.

Phase I: A time of infertility, beginning when a woman starts her menstrual bleeding and ending with the observation of mucus.

Phase II: The fertile time of the cycle. It is during this time that the woman ovulates and when conception may occur.

Phase III: The infertile time after ovulation.

Pituitary gland: A gland located at the base of the brain that releases various hormones that control the functions of other organs.

Postpartum: Of or occurring in the period of time after childbirth; after delivery.

Prem Rule: A rule developed by Dr. Konald A. Prem to calculate the Estimated Date of Childbirth (EDC); calculated by subtracting seven days from the first day of thermal shift, and then adding nine months. This method can be more closely linked to the actual day of ovulation than the Naegele Rule.

Premenopause: The natural life progression that occurs as a woman's fertile years gradually come to a close. It can begin as early as age 35, although the average age at the start of premenopause is 45. Often referred to by the medical community as *perimenopause.*

Pre-shift six: Six lower temperatures immediately preceding at least three temperatures that rise above them in a sustained pattern near Peak Day. Used in setting the Low Temperature Level (LTL).

Progesterone: A fertility hormone secreted by the corpus luteum that causes a woman's temperature to rise, prepares the uterus for the fertilized ovum, and helps sustain a pregnancy.

Prolactin: A pituitary hormone that stimulates and maintains the secretion of milk; referred to as "the mothering hormone." Higher levels of prolactin during breastfeeding play a role in the delay of ovulation.

Prostate gland: The male sexual organ that controls the release of urine from the bladder and provides a fluid to assist in the transport of sperm.

Puberty: The stage of adolescence in which an individual becomes physiologically capable of reproduction.

Responsible parenthood: The virtuous decisions by a married couple to plan or to postpone conception through the knowledge and practice of fertility awareness. Not to be confused with contraception.

Scrotum: The sac below the penis that contains the testicles.

Scant mucus: Mucus that is characterized by the lack of definition in both quantity and quality.

Self-gift: A choice to give oneself completely and totally, especially to a spouse, as reflective of Christ's act on the cross.

Semen: The fluid that is released through the penis during orgasm. Semen is made up of secretions of the reproductive glands and sperm.

Seminal fluid: A fluid produced by the seminal vesicles that assists in the transport of the sperm, and is expelled through the end of the penis when a man achieves sexual climax.

Seminal residue: Seminal fluid that sometimes remains in a woman's vaginal area after she has sexual intercourse.

Seminal vesicles: Sac-like pouches in the male that attach to the vas deferens and produce a sugar-rich fluid (fructose) that provides sperm with a source of energy and helps with the sperm's ability to move.

Sexual powers: The ability of men and women to unite in the marital embrace; an expression of God-like love using their entire persons (body and spirit).

Sperm: Male reproductive cells made by the testicles.

Spermicide: A sperm-killing agent, most often a cream or jelly, usually used as a contraceptive.

Sterilization: The process of rendering either male or female sterile or infertile.

Sympto-Thermal Method (STM): A method of fertility awareness that utilizes the observation of changes in the cervical mucus, basal body temperature and cervix to determine the fertile and infertile times of a woman's menstrual cycle.

Sympto-Thermal Rule: A rule to determine the infertile time of a woman's menstrual cycle following ovulation. Phase III begins on the evening of the third day of drying-up after Peak Day combined with three normal post-peak temperatures above the LTL, and the third temperature at or above the HTL, or the cervix closed and hard for three days. If the previous conditions are not met, then Phase III begins after waiting an additional post-peak day for another temperature above the LTL.

Temperature-Only Methods: Methods of natural family planning based upon Dr. G.K. Doering's studies of a woman's basal body temperature. The Couple to Couple League has based its Temperature-Only Rule on Doering's work.

Temperature-Only Rule: A formula used to determine the infertile time of a woman's menstrual cycle following ovulation using just temperature data. Phase III begins on the evening of the fourth day of normal temperatures above the Low Temperature Level (LTL). The last three temperatures must be on consecutive days, and at or above the High Temperature Level (HTL).

Testicles (or testes): The male sexual organs that are contained in the scrotum and produce sperm.

Thermal shift: At least three temperatures that are higher than the six preceding temperatures near Peak Day. Used in calculating the Sympto-Thermal Rule and Temperature-Only Rule.

Theology of the Body: A series of 129 individual addresses by Pope John Paul II given between 1979 and 1984.

Tubal ligation: A method of female sterilization in which the Fallopian tubes are surgically tied, cut or cauterized.

Tubal occlusion: A method of female sterilization in which tiny coils made of nickel are placed inside the Fallopian tubes which stimulate the growth of tissue that blocks the tubes.

Unintended pregnancy rate: Measured in terms of the number of women out of 100 who become pregnant in one year using a method intended to delay/postpone pregnancy.

User effectiveness: The effectiveness of a method intended to postpone/delay pregnancy based on *actual practice*; when calculating, all unintended pregnancies occurring during a study and all months or cycles are included, whether the method or rules were followed correctly or incorrectly.

Uterus: A hollow, pear-shaped organ in which a baby grows during the nine months of pregnancy; frequently called the womb.

Vagina: The female genital canal extending from the uterus to the vulva.

Vaginal sponge: A sponge that combines barrier and spermicidal methods of contraception, inserted vaginally prior to intercourse over the cervix to prevent conception.

Vas deferens: A narrow, muscular tube that connects the testicles to the urethra in the penis through which the sperm flow.

Vasectomy: Surgical excision of a part of the vas deferens, used as a method of male sterilization.

Vulva: The external parts of the vagina, including the labia.

Withdrawal: As a method of contraception, the act of removing the penis from a woman's vagina prior to ejaculation; also known as *coitus interruptus*.

Withdrawal bleed: The bleed that occurs monthly while using non-injectable hormonal contraceptives.

Index I

Hillebrand, Fr. Wilhelm, 41

Hogan, Rev. Richard M., x, 54, 106–107, 138, 140, 244

Hormonal contraception, 60, 223–227, 253

Hormonal contraceptive, 3, 223–227; combination pills, 223; Depo-Provera, 60, 222, 224, 253; Implanon, 223; implants, 223; injectable, 60; Jadelle, 223; Lunelle, 60, 224, 253; non-injectable, 60, 223, 254; NuvaRing, 223; patch, 60, 223; pill, 55, 60, 91–92, 140, 223; Progestasert, 223; progestin-only pills, 223

Hormone, 9–13, 32, 60, 78, 101, 141, 153, 223–224, 236, 247, 253–254; injectable, 60; mothering, 145; of love, 146; synthetic, 253

Humanae Vitae, 55–56, 107, 211, 253

Human body, 3–5, 25, 57–58, 68, 73, 106, 137–138, 244

Human Body...a sign of dignity and a gift, The, 54, 106

Human Chorionic Gonadotropin (hCG) hormone, 96, 253

I

Illness, 19, 111, 120, 126, 133–135

Implanon, *See Hormonal contraceptive*

Implantation, 96, 98, 140–141, 244, 252–253

Implants, *See Hormonal contraceptive*

Infertile time, ix, 3–4, 11, 31, 34, 46, 65, 78, 92–93, 102, 107, 253, 255

Infertility, ix, 3–4, 8, 32, 45–46, 59–60, 67, 74, 77, 84, 99, 101, 142, 209, 244, 253–254; and nutrition, 242; and smoking and alcohol, 243; postpartum, 143, 150

Injectable hormonal contraceptives, 224, 253; and mucus patches, 129

Injectable Patch Rule, 226

Intrauterine device (IUD), 141, 223, 253

In vitro fertilization, 56, 138, 140–141, 244, 253

Is NFP Good?, 54

J

Jadelle, *See Hormonal contraceptive*

Just reasons (for avoiding pregnancy), 108

K

Kase, Nathan G., 152

Kendall-Tackett, K., 147

Kippley, John and Sheila, 211

Knaus, Hermann, 119

L

Labia, 8, 21, 32, 237, 253

Last Dry Day Rule, 82–85, 114, 220, 224, 227, 245, 253

Lauwers, J., 144, 148

Lawrence, Ruth and Robert, 145

Less-fertile mucus, 32, 238, 253; after Peak Day, 240; and healthy mucus pattern, 127; and Post-Injectable Patch Rule, 222, 225, 246

LeVoir, John M., 54

Libido, 152, 228, 253; increased, 30

Low Temperature Level (LTL), 43, 44, 48, 50, 71, 168, 252, 253–255; determining, 74

Lunelle, *See Hormonal contraceptive*

Lust, 138

Luteal phase, 98–99, 101, 136, 154, 194, 196, 253

Luteinizing hormone (LH), 9, 12–13, 78, 95, 102, 252, 253

M

Macadam, P., 146–147

Male anatomy, 6

Marital intimacy, 89, 155

Masturbation, 138, 244

Measurable signs, 15–30

Medications, 19, 111, 124, 126, 136, 227–235; chart, 206

Medications & Mother's Milk, 228

Membership, CCL, 15, 158

Membership number, 15

Menarche, 10, 253

Mennella, J., 148

Menopause, 10, 152–154, 158, 253

Menstruation, 2, 8, 10–11, 16, 23, 32, 61, 67–68, 77–80, 98, 103–104, 113, 119, 124, 127, 131, 145, 150, 208–209, 223, 227, 242, 245, 251, 253; bleeding, 98; blood flow, 77; permanent cessation, 152

Mion, A., 100

Mirena, 223

Miscarriage, 102, 236, 242, 251

Missed temperatures, 73–76

Mixed breastfeeding, 144, 150

More-fertile mucus, 33, 209, 239, 253; and healthy mucus pattern, 127; and Post-Injectable Patch Rule, 222, 225, 246

Mucus, cervical, 67, 99, 101, 236–240; less-fertile, 34, 37; more-fertile, 34, 37, 70, 98, 99; pattern, 36; symbols, 37

Mucus characteristics, 23, 32, 36, 68, 85, 237, 253; how to observe, 23; how to record, 24; less-fertile, 33; more-fertile, 33

Mucus-Only Methods, 122, 220–221, 253

Mucus-Only Rule, 122–124, 131, 201, 221, 246, 248, 253–254

Mucus patches, 129, 204, 224; less-fertile, 254

Mucus pattern, 126; healthy, 127; patches, 129; scant, 128; unusual, 127

Mucus photos, 237

Mucus sensations, 20–21, 32, 68, 70, 79, 85, 209, 236, 237, 254; how to record, 22; less-fertile, 32; more-fertile, 33, 36

Mucus sign, 20, 50, 79, 83, 113, 220, 224, 248; interpreting, 32, 128, 130

Mucus symbols, 33, 254

N

Naegele Rule, 103–104, 115, 252, 254

NaproTECHNOLOGY, 122, 236, 244, 249

Natural Conception Regulation, 213, 220

Natural Family Planning (NFP), vii, ix, 4, 12, 31, 58, 92, 96, 155, 211, 254; benefits of, 155–157; types of, 253

New England Journal of Medicine, 95, 220

NFP-supportive physicians, 241

Non-injectable hormonal contraceptives, *See Hormonal contraceptive*

NuvaRing, *See Hormonal contraceptive*

O

Ogino, M.D., Kyusaku, 119

One More Soul, 241

On Human Life, 253. *See also Humanae Vitae*

Onis, M., 147, 150

Our Bodies, Ourselves, vii

Ova, 5, 7

Ovary, 7–12, 40, 252, 254

Ovulation, 4, 8–12, 20, 25, 27, 31–34, 36–37, 40–41, 45–46, 65, 67–71, 79–81, 95, 98–101, 103–104, 119, 208, 253–255; and pain, 30; delayed, 120, 145, 153

Ovum, 5, 252, 254

Oxytocin, 146, 254

P

Passarin, K., 100

Patches of mucus, 127

Patch Rule; mucus, 129, 224; non-injectables, 254; post-injectable, 222, 225–226, 246, 254

Patch, the, *See Hormonal contraceptive*

Peak Day, 36–38, 41, 70–71, 98, 100, 127, 224–225, 254–255; and scant mucus, 128

Penis, 6, 141, 252, 254, 255–256

Periano, 144, 147

Perimenopause, 152–154, 254

Period, *See Menstruation*

Phase I, 8, 84, 254

Phase I Guidelines, 79–80

Phase I rules, 88

Phase II, 8, 67, 75, 80, 99, 253–254

Phase III, 3, 8, 11, 17, 27, 34, 46, 74, 252, 254–255

Phase III rules, 246; beginner's first cycle, 59

Pill, the. *See Hormonal contraceptive*

Pituitary gland, 9–10, 139, 153, 252–254

Placenta, 253

Pope John Paul II, vii, 54, 57, 137, 211

Pope John XXIII, 55

Pope Paul VI, 55–56, 96, 211, 253

Pornography, 138

Post-Hormonal Rule, 60, 224, 227, 246; non-injectable, 221, 246

Postpartum, 28, 61, 111, 129, 131–132, 143, 145, 150–151, 208–209, 241–242, 254

Pregnancy; definition of, 140

Pregnancy, achieving, ix, 4, 105, 156; and biological clock, 207; and fertiliy monitors, 102; and technologies, 243; helps for, 100; hints for, 99; key observable signs, 98; practical helps, 242; signs of fertility, 99; tips for husbands, 242

Pregnancy, avoiding, 46, 78, 91, 107, 219–220

Prem, M.D., Konald A, 103, 211, 254

Premenopause, 28, 61, 111, 129, 131–132, 152–154, 158, 208–209, 254; and breakthrough bleeding, 208; and fertility, 243; hormonal changes, 153

Prem Rule, 103, 115, 194, 252, 254

Pre-shift six, 42, 44, 71, 74–75, 112–113, 124, 251, 253–254

Procreation, 107, 156

Progestasert, *See Hormonal contraceptive*

Progesterone, 9–13, 25, 27, 32, 36, 40, 69, 71, 77, 99, 253–254

Progestin-only pills, *See Hormonal contraceptive*

Prolactin, 145–146, 150, 232–235, 254–255